Cloud Na Development with Azure

A practical guide to build cloud-native apps on Azure cloud platform

Pavan Verma

www.bpbonline.com

First Edition 2024

Copyright © BPB Publications, India

ISBN: 978-93-55517-715

All Rights Reserved. No part of this publication may be reproduced, distributed or transmitted in any form or by any means or stored in a database or retrieval system, without the prior written permission of the publisher with the exception to the program listings which may be entered, stored and executed in a computer system, but they can not be reproduced by the means of publication, photocopy, recording, or by any electronic and mechanical means.

LIMITS OF LIABILITY AND DISCLAIMER OF WARRANTY

The information contained in this book is true to correct and the best of author's and publisher's knowledge. The author has made every effort to ensure the accuracy of these publications, but publisher cannot be held responsible for any loss or damage arising from any information in this book.

All trademarks referred to in the book are acknowledged as properties of their respective owners but BPB Publications cannot guarantee the accuracy of this information.

To View Complete
BPB Publications Catalogue
Scan the QR Code:

www.bpbonline.com

Dedicated to

My beloved parents, who constantly inspire me:

Shri Thakur Prasad Verma
Smt. Laxmi Verma

and

My wife **Anuradha** *and my daughter* **Palak**
to be always there to support me

About the Author

Pavan Verma is working as a Principal Engineer at McKinsey & Company with 20 years of industry experience, and previous to McKinsey, he worked with Accenture. Pavan has global experience working with Fortune 500 companies in defining and successfully executing digital business transformation initiatives.

Pavan has a depth of experience in building strategies and road maps for industries to move to a new cloud-native platform. Pavan has working experience on all major clouds: Azure, AWS, GCP, and RedHat, and has helped global customers based in Asia, Europe, and North America. Pavan has experience building large-scale customer-facing applications using Azure cloud services, delivering effortless and seamless customer experience.

Pavan did computer engineering at Kamla Nehru Institute of Technology, Sultanpur, and studied application security at the Massachusetts Institute of Technology. Pavan is pursuing an MBA from Boston University and likes to work with nature and play guitar in his free time.

About the Reviewers

❖ **Ankit** is a senior cloud data architect with Google and has over a decade of progressive work experience in Cloud, Data, AI and ethical machine learning practices. He works with customers to develop scalable, reliable and performant data and machine learning platforms and has worked across companies like Amazon, CVS, Deloitte, and Infosys. He is a technical reviewer for various books focused on data governance, ethical AI, AI governance, Data and AI platforms, Python for AI and other material related to promotion of AI ethically and responsibly in the society. He earned his masters from the esteemed Kelley School of Business and serves as the advisory board member for Institute of Business Analytics, Indiana University Bloomington.

❖ **Dhirendra Kumar** is a Kubernetes cloud Architect, Boston, USA, specializing in helping infrastructure architecting. He has been involved in other aspects of information technology, including software development, security, system automation, system architecture, and design since 2004, he has focused primarily on cloud-native solutions for customers.

I would like to thank my parents and son, Naitik, for the opportunity to contribute to this book.

❖ **Alok Shankar**, an Engineering Manager at Oracle's Health AI organization, is an expert and a thought leader in the field of cloud computing, Edge and distributed cloud, Healthcare IT and AI. With a distinguished career at Oracle, Microsoft, Cisco, Sumo Logic and more, he has made significant contributions to pioneer cloud services and technologies, notably in cloud edge device virtualization, infrastructure, and Software Defined Networks. A Carnegie Mellon alumnus, Alok is also a forward-thinking angel investor with Hustle Fund VC and serves on advisory boards for tech startups. Alok's work has not only garnered industry accolades but also contributed to advancements in cloud and edge computing.

Acknowledgement

I want to express my sincere gratitude to several people who have supported me while writing this book.

I want to express my utmost gratitude to my parents, who have been a constant source of inspiration for me to do good. My mother was my first teacher who believed in my potential, and my father was a mentor who guided me and showed me the right path to take. I am incredibly grateful to my wife, Anuradha, and daughter, Palak, for their unwavering motivation and support throughout the process of writing this book. Without their encouragement, this book would not have been possible. Their support means everything to me, and I am genuinely thankful for the motivation they provided at every step.

I am grateful to the companies that have given me the opportunity to learn about Azure Cloud through hands-on work and learning platforms. These experiences have provided me with a wealth of information to understand better and solidify my knowledge. I also want to express my gratitude to Ankit Virmani, Alok Shankar, and Dhirendra Kumar for their valuable technical feedback on this book.

I am thankful to the team at BPB Publication for their immense support in providing me with enough time to complete the book on Azure cloud computing, a vast and constantly evolving field. It required a lot of effort to cover all the essential topics related to Azure cloud services in the book. However, the BPB team made it possible by allowing me enough time to think through and explain each topic in detail. I appreciate their support and encouragement throughout the process of publishing the book.

Preface

Cloud and cloud-native development have become buzzwords in the technology industry because they offer many benefits to organizations that adopt them. There are many cloud service providers in the market, and Azure is a critical public cloud service provider. Azure is a powerful cloud computing platform with a wide range of services, and reading this book can help you gain an in-depth understanding of these services and how to use them effectively. Azure is one of the most popular cloud computing platforms, and having knowledge and skills in Azure can be a valuable asset in your career.

Suppose you are planning to take a certification exam in Azure. In that case, reading this book can help you prepare for the exam by providing a detailed understanding of the concepts and topics covered in the exam. Azure is constantly evolving, with new features and services being added regularly. Reading books on Azure Cloud can help you stay up-to-date with the latest developments in the platform and keep your skills current.

This book is aimed at helping developers, designers, and architects using Azure as a Cloud Service Provider (CSP). This book will cover the Azure platform's primary offerings and how those can be used for building highly scalable, secure, and reliable applications. The book will also cover real-life implementation examples, providing Azure services' realization and how they are being used. The book anticipates that readers will have some basic knowledge of computers and the cloud, but it does not expect advanced expertise.

This book is divided into 11 chapters. We will start with learning about the basics of cloud computing and then learn about the various Azure features. By reading this book, readers will learn about Azure Functions, AKS, Cosmos DB, Azure Event Grid, EventHub, and Service Bus. In the last section, we will cover the real-life scenarios and architectures of Azure and the services it uses. The details of the book and its chapters are listed below.

Chapter 1: Introduction to Azure Cloud and Cloud Native Development - explains what cloud computing is and what type of services it provides in terms of delivery of computing services, including servers, storage, databases, networking, software, and analytics, over the internet.

Chapter 2: Azure Services for Cloud Native Development - covers the details of different Azure Services it provides for Cloud Native Development and see how they help in the software development life cycle.

Chapter 3: Data Storage Services on Azure Cloud - explains the data storage services available on Azure Cloud and how they help in every type of data need of the organization.

Chapter 4: Azure Kubernetes and Container Registry - covers the concept of containerization and its orchestrations. We will also review how it helps the scalability and availability of the applications at scale.

Chapter 5: Developing Application on Azure - explores the best practices and concepts around cloud native and microservices development. We will discuss developing more resilient, secure, and scalable services.

Chapter 6: Monitoring and Logging Applications on Azure - covers information about the monitoring and logging services provided by Azure and how they help developers identify and remedy issues.

Chapter 7: Security and Governance in Azure - explains the security and governance services provided by Azure and the security best practices everyone should follow.

Chapter 8: Deploying Applications on Azure - explains the CI/CD concepts and how Azure Cloud helps build pipelines that provide agility and speed to the development and deployment of the applications.

Chapter 9: Advanced Azure Services - will cover the advanced Azure services like cognitive, AI, and IoT and see how they help organizations.

Chapter 10: Case Studies and Best Practices - this chapter will go through the real-life case studies implemented by top organizations and how they benefit.

Chapter 11: Cloud, Generative AI, and Future Trends - explains a critical topic: Generative AI. We will go through the basics of the general concepts and their use.

Coloured Images

Please follow the link to download the
Coloured Images of the book:

https://rebrand.ly/qf5movh

We have code bundles from our rich catalogue of books and videos available at **https://github.com/bpbpublications**. Check them out!

Errata

We take immense pride in our work at BPB Publications and follow best practices to ensure the accuracy of our content to provide with an indulging reading experience to our subscribers. Our readers are our mirrors, and we use their inputs to reflect and improve upon human errors, if any, that may have occurred during the publishing processes involved. To let us maintain the quality and help us reach out to any readers who might be having difficulties due to any unforeseen errors, please write to us at :

errata@bpbonline.com

Your support, suggestions and feedbacks are highly appreciated by the BPB Publications' Family.

Did you know that BPB offers eBook versions of every book published, with PDF and ePub files available? You can upgrade to the eBook version at www.bpbonline.com and as a print book customer, you are entitled to a discount on the eBook copy. Get in touch with us at :

business@bpbonline.com for more details.

At **www.bpbonline.com**, you can also read a collection of free technical articles, sign up for a range of free newsletters, and receive exclusive discounts and offers on BPB books and eBooks.

Piracy

If you come across any illegal copies of our works in any form on the internet, we would be grateful if you would provide us with the location address or website name. Please contact us at **business@bpbonline.com** with a link to the material.

If you are interested in becoming an author

If there is a topic that you have expertise in, and you are interested in either writing or contributing to a book, please visit **www.bpbonline.com**. We have worked with thousands of developers and tech professionals, just like you, to help them share their insights with the global tech community. You can make a general application, apply for a specific hot topic that we are recruiting an author for, or submit your own idea.

Reviews

Please leave a review. Once you have read and used this book, why not leave a review on the site that you purchased it from? Potential readers can then see and use your unbiased opinion to make purchase decisions. We at BPB can understand what you think about our products, and our authors can see your feedback on their book. Thank you!

For more information about BPB, please visit **www.bpbonline.com**.

Join our book's Discord space

Join the book's Discord Workspace for Latest updates, Offers, Tech happenings around the world, New Release and Sessions with the Authors:

https://discord.bpbonline.com

Table of Contents

1. Introduction to Azure Cloud and Cloud Native Development 1
    Introduction 1
    Structure 2
    Objectives 2
    Brief history of cloud computing and its evolution 2
    PaaS, SaaS, IaaS offerings 3
    Monolithic and microservice application architectures 6
        Azure cloud offerings and its features 7
    Benefits of using Azure Cloud for development 9
    Conclusion 10
    Questions 10

2. Azure Services for Cloud Native Development 13
    Introduction 13
    Structure 14
    Objectives 15
    Azure Compute 15
    Azure Identity and Access Management 17
    Azure Azure Active Directory 18
    Azure Functions 19
    Azure Event Hubs 19
    Azure Event Grid 21
    Azure Service Bus 21
    Azure Logic Apps 22
    Azure Apps Service 23
    Azure WebJobs 24
    Azure Mobile Services 25
    Azure Service Fabric 26
    Azure SignalR 27

  Conclusion 28

  Questions 29

3. Data Storage Services on Azure Cloud 31

  Introduction 31

  Structure 31

  Objectives 32

  Structured data and normalization forms 32

  Unstructured data 34

  Semi-structured data 35

  Azure data storage services 35

  Azure SQL Database 37

    Purchasing models 38

      Service tiers 39

      Compute tiers 39

  Azure Archive Storage 40

  Azure Cosmos DB 41

  Azure Table Storage 43

  Azure Cache for Redis 44

  Azure HDInsight 46

  Azure Files 47

  Azure Data Lake Storage 48

  Azure Blob Storage 50

  Azure Databricks 51

  Conclusion 54

  Questions 55

4. Azure Kubernetes and Container Registry 57

  Introduction 57

  Structure 57

  Objectives 58

  Containers 58

  Docker 59

Container orchestration	60
Kubernetes	61
Azure Kubernetes Service and Azure Container Registry	63
Azure Kubernetes Service	64
Azure Container Registry	65
Azure API Management	67
Azure API Gateway	68
Conclusion	69
Questions	70

5. Developing Application on Azure 71

Introduction	71
Structure	72
Objectives	72
Best cloud-native design practices and challenges	73
Microservices architecture and patterns	75
Twelve-factors applications	77
Containerization and deployment strategies	78
Building Microservices with AKS	80
Serverless development with Azure Functions	86
Using Cosmos DB for NoSQL databases	89
Building event-driven applications	92
Building workflows with Azure Logic Apps	93
Developing applications using Java and .Net	95
Java (Spring Boot)	*95*
NET (ASP.NET Core)	*97*
Conclusion	98
Questions	99

6. Monitoring and Logging Applications on Azure 101

Introduction	101
Structure	101
Objectives	102

Understanding Azure monitoring and logging services 102
High-Level Architecture 103
Azure Application Insights 104
    How to use Application Insights 106
Azure Log Analytics 107
Common Azure Cloud problems 110
Setting up monitoring with Azure Monitor 111
Troubleshooting common issues with Azure applications 113
Conclusion 115
Questions 116

7. Security and Governance in Azure 117
Introduction 117
Structure 118
Objectives 118
Understanding Azure security and governance features 119
Best practices for securing Azure applications 120
Identifying surface attacks 122
Threat modeling 124
Understanding Azure governance policies 126
Access control and identity management on Azure 127
Data governance 129
Conclusion 130
Questions 131

8. Deploying Applications on Azure 133
Introduction 133
Structure 134
Objectives 134
Introduction to DevOps and CI/CD 134
    DevOps 135
    Continuous integration and continuous deployment 135
        Continuous integration 136

Continuous deployment/continuous delivery	136
Key principles of DevOps	137
Understanding DevOps and CI/CD in Azure	138
Setting up a DevOps pipeline with Azure DevOps	139
Implementing an automated QA process	141
Azure DevOps and GitHub Actions	143
Components	*144*
Process	*144*
Using Azure Kubernetes Service	146
Azure Functions and Logic Apps	148
Best practices for deploying applications on Azure	150
Conclusion	152
Questions	153
9. Advanced Azure Services	**155**
Introduction	155
Structure	155
Objectives	156
Introduction to data analysis	156
Azure Machine Learning	158
Azure Machine Learning architecture	*158*
Data preparation	*159*
Model training	*159*
Model deployment	*160*
Monitoring and management	*160*
Experimentation and version control	*161*
Collaboration	*161*
Integration	*161*
Security and Compliance	*161*
Use cases	*162*
Azure Cognitive Services	162
Azure Synapse Analytics	165

Azure IoT Hub 167

Conclusion 169

Questions 170

10. Case Studies and Best Practices 171

Introduction 171

Structure 171

Objectives 171

Transforming a monolithic application 172

Cloud-native best practices 178

Real-world cloud-native applications 184

    Netflix 186

    Spotify 187

    Uber 187

    Amazon 188

    Microservices usage 188

    Airbnb 189

    Etsy 189

    Twitter 189

    LinkedIn 189

    Walmart 190

    Coca-Cola 190

Conclusion 190

Questions 191

11. Cloud, Generative AI, and Future Trends 193

Introduction 193

Structure 193

Objectives 194

Recap of key concepts and takeaways 194

    Virtualization 194

    On-demand self-service 194

    Auto scalability 195

> Service models 195
> Cloud deployment models.. 196
> Pay-as-you-go pricing 196
> Service Level Agreements 197
> Resource pooling.. 197
> Network access 197
> Security and Compliance 197
> Data center locations 197
> Elastic load balancing.. 197
> Redundancy and high availability... 197
> Data storage options.. 197
> Orchestration... 198
> DevOps and CI/CD.. 198
> Monitoring and management tools 198
> Data transfer and bandwidth costs 198

Generative AI: An overview 198
> Large language models 199
>> How LLMs help in generative AI and content creation 199

Azure Cloud and generative AI 202
> Azure Cloud Services for generative AI... 202
>> Azure Machine Learning Service 202
>> Azure Cognitive Services.. 203
>> Azure Databricks 204
>> Azure GPU Virtual Machines 204
>> Azure Kubernetes Service 204

Learning generative AI Azure services 204
> Access to generative AI services 205
> Integration with OpenAI models 205
> Scalable infrastructure 205
> Development and experimentation.. 205
> GPU Acceleration 205
> Comprehensive documentation and tutorials... 205

- *Scalability and ease of deployment* 205
- *Collaboration and integration* 206
- *Data management* 206
- *Security and Compliance* 206

Writing your first generative AI program 206

Future trends in cloud-native development 208
- *Edge computing* 208
  - *Advantages of edge computing* 209
- *Serverless computing* 210
- *Multi-cloud and hybrid cloud adoption* 210
- *AI and Machine Learning integration* 211
- *Quantum computing in the cloud* 212
- *Containerization and Kubernetes* 212
- *Serverless databases* 212
- *Security and compliance* 212
- *Green cloud computing* 212
- *Blockchain integration* 213
- *5G and cloud* 213
- *Serverless IoT* 213
- *Data analytics and big data* 214
- *Container security* 214
- *Mature cloud-native ecosystem* 214

Azure Cloud future trends 214
- *Azure Arc* 215
- *Azure Quantum* 215
- *Azure Percept* 216
- *Generative AI and Azure AI* 216
- *Azure Virtual Desktop* 217
- *Azure Data Explorer* 217
- *Azure IoT* 218

Conclusion 219

Questions 220

Index 221-228

CHAPTER 1
Introduction to Azure Cloud and Cloud Native Development

Introduction

Cloud computing refers to delivering computing services, including servers, storage, databases, networking, software, and analytics, over the internet known as the cloud. Rather than managing and maintaining physical servers and infrastructure on-premises, organizations can leverage cloud computing to access these resources as needed and pay only for what they use.

Microsoft Azure is a cloud computing platform and service offered by Microsoft. It provides a wide range of cloud services, including computing, analytics, storage, and networking, to enable businesses to build, deploy, and manage applications and services in the cloud.

Azure allows organizations to scale their computing resources up or down as needed, enabling them to respond quickly to changing business demands.

Azure's pay-as-you-go model enables organizations to pay only for the resources they use rather than investing in and maintaining expensive on-premises infrastructure.

Azure offers robust security features and compliance certifications to help protect data and applications.

Overall, Azure's value proposition lies in its ability to provide organizations with a flexible, cost-effective, reliable, and innovative cloud platform to meet their computing needs.

Structure

In this chapter, we are going to discuss cloud computing and its evolutions:

- Brief history of cloud computing and its evolution
- PaaS, SaaS and IaaS offerings
- Monolithic and microservice application architectures
- Benefits of Azure Cloud for development

Objectives

The objective of this chapter is an overview of cloud-native development and why it is essential.

Cloud-native development is a software development approach specifically designed for cloud computing architectures. It is focused on building applications using cloud services and leveraging cloud platforms' scalability, reliability, and agility. Cloud service provides various on-demand services, making code development and deployment processes efficient and seamless. The Cloud Native Computing Foundation defines it as the following:

Cloud-native technologies empower organizations to build and run scalable applications in modern, dynamic environments such as public, private, and hybrid clouds. Containers, service meshes, microservices, immutable infrastructure, and declarative APIs exemplify this approach.

The traditional development approach creates one code base containing everything and has one binary file for deployment. It was called monolithic because, over a while, code became so huge that it was causing boilerplate problems and required lots of budgets from organizations to maintain and run.

Brief history of cloud computing and its evolution

Cloud computing has its roots in the 1960s when the concept of time-sharing was first introduced. Time-sharing allowed multiple users to access a single computer simultaneously and was the precursor to modern cloud computing.

However, it was only in the late 1990s and early 2000s that the term **cloud computing** began to be used. Several companies started offering web-based applications and services hosted in the cloud - a term that describes the Internet.

One of the first cloud computing services was **Salesforce.com**, which launched in 1999 and offered a web-based **customer relationship management** (**CRM**) platform. In 2002, **Amazon Web Services** (**AWS**) launched its **Elastic Compute Cloud (EC2)** service, which allowed users to rent computing resources on demand.

Over the next decade, cloud computing continued to evolve and mature. In 2006, Amazon launched its **Simple Storage Service** (**S3**), which allowed users to store and retrieve data from anywhere on the internet. In 2008, Google launched its App Engine service, which allowed developers to build and deploy web applications on Google's infrastructure.

In 2009, the **National Institute of Standards and Technology** (**NIST**) released a definition of cloud computing that helped to standardize the terminology and concepts used in the industry. This definition included the five essential characteristics of cloud computing: On-demand self-service, broad network access, resource pooling, rapid elasticity, and measured service.

Today, cloud computing is a ubiquitous technology that organizations of all sizes and industries use. The major cloud providers, Amazon, Microsoft, and Google, offer a wide range of services that include **Infrastructure-as-a-Service** (**IaaS**), **Platform-as-a-Service** (**PaaS**), and **Software-as-a-Service** (**SaaS**) offerings. Additionally, cloud computing has enabled the rise of new technologies, such as containers and serverless computing, changing how developers build and deploy applications in the cloud:

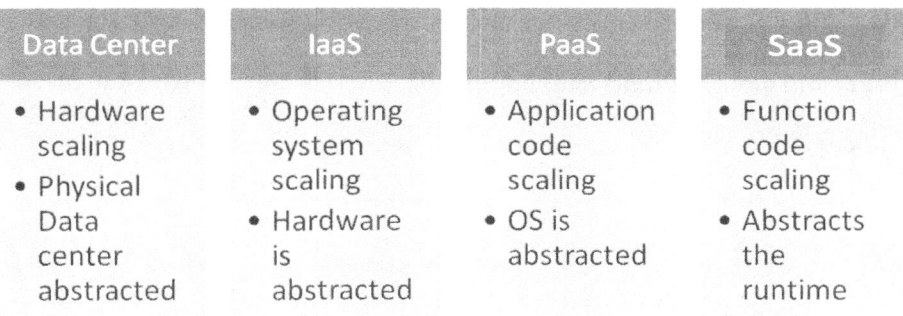

Figure 1.1: Cloud journey and evolution

PaaS, SaaS, IaaS offerings

Cloud service providers provide several models, but PaaS, SaaS, and IaaS are the three primary models of cloud computing services. Each of these models offers different levels of abstraction and functionality to meet the needs of different types of applications and users:

Responsibility	On Prem	IaaS	PaaS	SaaS
Application	Customer	Customer	Customer	CSP
Data	Customer	Customer	Customer	CSP
Runtime	Customer	Customer	CSP	CSP
Middleware	Customer	Customer	CSP	CSP
Operating System	Customer	Customer	CSP	CSP
Virtualization	Customer	CSP	CSP	CSP
Servers	Customer	CSP	CSP	CSP
Storage	Customer	CSP	CSP	CSP
Networking	Customer	CSP	CSP	CSP

CSP – Cloud Service Provider

Table 1.1: Different cloud-type offerings

Platform-as-a-Service (PaaS): PaaS provides a complete development and deployment environment in the cloud, allowing developers to build, test, and deploy applications without worrying about the underlying infrastructure. PaaS typically includes development tools, programming languages, databases, and other services necessary to build and run applications. Examples of PaaS offerings include AWS Elastic Beanstalk, Microsoft Azure App Service, and Google Cloud App Engine:

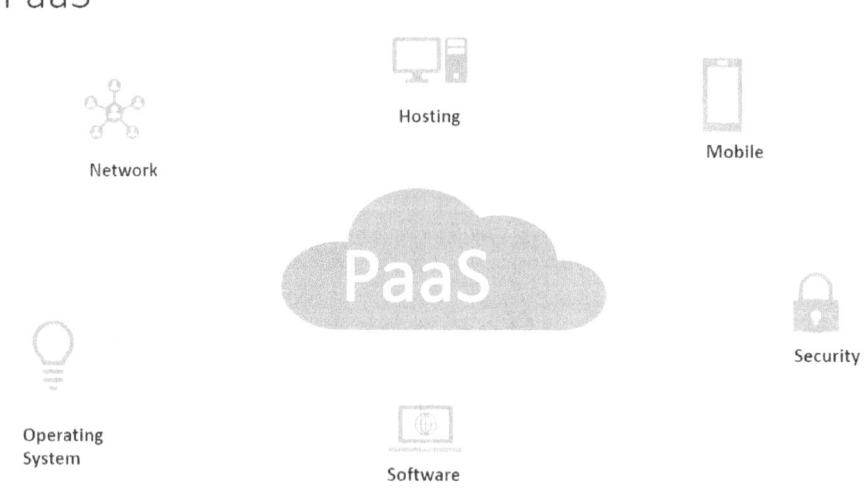

Figure 1.2: Platform as a Service (PaaS)

Software-as-a-Service (SaaS): SaaS provides complete applications delivered over the internet, eliminating users needing to install and maintain software on their devices. SaaS applications are typically accessed through a web browser or a mobile app and are often charged on a subscription basis. Examples of SaaS offerings include Salesforce, Dropbox, and Microsoft Office 365:

Figure 1.3: *Software as a Service (SaaS)*

Infrastructure-as-a-Service (IaaS): IaaS provides virtualized computing resources, including servers, storage, and networking, that can be rented on demand. IaaS users have complete control over the operating system, middleware, and applications that run on the infrastructure. IaaS offerings are typically charged based on usage and are often used by organizations that need to run complex workloads that require high levels of customization and control. Examples of IaaS offerings include **Amazon Web Services** (**AWS**), **Elastic Compute Cloud** (**EC2**), Microsoft Azure Virtual Machines, and Google Cloud Compute Engine:

Figure 1.4: *Infrastructure as a Service (IaaS)*

Monolithic and microservice application architectures

Monolithic architecture can be considered architecture where the whole building has been carved out from a single piece of stone. It is a traditional model of system development and architecture. In monolithic applications, as shown in *Figure 1.5*, everything UI, business logic, configuration, and data access components get bundled together as a single code unit. The problem with this approach is that for every small change, we need to build and deploy the entire package, and over time, when the code base keeps increasing, it becomes a bottleneck for the organizations. The team can not provide the agility and speed we need today.

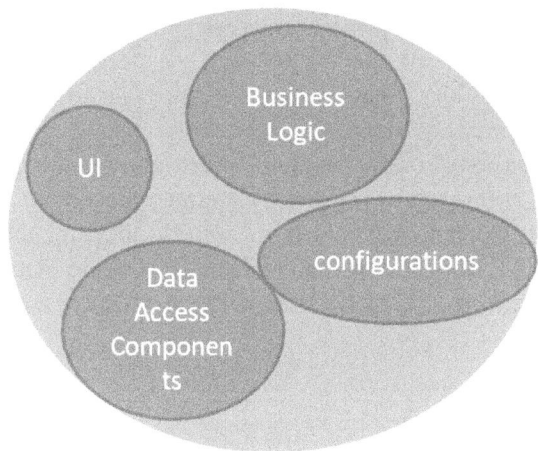

Figure 1.5: Monolithic architecture

Cloud-native development typically involves designing and developing applications as microservices, each independently deployable and scalable. This approach allows developers to build more resilient, adaptable, and efficient applications than traditional ones. Cloud-native development also emphasizes containerization and container orchestration tools like Docker and Kubernetes. Containers provide a lightweight and portable way to package applications, while container orchestration tools allow developers to easily manage and scale their applications across multiple hosts and clusters. Kindly refer to the following figure for microservices architecture:

Microservices Architecture

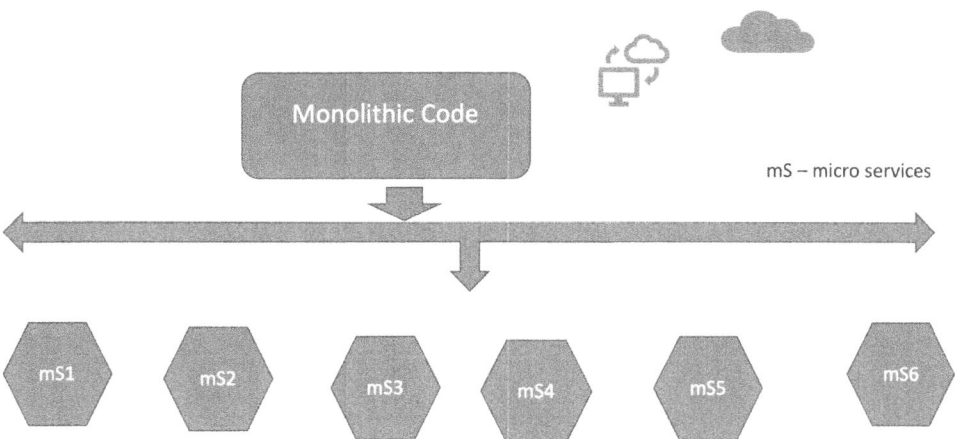

Figure 1.6: Microservices architecture

In the above diagram, we can see that one monolithic code has been refactored into multiple microservices. Every microservice is an isolated unit that can be built and deployed independently. As we have seen in monolithic applications, the whole unit needs to be made and deployed for a small change. In contrast, in the case of microservices, only the impacted service will be deployed. The rest of the services will be unimpacted, and cloud-native development supports the microservice architecture and provides the necessary platform to build, manage, and monitor the microservices.

Cloud-native development is essential because it helps organizations take advantage of the benefits of cloud computing, including greater flexibility, scalability, and cost-effectiveness. By building applications specifically designed for cloud platforms, organizations can avoid many scalability and availability challenges of traditional on-premises applications. Additionally, cloud-native development can help organizations reduce their time-to-market and accelerate their innovation cycles, allowing them to meet the needs of their customers better and stay ahead of the competition.

Azure cloud offerings and its features

Azure is a cloud computing platform and service offered by Microsoft. It provides a wide range of cloud offerings that enable organizations to build, deploy, and manage applications and services in the cloud. Some of the key Azure offerings include:

Virtual machines: Azure provides a range of virtual machines that can run applications and services in the cloud. These virtual machines support various operating systems, including Windows, Linux, and other open-source platforms.

With Azure virtual machines, users can deploy and manage machines running Windows Server, Linux, or other operating systems. These VMs can be used for various purposes, including hosting websites and web applications, running custom software, processing large datasets, and more.

Azure virtual machines are highly customizable and can be configured to meet various computing requirements. Users can choose from multiple VM sizes, which provide different amounts of CPU, memory, and storage resources. They can also choose from various storage options, including premium and standard storage, as well as managed disks and storage accounts.

In addition to these features, Azure virtual machines provide users with various management and monitoring tools. Users can monitor their VMs using Azure Monitor, which provides real-time performance metrics and logs monitoring. They can also use Azure Automation to automate everyday management tasks, such as scaling and patching.

Azure offers several **virtual machines** (**VMs**) to meet different computing needs. Here are some of the main types of Azure VMs:

General purpose: These VMs are designed for various workloads, such as web servers, small to medium-sized databases, and development and testing environments.

Compute optimized: These VMs are designed for high-performance computing workloads that require a high CPU-to-memory ratio, such as batch processing, gaming, and scientific modeling.

Memory-optimized: These VMs are designed for workloads that require high memory-to-CPU ratios, such as relational database servers, in-memory analytics, and big data solutions.

Storage optimized: These VMs are designed for workloads that require high disk throughput and **input/output (I/O) operations per second** (**IOPS**), such as big data solutions, data warehousing, and large transactional databases.

Graphical Processing Units (GPU): These VMs are designed for workloads that require GPUs, such as machine learning, gaming, and video rendering.

High-performance computing: These VMs are designed for high-performance computing workloads that require low-latency, high-throughput networking, such as molecular modeling, computational fluid dynamics, and financial risk modeling.

Each type of VM offers a variety of sizes with different amounts of CPU, memory, and storage resources. Users can select the VM type and size that best meets their computing needs. It is important to note that pricing, availability, and features may vary depending on the specific VM type and size.

App Service: Azure App Service is a PaaS offering that allows developers to build and deploy web and mobile applications quickly and easily. App Service supports a wide range of programming languages, including .NET, Java, PHP, and Python.

Azure Functions: Azure Functions is a serverless computing service that enables developers to run code on-demand without having to manage or provision infrastructure. This makes building event-driven applications that scale dynamically based on demand easy.

Azure SQL Database: Azure SQL Database is a fully managed relational database service that provides high availability, automatic backups, and automatic scaling. It supports the Microsoft SQL Server engine and open-source databases like MySQL and PostgreSQL.

Azure Cosmos DB: Azure Cosmos DB is a globally distributed, multi-model database service that provides high availability, low latency, and automatic scaling. It supports a wide range of NoSQL data models, including document, graph, key-value, and column-family.

Azure Kubernetes Service (AKS): AKS is a managed Kubernetes service that allows organizations to deploy and manage containerized applications at scale. AKS provides built-in integration with Azure services like Azure Container Registry and Azure Monitor.

Azure DevOps: Azure DevOps is a comprehensive set of tools that allows organizations to manage their entire software development lifecycle, from planning and coding to building, testing, and deployment. It includes features like **continuous integration/continuous deployment** (**CI/CD**), agile project management, and automated testing.

Overall, Azure provides a wide range of cloud offerings that enable organizations to build and deploy applications and services quickly and easily, with high scalability, reliability, and security levels.

Benefits of using Azure Cloud for development

Azure provides many offerings, making **software development life cycle (SDLC)** processes agile and efficient. There are several benefits of using Azure Cloud for development:

- **Scalability**: Azure can scale up or down resources as needed, which can help developers avoid overprovisioning or underprovisioning resources. Auto-scaling can achieve this scalability, allowing resources to scale automatically based on demand.
- **Cost savings**: With Azure, developers only pay for the resources they use, which can help organizations save on infrastructure costs. Azure also offers features like reserved instances, which can help organizations save up to 72% compared to pay-as-you-go pricing.
- **Availability**: Azure provides high availability and disaster recovery options, which can help developers ensure that their applications are always available to end-users. Azure provides global distribution, redundancy, and automatic failover capabilities to ensure that applications are available during a failure.

- **Security**: Azure provides built-in security features like identity management, access control, and threat detection, which can help developers ensure their applications are secure. Azure also complies with industry standards and regulations, including **International Organization for Standardization (ISO)**, **Health Insurance Portability and Accountability Act (HIPAA)**, and **Payment Card Industry Data Security Standard (PCI-DSS)**.
- **Integration**: Azure integrates with many tools and technologies, including popular programming languages like .NET, Java, and Python. Azure also integrates with other Microsoft services like Visual Studio, Azure DevOps, and Power BI.
- **Flexibility**: Azure provides a wide range of cloud offerings, including IaaS, PaaS, and SaaS, which can help developers choose the best service for their applications. Azure also supports various open-source technologies, including Linux and other popular open-source software.

Overall, Azure provides a wide range of benefits that can help developers build, deploy, and manage applications and services in the cloud with high levels of scalability, reliability, and security.

Conclusion

Moving to the cloud provides all organizations of any shape and size the speed and agility to move faster and be innovative at scale. Cloud computing is changing how different teams collaborate, communicate, and be relevant in today's fast-changing digital world.

Suppose any organization plans to move to the cloud. In that case, its think tank should first focus on how this journey can help transform the business by providing the proper agility and speed to the company instead of focusing on the cloud technicalities and implementation complexities involved.

Now, you have a basic understanding of cloud computing and can see its journey. As the field of cloud computing is continually evolving, it is always beneficial to keep up with the latest updates.

Before moving to the next chapter, we should consider the questions below, which will provide a good starting point and quick knowledge check about cloud-native development principles and how Azure Cloud can support cloud-native development.

In the next chapter, we will discuss the core services the Azure cloud platform provides that help develop cloud-native applications.

Questions

1. What is cloud-native development, and how does it differ from traditional application development?

2. What are the benefits of adopting a cloud-native approach in application development?

3. How does Azure Cloud support cloud-native development?

4. What are SaaS, PaaS, and IaaS in cloud computing?

5. What are the core components of cloud-native architecture, and how are they implemented in Azure Cloud?

6. What are containers, and how do they contribute to cloud-native applications on Azure?

7. Can you explain the concept of microservices and how they are utilized in Azure Cloud?

8. What are some best practices for designing and developing cloud-native applications on Azure?

Join our book's Discord space

Join the book's Discord Workspace for Latest updates, Offers, Tech happenings around the world, New Release and Sessions with the Authors:

https://discord.bpbonline.com

CHAPTER 2
Azure Services for Cloud Native Development

Introduction

Microsoft Azure provides a wide range of services for cloud-native development. In this chapter, we will cover the primary services being used for cloud-native development one by one. We will start with **Azure Compute Services,** a set of cloud-based services from Microsoft Azure that allow users to run and manage applications and workloads in the cloud. These services provide scalable and flexible computing resources that can be quickly provisioned and operated, enabling users to focus on developing their applications without worrying about infrastructure management. Next, we will go through the Azure **Identity and Access Management (IAM)** and **Azure Active Directory (AAD)** services; both are cloud-based identity management services from Microsoft Azure. While both services are focused on identity management, they serve different purposes. IAM provides an access control framework to protect the data and resources. More than network firewalls and perimeters are required in a cloud environment to provide security. Developing a secure application is one of the core motivations for using the Azure cloud. Azure App Service offers a set of tools to help with it. **Azure App Service** is a fully managed platform for building and deploying web applications, while Azure functions provide serverless computing power. Azure WebJobs is a feature of Azure App Service that enables developers to run background processing tasks on-demand or on a schedule. In modern application architecture, new platforms are being built using event-driven architecture. Azure Cloud provides services for an application that handles large volumes of event data.

Azure Event Hubs is a cloud-based event streaming platform and messaging service that allows developers to build and process real-time data streaming applications to process and analyze large amounts of data generated from various sources, such as IoT devices, social media platforms, and other distributed systems. **Azure Service Bus** is a messaging service that allows applications and services to communicate with each other through the exchange of messages. Service Bus supports queue and topic-based messaging patterns and provides features such as message filtering, message sessions, and dead-letter queues. Service Bus is ideal for scenarios that require reliable messaging, guaranteed message delivery, and transactional processing. On the other hand, Azure Event Grid is an event-driven service that provides a publish/subscribe messaging pattern for real-time event processing. Event Grid allows developers to build event-driven architectures by reacting to events generated by various Azure services or custom events. The Azure Mobile Apps service supports mobile app development, which provides a more advanced and flexible solution for building mobile app backends in the cloud. Two other essential services that are important to note. First, **Azure Service Fabric** is a distributed systems platform from Microsoft Azure that simplifies the development, deployment, and management of microservices-based applications. It provides a reliable and scalable infrastructure for building and running cloud-native applications. Second, **Azure SignalR** Service provides a scalable and reliable platform for building real-time web applications using the SignalR library. It simplifies adding real-time functionality to web applications by providing a managed service for hosting and managing the SignalR hub.

Structure

In this chapter, we will go through the following topics in detail, and these services are very foundational in providing services to develop cloud-native solutions:

- Azure Compute
- Azure Identity and Access Management
- Azure Azure Active Directory
- Azure Functions
- Azure Event Hubs
- Azure Service Bus
- Azure Event Grid
- Azure Logic Apps
- Azure Apps Service
- Azure Mobile Services
- Azure Web Jobs

- Azure Service Fabric
- Azure SingalR

Objectives

This chapter aims to provide the details of different cloud services offered by Azure. It starts with selecting the computing system on which services will be hosted. After that, we will go through the other services for building functional services like Azure Functions. We will learn to secure the services by implementing RBAC using Azure IAM and Azure AD.

Different event-capturing services like EventHub, EventGrid, and Azure ServiceBus are the foundational components of event-driven architecture. There are other services like Azure Mobile Services for building mobile platforms and web jobs for developing batch jobs.

Azure Compute

Azure is a cloud computing platform created by Microsoft that offers a wide range of services, including computing services. Here are some of the computing services provided by Azure:

Virtual machines (VM): Azure provides VMs that allow you to run a wide range of operating systems, including Windows and Linux. You can choose from various sizes and configurations to meet your needs.

Azure Virtual Machines is a cloud-based service provided by Microsoft Azure that enables you to create and manage virtual machines in the cloud. It provides a scalable and flexible platform for running applications and services, allowing you to deploy and manage virtual machines easily for a wide range of use cases.

Here are some key features of Azure Virtual Machines:

Type	Sizes	Description
General purpose	B, Dsv3, Dv3, Dasv4, Dav4, DSv2, Dv2, Av2, DC, DCv2, Dpdsv5, Dpldsv5, Dpsv5, Dplsv5, Dv4, Dsv4, Ddv4, Ddsv4, Dv5, Dsv5, Ddv5, Ddsv5, Dasv5, Dadsv5	Balanced CPU-to-memory ratio. Ideal for testing and development, small to medium databases, and low to medium traffic web servers.

Type	Sizes	Description
Compute optimized	F, Fs, Fsv2, FX	High CPU-to-memory ratio. Good for medium-traffic web servers, network appliances, batch processes, and application servers.
Memory optimized	Esv3, Ev3, Easv4, Eav4, Epdsv5, Epsv5, Ev4, Esv4, Edv4, Edsv4, Ev5, Esv5, Edv5, Edsv5, Easv5, Eadsv5, Mv2, M, DSv2, Dv2	High memory-to-CPU ratio. Great for relational database servers, medium to large caches, and in-memory analytics.
Storage optimized	Lsv2, Lsv3, Lasv3	High disk throughput and IO ideal for Big Data, SQL, NoSQL databases, data warehousing and large transactional databases.
GPU	NC, NCv2, NCv3, NCasT4_v3, ND, NDv2, NV, NVv3, NVv4, NDasrA100_v4, NDm_A100_v4	Specialized virtual machines targeted for heavy graphic rendering and video editing, as well as model training and inferencing (ND) with deep learning. Available with single or multiple GPUs.
High performance compute	HB, HBv2, HBv3, HBv4, HC, HX	Azure cloud's fastest and most powerful CPU virtual machines with optional high-throughput network interfaces (RDMA).

Table 2.1: Type of virtual machines

Multiple operating system support: Azure Virtual Machines support various operating systems, including Windows, Linux, and FreeBSD.

Scalability: Azure Virtual Machines can scale up or down based on demand, allowing you to adjust to changing workload requirements quickly.

High availability: Azure Virtual Machines provide high availability and redundancy features, including load balancing and automatic failover.

Security and compliance: Azure Virtual Machines provide built-in security and compliance features, including network security groups and encryption at rest.

Easy management and monitoring: Azure Virtual Machines provides easy management and monitoring tools, including the Azure Portal, Azure PowerShell, and Azure CLI.

Integration with other Azure services: Azure Virtual Machines integrates seamlessly with other Azure services, including Azure Storage and Azure Networking.

Azure Kubernetes Service (AKS): AKS is a managed Kubernetes service that allows you to deploy, manage, and scale containerized applications in the cloud.

Azure Functions: Azure Functions is a serverless computing service that allows you to run event-driven code without worrying about the underlying infrastructure.

Azure Batch: Azure Batch is a managed service that allows you to run large-scale parallel and **high-performance computing** (**HPC**) applications in the cloud.

Azure Container Instances (ACI): ACI is a serverless container platform that allows you to run containers in the cloud without managing the underlying infrastructure.

These are just a few of the computing services provided by Azure. Depending on your specific needs, many other services and features are available to help you build and run your applications in the cloud.

Azure Identity and Access Management

Azure **Identity and Access Management** (**IAM**) is a set of tools and services in the Azure platform that enable you to manage identities and control access to resources in your Azure environment.

Access management is a two-step process to access the services and data on the cloud called authentication and authorization. Authentication tells who can access the services and data, while authorization ensures what can be accessed.

Here are some key features of Azure IAM:

Role-based access control (RBAC): RBAC is a permissions model allowing users and groups access to Azure resources based on their roles and responsibilities.

Conditional Access: Conditional Access allows you to apply access policies based on conditions like user location, device state, and risk levels to ensure that only authorized users can access resources.

Multi-factor authentication (MFA): MFA provides an extra layer of security by requiring users to provide additional verification when signing in.

Azure Privileged Identity Management (PIM): PIM provides just-in-time access to privileged roles in Azure, allowing users to activate their access only when needed and reducing the risk of misuse.

Azure AD Connect: Azure AD Connect is a tool that synchronizes on-premises directories with Azure AD, enabling a hybrid identity solution.

Azure IAM can ensure that your organization's resources are secure and accessible only to authorized users.

Azure Azure Active Directory

Azure Azure Active Directory (AAD) is a cloud-based identity and access management service with a centralized location to manage identities, authentication, and authorization for cloud and on-premises resources. Azure AD supports modern authentication and authorization scenarios such as **Single Sign-On (SSO)**, **Multi-factor authentication (MFA)**, Conditional Access, and Identity Protection. Please refer to the following figure:

Figure 2.1: *Azure Active Directory*

Some key features of Azure AD include:

- **Single Sign-On (SSO)**: Azure AD allows users to sign in once and access multiple cloud and on-premises applications without signing in again.

- **Multi-factor authentication (MFA):** Azure AD provides MFA capabilities to add a layer of security to sign-in events.

- **Conditional Access**: This allows administrators to set access policies based on device type, location, user group, and risk level.

- **Application Proxy**: Azure AD Application Proxy allows users to access on-premises web applications without a VPN.

- **Identity Protection**: Azure AD Identity Protection uses machine learning to detect and prevent identity-based attacks, such as password spray and brute force attacks.

- **Self-service password reset**: Azure AD allows users to reset their passwords or unlock their accounts using self-service capabilities, reducing the burden on IT support.

By using Azure AD, organizations can centralize identity management and reduce the risk of security breaches by enforcing access policies and monitoring user activity.

Azure Functions

Azure Functions is a serverless computing service provided by Microsoft Azure that enables developers to build and run event-driven applications and microservices without the need to manage infrastructure. With Azure Functions, developers can create serverless functions that automatically scale on demand to meet workload requirements.

Here are some key features of Azure Functions:

Event-driven computing: Azure Functions can be triggered by many events, including HTTP requests, timer-based events, message queues, etc.

Pay-per-use pricing model: Azure Functions offers a pay-as-you-go pricing model, where you only pay for the time your function executes and the resources consumed.

Multi-language support: Azure Functions supports multiple programming languages, including C#, Java, JavaScript, PowerShell, and Python.

Integration with Azure services: Azure Functions integrates with a wide range of Azure services, including Azure Blob Storage, Azure Event Hubs, Azure Service Bus, and more.

Easy deployment and management: Azure Functions can be easily deployed and managed using Azure Portal, Azure CLI, or Azure DevOps.

Serverless architecture: With Azure Functions, developers do not have to worry about managing servers, operating systems, or infrastructure. This allows developers to focus on building applications and not worry about infrastructure management.

Azure Functions provides a simple and cost-effective way to build and run serverless applications, making it easier for developers to develop and deploy their code.

Azure Event Hubs

Azure Event Hubs is a cloud-based event processing service provided by Microsoft Azure that enables the processing and analyzing of large amounts of event data. It provides an infrastructure where you can design a scalable system that processes millions of data daily, such as capturing the IoT messages from many devices. It is a fully managed service that enables you to ingest, store, and analyze millions of events per second.

Here are some key features of Azure Event Hubs:

- **High-throughput event processing**: Azure Event Hubs is designed for high-throughput event ingestion, processing, and streaming. It can handle millions of events per second and provides low-latency data delivery.

- **Event streaming and data integration**: Azure Event Hubs provides a unified event streaming platform that enables you to integrate with various data sources, including applications, devices, and other services.

- **Scalability and availability**: Azure Event Hubs provide high scalability and availability through multiple data centers and zones, ensuring your data is always available and safe.

- **Easy integration with Azure services**: Azure Event Hubs integrates seamlessly with various Azure services, including Azure Functions, Azure Stream Analytics, and Azure Logic Apps.

- **Security and compliance**: Azure Event Hubs provides robust security and compliance features, including role-based access control, encryption at rest, and in-transit encryption.

- **Real-time data insights**: Azure Event Hubs enables real-time data insights through integration with Azure Stream Analytics, which provides a powerful way to analyze and process data in real-time.

Azure Event Hubs is a powerful event processing service that provides scalability, reliability, and real-time insights, making it an ideal choice for processing and analyzing large amounts of event data; refer to the following figure:

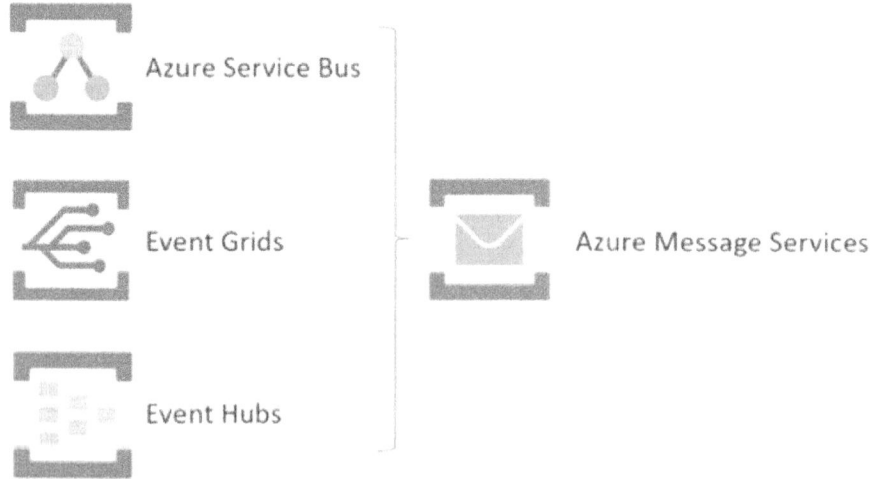

Figure 2.2: Azure Event handling Service Bus, Event Grids, and Event Hubs

Azure Event Grid

Azure Event Grid is a fully managed event routing service provided by Microsoft Azure that simplifies the creation of event-based applications and workflows. It allows you to easily subscribe to and react to events from various sources, including Azure services, third-party SaaS applications, and custom applications. It will enable you to add the filtering logic and rules that can be applied to the messages received and route them further to different services.

Here are some key features of Azure Event Grid:

- **Event-based architecture**: Azure Event Grid is based on an event-driven architecture, where events are generated and consumed by various services and applications. This makes it easy to create and manage event-driven workflows.
- **Multi-cloud support**: Azure Event Grid supports multiple cloud environments, including Azure, AWS, and Google Cloud. This allows you to integrate with services from different cloud providers and create hybrid workflows.
- **Built-in integration with Azure services**: Azure Event Grid provides built-in integration with various Azure services, including Azure Functions, Azure Logic Apps, Azure Automation, and more.
- **Simple event routing**: Azure Event Grid makes it easy to route events to different endpoints, including Azure Functions, Webhooks, and Azure Event Hubs.
- **Scalability and reliability**: Azure Event Grid provides high scalability and reliability through a serverless architecture that automatically scales based on demand.
- **Cost-effective**: Azure Event Grid offers a pay-per-event pricing model, where you only pay for the events you consume, making it a cost-effective solution for event-based workflows.

Azure Event Grid is a powerful event-routing service that simplifies the creation of event-driven applications and workflows, making it an ideal choice for organizations that want to create event-based architectures.

Azure Service Bus

Azure Service Bus is a cloud-based messaging service provided by Microsoft Azure that enables reliable, scalable, and secure communication between applications and services. It provides a fully managed messaging infrastructure that lets you decouple your applications and services, making them more scalable, flexible, and resilient.

Here are some key features of Azure Service Bus:

- **Message queueing**: Azure Service Bus provides capabilities that enable you to send, receive, and process messages reliably and asynchronously.

- **Publish/subscribe messaging**: Azure Service Bus supports the publish/subscribe messaging pattern, where messages can be posted to one or more topics, and subscribers can receive messages from those topics.

- **Message routing**: Azure Service Bus provides powerful message routing capabilities that enable you to route messages based on various criteria, including message properties, content-based routing, and more.

- **Transactional support**: Azure Service Bus supports distributed transactions, enabling you to ensure data consistency and reliability across multiple systems.

- **Security and compliance**: Azure Service Bus provides robust security and compliance features, including encryption at rest and in transit, role-based access control, and compliance with various industry standards.

- **Hybrid connectivity**: Azure Service Bus provides hybrid connectivity capabilities that allow you to connect your on-premises applications and services with cloud-based applications and services.

- **Load balancing**: Azure service bus manages load balancing across competing workers to provide better service reliability.

Azure Service Bus is a powerful messaging service that provides reliable, scalable, and secure communication between applications and services. Its rich feature set makes it an ideal choice for enterprise-level messaging scenarios that require high reliability, scalability, and security.

Azure Logic Apps

Azure Logic Apps is a cloud-based integration and workflow automation service provided by Microsoft Azure. It allows you to create scalable and reliable workflows that integrate with various services within and outside Azure using a visual designer or code-based workflow definitions.

Here are some key features of Azure Logic Apps:

- **Visual designer**: Azure Logic Apps provides a drag-and-drop graphic designer that enables you to create and manage workflows easily without writing code.

- **Built-in connectors**: Azure Logic Apps provides many built-in connectors for various services, including Azure services, Microsoft 365, Salesforce, and more.

- **Custom connectors**: Azure Logic Apps allows you to create custom connectors to integrate with any RESTful API.

- **Serverless architecture**: Azure Logic Apps provides serverless architecture, which means you only pay for what you use, and the service automatically scales to meet demand.

- **Monitoring and diagnostics**: Azure Logic Apps provide built-in monitoring and diagnostics capabilities that allow you to monitor the performance and health of your workflows.

- **Integration with Azure services**: Azure Logic Apps integrates seamlessly with various Azure services, including Azure Event Grid, Azure Service Bus, Azure Functions, and more.

Azure Logic Apps is a powerful workflow automation service that provides a flexible and scalable way to integrate various services and automate workflows. Its visual designer and built-in connectors make it easy to use, while its serverless architecture and integration with Azure services make it a powerful tool for building complex workflows.

Azure Apps Service

Azure App Service is a fully managed **Platform-as-a-Service (PaaS)** offered by Microsoft Azure that enables you to build, deploy, and scale web and mobile applications quickly. It provides a fully managed platform for building, deploying, and scaling web applications and APIs. It provides the components to build and deploy the cloud application. It comes with three pricing tiers: Basic, standard, and premium; based on the chosen pricing tier, Azure will provide the service offered at that level.

Here are some key features of Azure App Service:

- **Multiple languages and frameworks**: Azure App Service supports various programming languages, including .NET, Java, Python, Node.js, and more. It also supports frameworks such as ASP.NET, Spring, Flask, and Express.

- **Scalability and high availability**: Azure App Service provides a scalable and high-availability platform that can automatically scale up or down based on demand.

- **DevOps integration**: Azure App Service provides deep integration with DevOps tools, including Azure DevOps, GitHub, and Visual Studio Team Services.

- **Deployment slots**: Azure App Service allows you to create deployment slots, which enable you to deploy and test new versions of your application before promoting them to production.

- **Security and compliance**: Azure App Service provides built-in security features, including SSL/TLS encryption, OAuth authentication, and role-based access control. It also complies with various industry standards, including HIPAA, ISO 27001, and more.

- **Integration with other Azure services**: Azure App Service integrates seamlessly with other Azure services, including Azure SQL Database, Azure Cosmos DB, Azure Event Grid, and more.

Azure App Service is a powerful platform for building and deploying web and mobile applications. Its support for multiple languages and frameworks, scalability, DevOps integration, and security features make it an ideal choice for organizations of all sizes.

Azure WebJobs

Azure WebJobs is a feature of Azure App Service that allows you to run long-running tasks, such as background processes or scheduled jobs, as part of your web application. It provides an easy way to perform tasks in the background of your web application without requiring you to create a separate application or infrastructure to run these tasks; refer to the following figure:

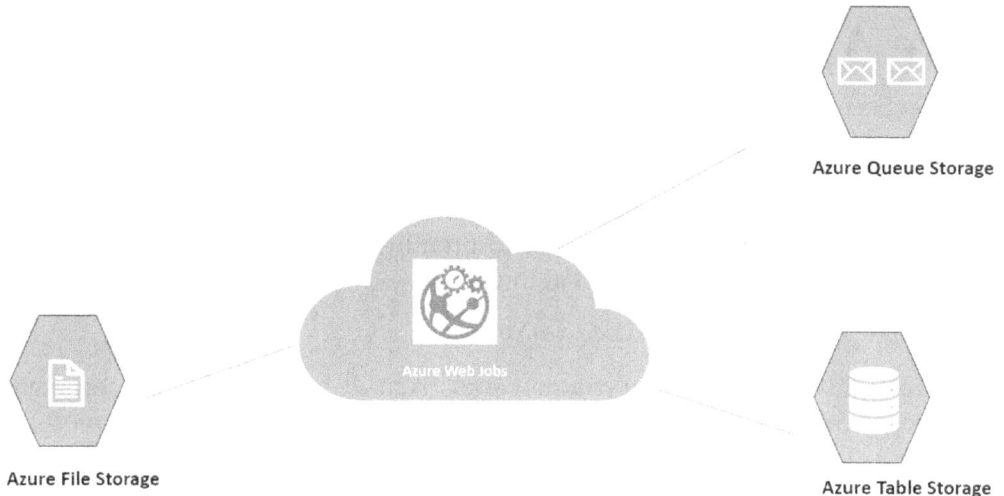

Figure 2.3: Azure WebJobs

Here are some key features of Azure WebJobs:

- **Support for multiple languages and platforms**: Azure WebJobs supports various languages, including .NET, Node.js, Python, PHP, and more.

- **Easy deployment and scaling**: Azure WebJobs can be scaled just like any other Azure App Service, making it easy to manage and scale your background tasks.

- **Integration with Azure Functions**: Azure WebJobs can be integrated with Azure Functions to provide even more flexibility and power for running background tasks.

- **Multiple triggering options**: Azure WebJobs supports numerous triggering options, including time-based triggers, file-based triggers, and message-based triggers.

- **Automatic monitoring and logging**: Azure WebJobs provides automated monitoring and logging, so you can easily monitor the status and health of your background tasks.

- **Integration with Azure App Service**: Azure WebJobs integrates seamlessly with Azure App Service, so you can quickly run your background tasks alongside your web application.

Azure WebJobs is a powerful feature of Azure App Service that allows you to run long-running tasks efficiently as part of your web application. Its support for multiple languages, easy deployment and scaling, and integration with Azure Functions make it an ideal choice for organizations needing background tasks as part of their web applications.

Azure Mobile Services

Azure Mobile Services is a cloud-based service provided by Microsoft Azure that enables you to build and deploy mobile backends for your mobile applications. It provides a scalable and reliable platform for building mobile apps on various platforms, including iOS, Android, and Windows.

Here are some key features of Azure Mobile Services:

- **Easy integration with mobile platforms**: Azure Mobile Services provides easy integration with various mobile platforms, including iOS, Android, and Windows.

- **Scalability and high availability**: Azure Mobile Services provides a scalable and high-availability platform that can automatically scale up or down based on demand.

- **Support for multiple languages**: Azure Mobile Services supports various programming languages, including .NET, Node.js, and Java.

- **Built-in authentication and authorization**: Azure Mobile Services provides built-in authentication and authorization capabilities, including support for social media authentication, Active Directory, and more.

- **Integration with Azure services**: Azure Mobile Services integrates seamlessly with various Azure services, including Azure Storage, Azure Notification Hubs, and Azure Cosmos DB.

- **Monitoring and diagnostics**: Azure Mobile Services provides built-in monitoring and diagnostics capabilities that allow you to monitor the performance and health of your mobile backend.

Azure Mobile Services is a powerful platform for building and deploying mobile backends. Its easy integration with mobile platforms, scalability, built-in authentication and authorization, and integration with other Azure services make it an ideal choice for organizations that must build and deploy mobile apps quickly and easily.

Azure Service Fabric

Azure Service Fabric is a distributed systems platform offered by Microsoft Azure that enables you to build, deploy, and manage highly scalable and reliable microservices-based applications. It provides a flexible and robust platform for building modern cloud applications that run on-premises or in the cloud. Azure Service Fabric is shown in the following figure:

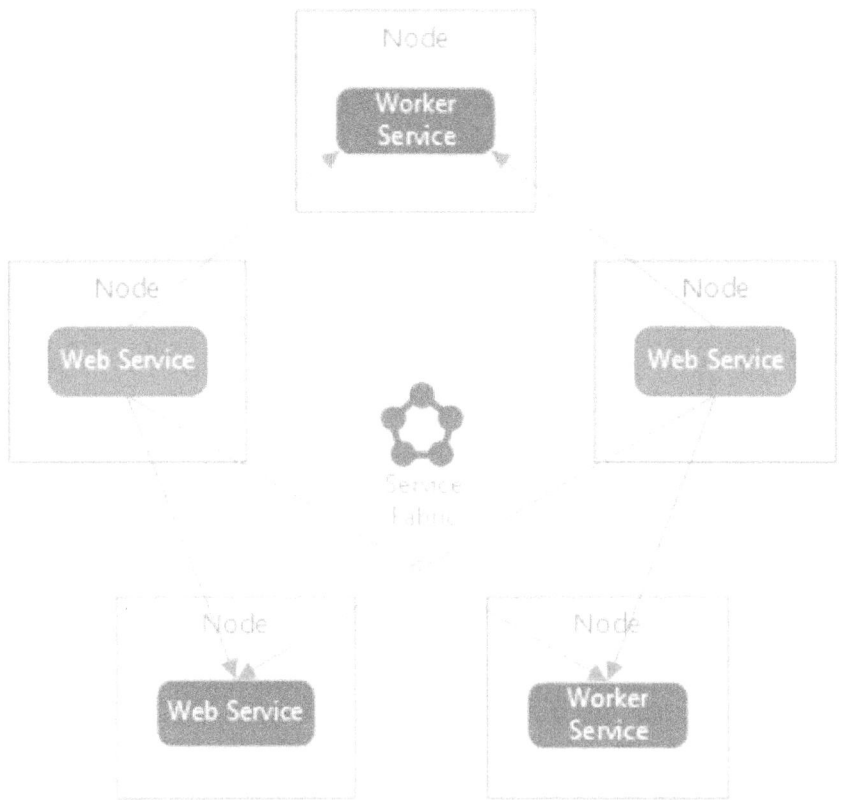

Figure 2.4: Azure Service Fabric

Here are some key features of Azure Service Fabric:

- **Microservices architecture**: Azure Service Fabric is designed to support a microservices architecture, which enables you to break down your application into smaller, independently deployable, and scalable components.

- **Scalability and high availability**: Azure Service Fabric provides a scalable and high-availability platform that can automatically scale up or down based on demand.

- **Support for multiple programming languages**: Azure Service Fabric supports various programming languages, including .NET, Java, and C++.

- **Built-in diagnostics and monitoring**: Azure Service Fabric provides built-in diagnostics and monitoring capabilities that allow you to monitor the health and performance of your microservices.

- **Container support**: Azure Service Fabric supports Docker containers, enabling you to deploy and manage containerized applications.

- **Integration with other Azure services**: Azure Service Fabric integrates seamlessly with other Azure services, including Azure Cosmos DB, Azure Event Hubs, and Azure IoT Hub.

Azure Service Fabric is a powerful platform for building and deploying highly scalable and reliable microservices-based applications. Its support for microservices architecture, scalability, multiple programming languages, built-in diagnostics and monitoring, container support, and integration with other Azure services make it an ideal choice for organizations that need to build modern cloud applications that can run on-premises or in the cloud.

Azure SignalR

Azure SignalR is a cloud-based service by Microsoft Azure that enables you to build real-time web applications using web sockets. It provides a scalable and reliable platform for building applications that require real-time communication and messaging between clients and servers; Azure SignalR is shown in the following figure:

Figure 2.5: Azure SignalR

Here are some key features of Azure SignalR:

- **Support for multiple client platforms**: Azure SignalR supports various platforms, including web browsers, mobile devices, and desktop applications.

- **Real-time communication**: Azure SignalR enables real-time communication between clients and servers, allowing faster response times and improved user experiences.

- **Scalability and high availability**: Azure SignalR provides a scalable and high-availability platform that can automatically scale up or down based on demand.

- **Security and authentication**: Azure SignalR provides built-in security and authentication capabilities, including OAuth and OpenID Connect support.

- **Integration with Azure services**: Azure SignalR integrates seamlessly with other Azure services, including Azure Functions and Azure App Service.

- **Serverless support**: Azure SignalR supports serverless architectures, allowing you to build applications without worrying about infrastructure.

Azure SignalR is a powerful platform for building real-time web applications that require real-time communication and messaging between clients and servers. Its support for multiple client platforms, real-time communication, scalability and high availability, security and authentication, integration with Azure services, and serverless support make it an ideal choice for organizations that need to build real-time web applications quickly and easily.

Conclusion

Azure provides a wide variety of services for development needs. It provides services for developing, deploying, and monitoring the applications. We discussed those services and their features in detail. Here is the summary for those services:

Azure Computer Services provides a way to build the compute services where we can deploy and run the workloads. Azure App Service is a fully managed platform for building, deploying, and scaling web applications. It supports multiple programming languages and frameworks, such as .NET, Java, Node.js, Python, and more.

Azure Functions is a serverless compute service that enables event-driven, on-demand execution of code in various languages. Azure Logic Apps: Azure Logic Apps provides a visual designer for building workflows and orchestrating business processes. It lets you connect and integrate multiple systems and services using pre-built connectors. Logic Apps supports event-driven architectures and enables seamless integration with SaaS applications, on-premises systems, and other Azure services.

Azure Service Bus is a messaging service that enables reliable and secure communication between distributed applications. It supports publish/subscribe and message queue patterns, allowing decoupled and asynchronous communication. Service Bus provides features like message ordering, duplicate detection, and dead-lettering for complex messaging scenarios. Azure Event Grid is an event service that simplifies building event-driven architectures. It allows you to route events from Azure services and custom sources to event handlers or endpoints. Event Grid supports a publish/subscribe model and integrates with Azure Functions, Logic Apps, and Azure Event Hubs.

These Azure services provide developers with powerful tools and capabilities for building cloud-native applications. They enable scalability, flexibility, and integration with other Azure services, allowing developers to focus on application logic and functionality while leveraging Azure's managed services and infrastructure.

In the next chapter, we will discuss the different database services Azure Cloud provides, which are very important because databases are a critical component of any organization.

Questions

We have gone through many services in this chapter, like how to create virtual machines depending on the need. Let us do a quick knowledge check.

1. What is Microsoft Azure, and what does it offer?
2. How does Azure compare to other cloud providers like AWS and Google Cloud?
3. What are Azure Virtual Machines, and how do they work?
4. Can I use my custom operating system image on Azure VMs?
5. What are Azure App Services, and how do they differ from virtual machines?
6. How does Azure Active Directory work, and what is its role in Azure services?
7. What is Azure IAM, and how is it used to secure Azure services?

Join our book's Discord space

Join the book's Discord Workspace for Latest updates, Offers, Tech happenings around the world, New Release and Sessions with the Authors:

https://discord.bpbonline.com

CHAPTER 3
Data Storage Services on Azure Cloud

Introduction

In the enterprise landscape, various types of data are created for different applications and in different forms. We can classify the data into three large families: structured, unstructured, and semi-structured.

Structure

In this chapter, we will learn the following topics:

- Structured data and normalization forms
- Unstructured data
- Semi-structured data
- Azure data storage services
- Azure SQL Database
- Azure Archive Storage
- Azure Cosmos DB
- Azure Table Storage

- Azure Cache for Redis
- Azure HDInsight
- Azure Files
- Azure Data Lake Storage
- Azure Blob Storage
- Azure Databricks

Objectives

For all the systems we build, the goal of any system being constructed is to understand how data is stored and processed. Most systems produce large-scale data, which can be categorized into relational and non-relational formats. The relational data format is the traditional way of managing the data where every data is in a well-defined format and adequately related. Usually, there will be a well-defined schema that will have collections of tables. Every table will have one unique definition for every row, and referential keys will be defined for other tables. Table relations will follow normalization forms, mainly in 3rd standard form, which we will discuss later in this chapter.

Non-relational data can be defined in two formats: semi-structured and unstructured. Semi-structured data is data where we have at least some labels that can be associated with it. One of the examples is the JSON payload data, where every JSON payload will have defined attributes. Unstructured data is like device log files and images, which have data but do not have associated labels. A lot of effort goes into determining the labels for this data to be used after the processing.

Most enterprises also build a data lake where all the systems dump their data for analytics. Azure also provides services that extract insights from all these lakes, which helps organizations make the right business decisions. We also need to build data pipelines to connect all these data sources and control the flow of the information.

To manage the data at the enterprise level, we must decide what types of machines or computing devices we need to support the systems effectively.

Structured data and normalization forms

Structured data is organized and formatted in a predefined manner and typically stored in fixed fields within a database or spreadsheet. It follows a specific data model and has a well-defined schema, which means that the structure and format of the data are known in advance. Structured data is typically organized into rows and columns, making it easy to search and analyze. Examples of structured data include transactional data in a relational database, spreadsheets with tabular data, and data represented in XML or JSON with a defined structure. This is the classical way of organizing the data, where we group the data into object entities and associate properties and then try to establish the entity relationships in the form of **has-a** and **is-a**. The inheritance relationship between tables can shown as is-a relationship. For example, if a Car is a parent object, we can say that *Honda is a car*. Similarly, a relationship shows the association of the objects; one example is that the class has students.

Another essential property of relational databases is the ACID properties, which are the most critical part of the database. ACID stands for **atomicity**, **consistency**, **isolation**, and **durability**:

- **Atomicity**: Atomicity is related to transactions. If a transaction commits the data in four tables, atomicity ensures that all four tables will be updated or none. This update to the database is called a transaction, and it either commits or aborts.

- **Consistency**: It ensures that any changes to values are consistent with changes to other values in the same instance.

- **Isolation**: Isolation is needed when concurrent transactions happen, and the database must ensure that every transaction occurs in an isolated context to avoid impacting the other transaction.

- **Durability**: Maintaining updates of committed transactions is essential. These updates must always be recovered. The ACID property of durability addresses this need. Durability refers to the ability of the system to recover committed transaction updates if either the system or the storage media fails.

Another essential property of the relational database is the normalization forms. The database normalization forms, also known as standard forms, are guidelines that help ensure the efficiency, integrity, and flexibility of a relational database. Normalization involves breaking down a database schema into smaller, well-structured tables that minimize data redundancy and dependency. The most commonly recognized normalization forms are as follows:

- **First normal form (1NF)**: It eliminates duplicate data and ensures atomicity. Each column in a table contains only atomic values (indivisible values) and it cannot have multiple values. We define each table's primary key and ensure all the associated columns are linked with that key. It provides that each row in a table is unique.

- **Second normal form (2NF)**: For any data to be in the second normal form, we must ensure that data is already in the first normal form. All no-key attributes depend on the primary key, ensuring data is appropriately structured and eliminating partial discrepancies. We need to separate the properties of all entities in different tables so that there are no repeat rows.

- **Third normal form (3NF)**: For data to be in third normal form, ensure that it meets the requirements of the 2NF. This eliminates transitive discrepancies, ensuring that data is not redundantly stored. In this form, no non-key attribute should depend on another non-key attribute.

- **Boyce-Codd normal form (BCNF)**: This eliminates all non-trivial functional discrepancies and meets the requirements of 3NF. Every determinant (attribute that determines the values of other attributes) is a candidate key.
- **Fourth normal form (4NF)**: This eliminates multi-valued discrepancies and meets the requirements of BCNF. No table should have more than one multi-valued dependency.
- **Fifth normal form (5NF)**: This eliminates joint discrepancies and meets the requirements of 4NF. The candidate keys imply all common dependencies.

There are additional normal forms beyond 5NF, such as **domain-key normal form (DK/NF)**, **sixth normal form (6NF)**, and so on. These higher normal forms address more specialized and complex scenarios and are commonly less encountered in practice:

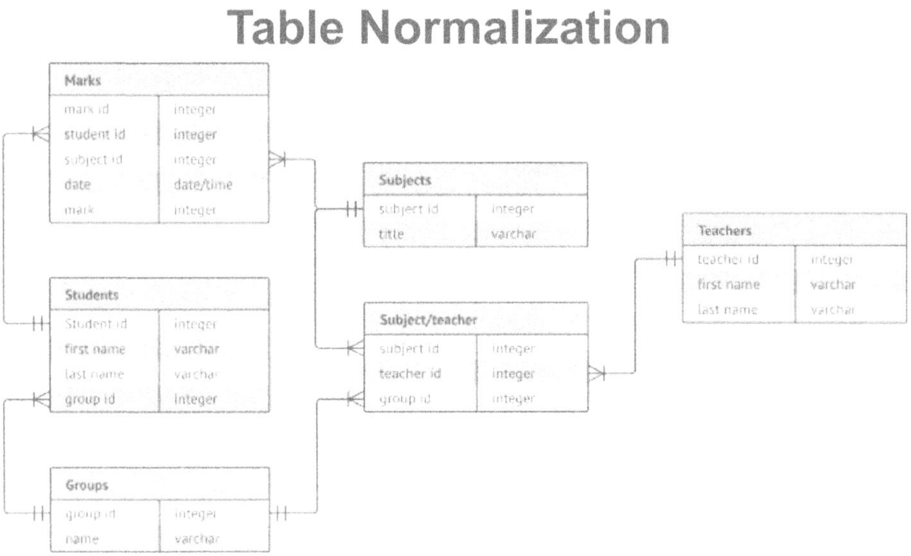

Table Normalization

Figure 3.1: Depiction of normalization

It is important to note that normalization is not always a strict requirement and can depend on the specific needs and characteristics of the data and the database system in use. Over-normalization can lead to increased complexity and decreased performance, so balancing normalization and denormalization is often necessary to optimize database design.

Unstructured data

Unstructured data refers to data that does not have a predefined or organized format. It does not follow a specific data model or have a predetermined schema. Unstructured data is typically human-generated and often found in text documents, emails, social media posts, audio files, video files, images, etc. Unlike structured data, unstructured data does not fit neatly into rows and columns. It is usually free-form and lacks a standardized format, making it challenging to analyze using traditional methods.

Examples of unstructured data include emails, social media posts, customer reviews, audio recordings, video files, sensor data, and documents like PDFs or Word files.

Semi-structured data

Semi-structured data lies between structured and unstructured data. It has some organizational structure but does not conform to a strict schema. It contains tags, markers, and other indicators that provide some level of organization and make it partially searchable and analyzable.

Examples of semi-structured data include data represented in XML or JSON files, log files, web pages, and documents with defined sections and headers.

Note: The distinction between structured, semi-structured, and unstructured data is not always black and white. Data can exist on a spectrum, with varying degrees of structure and organization. Additionally, data can be transformed from unstructured to structured or vice versa through data processing and extraction techniques.

Azure data storage services

Data storage is a critical aspect of cloud computing, and Microsoft Azure offers a wide range of data storage services that cater to different needs and requirements. This segment will provide an overview of the various data storage services available on the Azure cloud platform, including Azure Storage, Azure Disk Storage, Azure Data Lake Storage, Azure Database Services, and Azure Backup and Site Recovery.

Microsoft Azure Storage is a cloud storage solution that provides highly available, massively scalable, durable, and secure storage for various data objects in the cloud. Azure Storage data objects are accessible from anywhere worldwide over HTTP or HTTPS via a REST API. Azure Storage also offers client libraries for developers building applications or services with .NET, Java, Python, JavaScript, C++, and Go1. Developers and IT professionals can use Azure PowerShell and Azure CLI to write scripts for data management or configuration tasks. The Azure portal and Azure Storage Explorer provide user-interface tools for interacting with Azure Storage.

Azure provides various data storage services to help organizations manage their data efficiently. Organizations can choose the service that best fits their requirements and budget. Some of the data storage services offered by Azure are as follows:

- **Azure Blob Storage**: Blob storage stores unstructured data such as text, images, videos, and audio files. It is highly scalable and can handle large amounts of data. Blob storage also offers various tiers to help organizations optimize storage costs.

- **Azure Files**: Azure Files is a fully managed file share service in the cloud, which allows organizations to create SMB file shares that can be accessed from anywhere. It provides snapshots, encryption, and backup to protect data.

- **Azure Data Lake Storage**: Azure Data Lake Storage is a scalable and secure data repository for big data analytics workloads. It allows organizations to store and analyze large amounts of data in various formats like text, images, and videos.

- **Azure Cosmos DB**: Cosmos DB is a globally distributed, multi-model database service that supports multiple data models, including document, key-value, graph, and column family. It provides high availability, low latency, and automatic scaling to ensure consistent performance.

- **Azure SQL Database**: Azure SQL Database is a fully managed relational database service that provides features like automatic tuning, backup, and disaster recovery. It supports various languages and platforms and provides high availability and security.

- **Azure Archive Storage**: Archive Storage is a low-cost, long-term storage solution for infrequently accessed data. It provides features like encryption, compliance, and data retention policies to ensure data protection.

- **Azure Table Storage**: Azure Table Storage is a NoSQL key-value store that can handle large amounts of semi-structured data. It supports automatic scaling and provides features like encryption and replication to ensure data protection.

- **Azure Cache for Redis**: Azure Cache for Redis is an in-memory data store that can handle large amounts of data and provide high throughput and low latency. It supports automatic scaling and can be a caching layer for various applications.

- **Azure HD Insight**: Azure HDInsight is a fully managed cloud service that enables organizations to process big data workloads using popular open-source frameworks like Hadoop, Spark, Hive, and HBase. It provides a fast, cost-effective, and scalable solution for storing, processing, and analyzing large volumes of data:

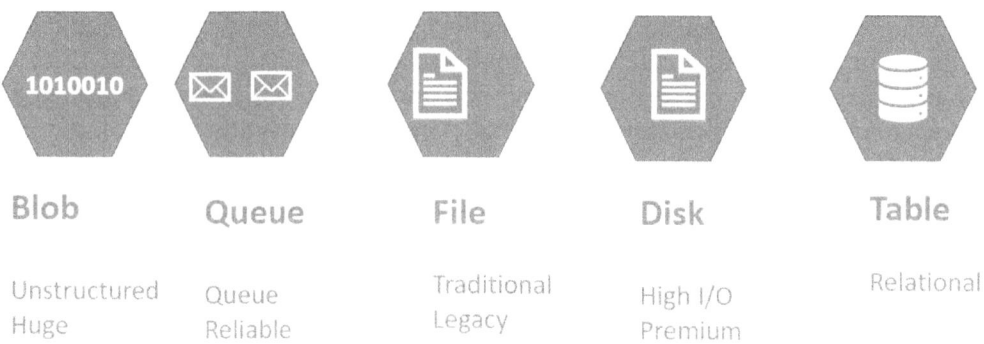

Figure 3.2: Type of data storage techniques

Different use cases for using various Azure Database services are shown in *Figure 3.3*:

	Azure Storage	Azure Cosmos DB	Azure SQL Databases	Azure Databases for PostgreSQL and MySQL	Azure SQL Data Warehouse	Azure Data Lake Store
Relational data			X	X	X	
Non-relational data	X	X				X
Advanced querying		X	X	X	X	X
Large amounts of data					X	X
Optimized for OLAP*					X	X
Optimized for OTLP**	X	X	X	X		
Use Microsoft tools	X	X	X		X	X
Use open-source tools				X		

* OLAP stands for Online Analytical Processing, which is the processing and analyzing of data

Figure 3.3: *Azure data storage types*

Azure SQL Database

Azure SQL Database is a fully managed relational database service with features like automatic tuning, backup, and disaster recovery. It supports various languages and platforms and provides high availability and security:

Figure 3.4: *Azure SQL Database*
Source: azure.microsoft.com

Azure SQL Database is a fully managed **Platform as a Service (PaaS)** relational database service provided by Microsoft Azure with 99.99% availability. It is a cloud-based implementation of Microsoft SQL Server designed to provide high availability, scalability, and security for your applications and data. Azure SQL Database eliminates the need for managing and maintaining the underlying infrastructure, allowing you to focus on developing your applications.

Some key features and benefits of Azure SQL Database are as follows:

- **Managed service**: Azure SQL Database is a fully managed service, which means that Microsoft handles tasks such as hardware provisioning, software patching, and database backups. This frees you from administrative tasks and lets you focus on your application development.

- **Scalability**: Azure SQL Database allows you to quickly scale your database resources up or down based on your application's needs. You can increase or decrease your database's computing power and storage capacity without downtime.

- **High availability**: Azure SQL Database ensures high availability through its built-in redundancy and automatic failover capabilities. It replicates your database to multiple data centers, protecting against hardware failures or data center outages.

- **Security**: The Azure SQL Database offers robust security features to protect your data. It supports features such as rest and transit encryption, database firewall rules, authentication mechanisms, and threat detection.

- **Compatibility**: Azure SQL Database is based on the same SQL Server Database Engine, meaning existing SQL Server applications can easily be migrated to Azure SQL Database without significant changes.

- **Integration with Azure Services**: Azure SQL Database seamlessly integrates with other Azure services such as Azure Active Directory, Azure Data Factory, Azure Logic Apps, and Azure Functions, enabling you to build end-to-end solutions.

- **Cost efficiency**: Azure SQL Database offers flexible pricing options based on your database usage. You can choose between provisioned resources or a serverless option that automatically scales based on demand, helping you optimize costs.

Purchasing models

Cost is one of the critical motivations for the organization to adopt the cloud. Selecting the exemplary service and model is essential for cloud engineers and architects. The technical team assesses the need for CPU, memory, and processing requirements, and based on that, they formulate the requirement for what needs to be purchased. Azure provides two types of purchasing models for the Azure SQL Database.

Azure SQL Database offers the following purchasing models:

- **The vCore-based purchasing model**: vCore is called **virtual core**, which represents a logical CPU unit, and it lets you choose the number of vCores, the amount of memory, and the amount and speed of storage. The vCore-based purchasing model also allows you to use Azure Hybrid Benefit for SQL Server to gain cost savings by leveraging your existing SQL Server licenses.

- **The DTU-based purchasing model**: DTU is called **database transaction unit**, and it offers a blend of compute, memory, and I/O resources in three service tiers to support light to heavy database workloads. Compute sizes within each tier provide a different mix of these resources to which you can add additional storage.

Service tiers

Based on the purchasing model decided on vCore versus DTU, different types of service tiers need to be selected.

Service tiers offered by the vCore-based purchasing model are as follows:

- **The general-purpose service tier** is designed for typical workloads. It offers budget-oriented balanced compute and storage options.

- **The business critical service tier** is designed for OLTP applications with high transaction rates and low latency I/O requirements. It offers the most increased resilience to failures by using several isolated replicas.

- **The Hyperscale service tier** is designed for most business workloads. Hyperscale provides excellent flexibility and high performance with independently scalable compute and storage resources. It offers higher resilience to failures by allowing the configuration of more than one isolated database replica.

Service tiers offered by the DTU-based purchasing model are as follows:

The Standard service tier is designed for typical workloads. It offers budget-oriented balanced compute and storage options.

Compute tiers

The vCore-based purchasing model provides two different compute tiers for Azure SQL Database, the provisioned compute tier and the serverless compute tier. The DTU-based purchasing model offers just the provisioned compute tier.

The provisioned compute tier provides a specific amount of compute resources that are continuously provisioned independent of workload activity and bills for the amount of compute provisioned at a fixed price per hour.

The serverless compute tier automatically scales compute resources based on workload activity and bills for the computing used per second. The serverless compute tier is generally available in the general-purpose service tier and is currently in preview in the Hyperscale service tier.

Azure SQL Database provides different deployment options, including single databases, elastic pools for managing multiple databases with varying workloads, and managed instances for more advanced migration scenarios. It also supports various deployment models, such as the general-purpose, memory-optimized, and business-critical, each tailored for different performance and feature requirements. A single database represents a fully managed, isolated database. You might use this option if modern cloud applications and microservices need a single reliable data source. A single database is similar to a contained database in the SQL Server Database engine. An elastic pool is a collection of single databases with shared resources, such as CPU or memory. Single databases can be moved into and out of an elastic pool.

Azure SQL Database is a powerful and flexible solution for hosting your relational databases in the Azure cloud, providing the scalability, availability, security, and manageability needed to support your applications and data.

Azure Archive Storage

Azure Archive Storage is a solution provided by Microsoft Azure that is designed for long-term data retention at a low cost. It is suitable for scenarios where data needs to be stored for a long time but accessed infrequently:

Figure 3.5: *Azure Archive Storage*
Source: azure.microsoft.com

Some key features of Azure Archive Storage are as follows:

- **Cost-effective**: Azure Archive Storage is a low-cost storage option compared to other storage tiers in Azure. It offers significant savings for rarely accessed data but still requires long-term retention.

- **Data durability**: Azure Archive Storage provides high durability for your data. It replicates your data across multiple Azure data centers to ensure data resiliency and protection against hardware failures.

- **Long-term retention**: It is optimized for long-term data retention, typically for data accessed less than once a month. Examples of suitable use cases include compliance data, regulatory backups, archival data, and large data sets for research purposes.

- **Access latency**: Retrieving data from Azure Archive Storage has higher latency than other storage tiers. The retrieval time can range from hours to several minutes, depending on the specific retrieval method used.

- **Tiering and lifecycle management**: Azure Archive Storage integrates with Azure Blob Storage and supports tiering and lifecycle management features. You can use lifecycle policies to automatically transition data from hot or cool tiers to the archive tier based on defined rules and policies.

- **Security and compliance**: Azure Archive Storage provides security features such as encryption at rest and in transit. It also integrates with Azure Active Directory for authentication and offers granular access control through **shared access signatures (SAS)** or Azure **role-based access control (RBAC)**. It helps meet regulatory compliance requirements for data storage and management.

- **Scalability**: Azure Archive Storage is a highly scalable solution that allows you to store petabytes of data. You can quickly scale up or down based on your storage requirements without downtime.

It is important to note that while Azure Archive Storage offers cost-effective long-term retention, it is not designed for frequent or immediate access to data. If you anticipate the need for frequent access, consider other Azure Storage options like Azure Blob Storage or Hot/Cool tiers. Azure Archive Storage can be accessed programmatically using Azure Storage REST APIs, Azure PowerShell cmdlets, Azure CLI, or through client libraries in various programming languages.

Overall, Azure Archive Storage is a cost-effective and reliable solution for storing large volumes of data that require long-term retention and infrequent access. It helps organizations meet compliance requirements, optimize costs, and efficiently manage their data over time.

Azure Cosmos DB

Azure Cosmos DB is a globally distributed, multi-model database service provided by Microsoft Azure. It is designed to provide low latency, elastic scalability, and high availability for modern, cloud-native applications:

Figure 3.6: Azure Cosmos Database
Source: azure.microsoft.com

Some key features of Azure Cosmos DB are as follows:

- **Globally distributed**: Azure Cosmos DB enables you to replicate and distribute your data across multiple Azure regions worldwide. This global distribution ensures low-latency access to data for users in different geographic locations, improves availability, and provides resilience against regional outages.

- **Multi-model database**: Azure Cosmos DB supports multiple data models, including document, key-value, graph, columnar, and table, allowing you to choose the most appropriate model for your application's data. This flexibility enables you to build diverse and complex applications using a single database service.

- **Scalability**: Azure Cosmos DB provides horizontal scalability by automatically partitioning your data across multiple physical partitions. This allows your application to scale seamlessly to handle increasing workloads without any manual intervention or downtime.

- **Low-latency access**: Azure Cosmos DB offers single-digit millisecond read and write latencies globally. It achieves this by utilizing multi-region replication and employing technologies like automatic indexing, SSD storage, and a highly optimized query execution engine.

- **SLA-backed availability**: Azure Cosmos DB guarantees high availability with comprehensive **Service Level Agreements (SLAs)**. It provides 99.999% uptime for both read and write operations, ensuring that your applications are always accessible to users.

- **Consistency models**: Azure Cosmos DB supports various consistency models, including robust and bounded staleness, session, consistent prefix, and eventual consistency. This allows you to choose the appropriate consistency level based on your application requirements.

- **Security and compliance**: Azure Cosmos DB provides robust security features to protect your data. It integrates with Azure Active Directory for authentication and authorization. It also supports rest and transit encryption, compliance certifications such as ISO, SOC, and GDPR, and fine-grained access control using role-based access control.

- **Integration and extensibility**: Azure Cosmos DB integrates well with other Azure services, including Azure Functions, Azure Logic Apps, and Azure Synapse Analytics. It also provides SDKs and APIs for popular programming languages, enabling developers to build and interact with their applications easily.

- **Analytical capabilities**: Azure Cosmos DB provides integrated analytical capabilities through the integration with Azure Synapse Link. This allows you to perform real-time analytics on operational data without complex **extract, transform, and load** (**ETL**) processes.

Azure Cosmos DB is widely used for various applications, including e-commerce, gaming, IoT, social media, etc. It offers a flexible, globally distributed, and highly scalable database solution that can meet the demands of modern, data-intensive applications.

Azure Table Storage

Azure Table Storage is a NoSQL key-value store provided by Microsoft Azure. It is a scalable and highly available service designed for storing structured data in tables. Azure Table Storage is a part of the Azure storage service and is suitable for applications that require fast and efficient access to large amounts of data:

Figure 3.7: Azure Table Storage
Source: azure.microsoft.com

Some of the key features and characteristics of Azure Table Storage are as follows:

- **NoSQL key-value store**: Azure Table Storage is a NoSQL database service that stores data in a key-value format. Each data item is identified by a partition key and a row key, which forms a unique primary key together. This allows for fast and efficient data retrieval based on specific keys.

- **Scalability and performance**: Azure Table Storage is designed to scale horizontally to handle large amounts of data and high request rates. It automatically partitions data across multiple storage nodes to ensure performance and throughput. You can quickly scale up or down as per your application needs.

- **Schema-less and flexible**: Azure Table Storage is schema-less, meaning you can store entities with different properties within the same table. You can add or modify properties dynamically without affecting existing data. This flexibility is beneficial when dealing with evolving data structures.

- **Cost-effective**: Azure Table Storage offers a cost-effective solution for storing large amounts of structured data. The storage costs are relatively low compared to other Azure storage services.

- **High availability and durability**: Azure Table Storage replicates data within the same data center and provides geo-replication options to ensure data availability and durability. It automatically handles replication and failover, providing reliable access to your data.

- **Simple RESTful API**: Azure Table Storage can be accessed through a simple RESTful API, making it easy to integrate into applications. SDKs are also available for various programming languages, providing a more convenient programming experience.

- **Limited query capabilities**: Azure Table Storage offers basic querying capabilities, allowing you to filter, project, and order data based on the partition and row keys. However, it does not provide advanced querying features like complex joins or secondary indexes. You may need to use additional services or implement your data processing logic to perform complex queries.

- **Integration with Azure services**: Azure Table Storage seamlessly integrates with other Azure services, such as Azure Functions, Azure Logic Apps, and Azure Data Factory, enabling you to build end-to-end solutions.

Azure Table Storage is suitable for applications that require fast and scalable storage of structured data, such as IoT data, logging data, user profiles, and session management. It provides a cost-effective and flexible solution for managing large-scale data sets.

Azure Cache for Redis

Azure Cache for Redis is a fully managed, in-memory data caching service provided by Microsoft Azure. It is based on the popular open-source Redis database and is designed to improve application performance by storing frequently accessed data in memory:

Figure 3.8: *Azure Cache for Redis*
Source: azure.microsoft.com

Some of the key features and characteristics of Azure Cache for Redis are as follows:

- **In-memory data caching**: Azure Cache for Redis stores data in memory, which enables fast access and reduces the need to fetch data from disk-based storage systems. Caching frequently accessed data significantly improves application performance and reduces latency.

- **Fully managed service**: Azure Cache for Redis is a fully managed service, which means that Microsoft handles tasks such as infrastructure provisioning, setup, patching, and maintenance. This allows developers to focus on application logic rather than managing the underlying Redis infrastructure.

- **High performance**: Redis is known for its high-performance capabilities. Azure Cache for Redis leverages this by providing low-latency data access, high throughput, and high concurrency. It supports various data types, including strings, hashes, lists, and sorted sets, allowing for versatile data caching scenarios.

- **Scalability**: Azure Cache for Redis offers horizontal scalability to handle increasing workloads. You can quickly scale up or down by adjusting the cache size, and the service automatically manages data distribution across multiple cache nodes.

- **Persistence and data durability**: Azure Cache for Redis provides options for persistence, allowing you to persist data to disk for durability. It supports point-in-time snapshots and **append-only file (AOF)** persistence, protecting data against unexpected failures.

- **Advanced caching features**: Azure Cache for Redis offers a rich set of features to enhance caching functionality. These include support for cache expiration, eviction policies, pub/sub messaging, transactions, Lua scripting, and geospatial indexing. These advanced features help to build a highly available, scalable, and efficient cache that is not stale.

Azure HDInsight

Azure HDInsight is a cloud-based big data analytics service provided by Microsoft Azure. It allows you to efficiently process and analyze large volumes of data using popular open-source frameworks such as Apache Hadoop, Apache Spark, Apache Hive, Apache Kafka, and more:

Figure 3.9: Azure HDInsight
Source: azure.microsoft.com

Some of the key features and characteristics of Azure HDInsight are as follows:

- **Fully managed service**: Azure HDInsight is a fully managed service, meaning that Microsoft manages the underlying infrastructure, including provisioning, configuration, and monitoring. This allows you to focus on analyzing your data and deriving insights rather than addressing the infrastructure.

- **Support for open-source frameworks**: Azure HDInsight supports many open-source big data frameworks, including Hadoop, Spark, Hive, HBase, Storm, Kafka, and others. This enables you to use these frameworks' familiar tools and libraries to process and analyze your data.

- **Scalability**: HDInsight provides elastic scalability, allowing you to scale your cluster up or down based on your processing needs. You can easily add or remove nodes to handle varying workloads and optimize resource utilization.

- **Integration with Azure services**: HDInsight seamlessly integrates with other Azure services, such as Azure Storage, Azure Data Lake Storage, Azure Data Factory, Azure Machine Learning, and Power BI. This enables you to build end-to-end data pipelines and leverage the capabilities of these services in conjunction with HDInsight.

- **Security and compliance**: HDInsight provides robust security features to protect your data. It integrates with Azure Active Directory for authentication and supports encryption at rest and in transit. It also helps you meet regulatory compliance requirements such as GDPR, HIPAA, and ISO.

- **Multiple data processing engines**: HDInsight offers a variety of data processing engines, including Hadoop, Spark, and Hive. Each engine has its strengths and is optimized for different use cases. You can choose the appropriate engine based on your specific requirements.

- **Built-in monitoring and management**: HDInsight provides built-in monitoring and management capabilities through the Azure portal, Azure Monitor, and Azure Log Analytics. You can monitor cluster health, performance, and job execution metrics to gain insights into the behavior of your big data workloads.

- **Broad ecosystem and tooling**: HDInsight is compatible with a vast ecosystem of tools and libraries built around the Apache Hadoop and Spark ecosystems. This includes data exploration tools, data integration tools, machine learning frameworks, and visualization tools.

Azure HDInsight is commonly used for various big data analytics scenarios such as batch processing, real-time analytics, machine learning, data exploration, and ETL workflows. It offers a robust and scalable platform to process and derive insights from large volumes of data cost-effectively.

Azure Files

Azure Files is a cloud-based file storage service provided by Microsoft Azure. It offers fully managed file shares accessed from multiple **virtual machines** (**VMs**) and on-premises systems. Azure Files delivers a scalable and highly available solution for storing and sharing files across different platforms and locations:

Figure 3.10: Azure Files
Source: azure.microsoft.com

Some of the key features and characteristics of Azure Files are as follows:

- **Fully managed**: Azure Files is a fully managed service, which means that Microsoft handles the underlying infrastructure, including hardware provisioning, software updates, and maintenance. This allows you to focus on using the file shares without worrying about the backend management tasks.

- **File sharing**: Azure Files allows you to create file shares that can be accessed simultaneously by multiple VMs or on-premises systems. This makes it suitable for shared file storage scenarios, such as centralized application configuration files, user home directories, and collaboration platforms.

- **Standard and premium tiers**: Azure Files offers both traditional and premium tiers. The standard tier provides cost-effective storage for general-purpose file shares. In contrast, the premium tier is optimized for high-performance workloads that require low latency and high **input/output operations per second** (**IOPS**).

- **Support for SMB and NFS protocols**: Azure Files supports the industry-standard **Server Message Block** (**SMB**) protocol, allowing you to mount file shares as network drives on Windows and Linux VMs. It also supports the **Network File System** (**NFS**) protocol, which enables file access from Unix/Linux systems.

- **Data redundancy and high availability**: Azure Files automatically replicates your data within a storage account to provide redundancy and protect against hardware failures. It also offers built-in high availability, ensuring that your file shares are accessible even in the event of a failure in the underlying infrastructure.

- **Scalability**: Azure Files scales seamlessly to meet your storage needs. You can easily increase or decrease the size of your file shares and choose the appropriate performance tier based on your application requirements.

- **Integration with Azure services**: Azure Files integrates well with other Azure services. Azure File Sync can synchronize on-premises file servers with Azure Files, enabling hybrid scenarios. It also integrates with Azure Active Directory for authentication and provides granular access control through **shared access signatures** (**SAS**) and Azure RBAC.

- **Backup and disaster recovery**: Azure Files provide built-in backup and restore capabilities, allowing you to create snapshots of file shares for point-in-time recovery. You can also replicate file shares across Azure regions for disaster recovery purposes.

Azure Files is commonly used in various scenarios, including application data sharing, content management, shared drives, and migrating on-premises file shares to the cloud. It provides a reliable and scalable solution for storing and accessing files from different platforms and locations.

Azure Data Lake Storage

Azure Data Lake Storage is a scalable and secure cloud-based storage service provided by Microsoft Azure. It is designed to handle big data analytics workloads and provides a central repository for storing, processing, and analyzing large volumes of structured and unstructured data:

Figure 3.11: Azure Data Lake Storage
Source: azure.microsoft.com

Some of the key features and characteristics of Azure Data Lake Storage are as follows:

- **Scalability and performance**: Azure Data Lake Storage is built to handle massive data. It offers virtually unlimited storage capacity, allowing you to scale your data lake as your data grows. It provides high throughput and low latency for data access, enabling fast and efficient data processing.

- **Data Lake architecture**: Data Lake Storage follows a hierarchical file system, which means you can organize your data into folders and subfolders. This structure allows for efficient data organization, management, and access control.

- **Unified storage**: Data Lake Storage provides a unified storage experience, enabling you to store and analyze structured, semi-structured, and unstructured data. It supports various data formats such as CSV, JSON, Parquet, Avro, etc. This flexibility allows you to work with different data types in a single storage platform.

- **Integration with big data tools**: Data Lake Storage seamlessly integrates with various Azure big data and analytics services, such as Azure Databricks, Azure HDInsight, Azure Synapse Analytics, and Azure Machine Learning. It enables you to perform complex data processing, analytics, and machine learning tasks on your data using these services.

- **Security and compliance**: Data Lake Storage provides robust security features to protect your data. It integrates with Azure Active Directory for authentication and supports Azure RBAC for fine-grained access control. It also offers encryption at rest and in transit. It also helps meet regulatory compliance requirements with certifications such as GDPR, HIPAA, and ISO.

- **Data Lake Analytics**: Azure Data Lake Storage can be combined with Azure Data Lake Analytics to execute distributed and parallel data processing jobs using U-SQL, a SQL-like language. This allows you to run scalable analytics on large data sets stored in Data Lake Storage without the need for managing and provisioning infrastructure.

- **Data lifecycle management**: Data Lake Storage provides features for managing data lifecycle, including the ability to set expiration policies, automate data retention, and delete or archive data based on defined rules. This helps optimize storage costs and ensures compliance with data retention policies.

- **Data sharing and collaboration**: Data Lake Storage enables easy sharing and collaboration with internal and external users. You can grant granular access permissions to specific data files or folders, control Azure AD user or group-level access, and securely share data with external partners using Azure B2B collaboration.

Azure Data Lake Storage is commonly used in various big data analytics scenarios, such as data exploration, data preparation, data warehousing, machine learning, and real-time analytics. It provides a highly scalable and flexible storage solution for managing and analyzing large volumes of data securely and efficiently.

Azure Blob Storage

Azure Blob Storage is a cloud-based object storage service provided by Microsoft Azure. It is designed to store and manage unstructured data such as text files, images, videos, documents, backups, and logs. Azure Blob Storage offers reliable, scalable, and secure storage for a wide range of applications and use cases:

Figure 3.12: *Azure Blob Storage*
Source: *azure.microsoft.com*

Some of the key features and characteristics of Azure Blob Storage are as follows:

- **Blob storage**: Azure Blob Storage is optimized for storing and accessing large amounts of unstructured data, known as blobs. It provides a simple REST-based API for creating, reading, and updating blobs and managing metadata and properties associated with the blobs.

- **Scalability and durability**: Azure Blob Storage scales horizontally to accommodate growing storage requirements. It automatically handles data replication within a storage account to ensure durability and high availability. You can quickly scale up or down the storage capacity without downtime.

- **Multiple storage tiers**: Azure Blob Storage offers different storage tiers to optimize cost and performance based on your data access patterns. The tiers include Hot, Cool, and Archive. Hot tier provides high-performance storage for frequently accessed data, Cool tier offers lower-cost storage for infrequently accessed data, and Archive tier provides the lowest-cost storage for long-term retention.

- **Blob lifecycle management**: Azure Blob Storage includes blob lifecycle management, which allows you to define rules for automatically transitioning blobs between different storage tiers or deleting them based on age or other criteria. This helps optimize storage costs and automate data lifecycle management.

- **Security and encryption**: Azure Blob Storage ensures the security of your data with features such as encryption at rest and in transit. It supports Azure Active Directory integration for fine-grained access control and authentication. Additionally, you can enable Azure Private Link to access your storage account securely over a private network connection.

- **Integration with Azure services**: Azure Blob Storage seamlessly integrates with other Azure services. It can be used as a data source or destination for services like Azure Functions, Azure Logic Apps, Azure Data Factory, and Azure Stream Analytics. This enables you to build end-to-end data pipelines and perform data processing or analysis on your blobs.

- **Static website hosting**: Azure Blob Storage allows you to host static websites directly from a storage account. You can upload HTML, CSS, JavaScript files, and other static content and make it publicly accessible as a website. This feature helps host simple web applications, static content, or static documentation.

- **Data movement and migration**: Azure Blob Storage provides tools and utilities for efficiently moving data into and out of Blob storage. Azure Data Box and Azure Data Box Edge are physical appliances that can be used to transfer large amounts of data to or from Blob storage securely and quickly.

Azure Blob Storage is widely used for various scenarios, including backup and restore, data archiving, media storage and streaming, content distribution, data lakes, and serving static web content. It offers a reliable and scalable solution for storing and managing unstructured data in the cloud.

Azure Databricks

Azure Databricks is a fast, scalable, and collaborative Apache Spark-based analytics platform provided as a fully managed service on Microsoft Azure. It combines the power of Apache Spark with a simplified and integrated development environment, making it easier for data scientists, data engineers, and analysts to collaborate and build advanced analytics solutions; refer to the following figure:

Figure 3.13: Azure Databricks
Source: azure.microsoft.com

A complete stream processing pipeline is depicted in this reference architecture. There are four stages to this kind of pipeline: Ingested, processed, stored, and analyzed. Reporting the pipeline takes data from two sources, joins related records from each stream, enriches the result, and calculates a real-time average for this reference architecture. The outcomes are kept for later examination:

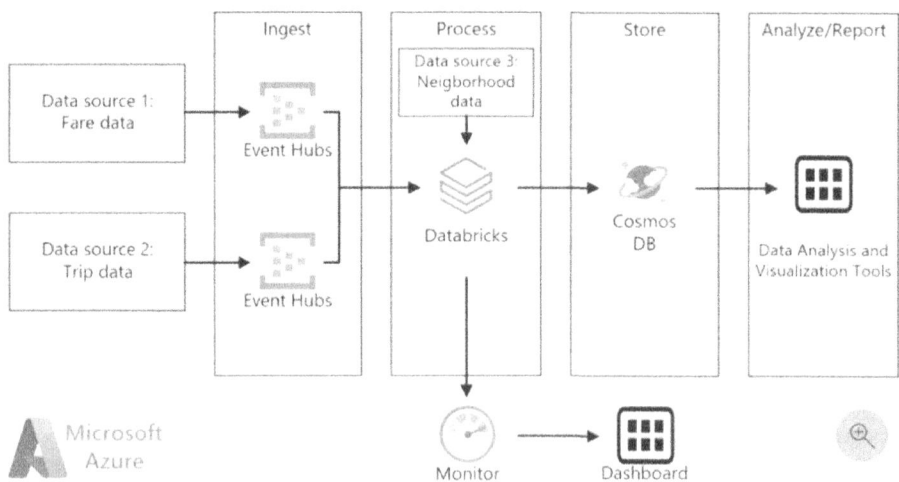

Figure 3.14: Azure Architecture for Databricks
Source: azure.microsoft.com

The parts of the architecture are as follows:

- **Sources of data:** Two data sources in this architecture simultaneously produce data streams. Information about rides and fare information can be found in the first stream. A simulated data generator that reads from a set of static files and sends the data to Event Hubs is included in the reference architecture. In an actual application, taxi cab-mounted devices would serve as the data sources.

- **Sky Blue occasion centers**: Event Hubs is a service for importing events. This architecture utilizes two Event Hub instances, one for each data source. Each data source sends A stream of data to the appropriate event hub.

- **Databricks from Azure**: Databricks is a Microsoft Azure cloud services-optimized analytics platform based on Apache Spark. The taxi ride and fare data are correlated using Databricks, and the enriched correlated data are supplemented with neighborhood data stored in the Databricks file system.

- **DB for Azure Cosmos**: A series of records are written to Azure Cosmos DB for Apache Cassandra as the result of an Azure Databricks job. Azure Cosmos DB for Apache Cassandra is utilized because it allows for the modeling of time series data. By using the two analytics engines that are accessible from your Azure Synapse workspace, Azure Synapse Link for Azure Cosmos DB enables you to run near real-time analytics over operational data in Azure Cosmos DB without affecting the performance or cost of your transactional workloads like Spark Pools and SQL Serverless.

- **Azure Analytics log**: Azure Monitor stores application log data in a Log Analytics workspace. To find problems with the application, Log Analytics queries can be used to examine log messages and analyze and visualize metrics.

The different components and features of Azure Databricks are as follows:

- **Workspace**: The Azure Databricks Workspace is a web-based environment that provides a collaborative platform for teams to manage their notebooks, code, and data. It offers version control, collaboration tools, and project management capabilities.

- **Apache Spark**: Azure Databricks leverages Apache Spark, an open-source distributed computing framework, to perform fast and scalable data processing and analytics. It supports various Spark components, including Spark SQL, Spark Streaming, a **machine learning library** (**MLlib**), and **graph processing** (**GraphX**).

- **Notebooks**: Notebooks are a crucial feature of Azure Databricks, allowing users to create interactive documents that combine code (in languages like Python, Scala, or R), visualizations, and narrative text. Notebooks are used for exploratory data analysis, building and sharing models, and creating production workflows.

- **Cluster management**: Azure Databricks simplifies cluster management by automatically provisioning and managing Apache Spark clusters. Users can easily scale clusters up or down to meet processing requirements, and Azure Databricks optimizes resource utilization based on workload demands.

- **Integrations**: Azure Databricks integrates with various Azure services and tools, including Azure Data Lake Storage, Azure Blob Storage, Azure SQL Database, Azure Cosmos DB, Azure Event Hubs, Azure Machine Learning, and more.

These integrations enable seamless data ingestion, data processing, and model deployment.

- **Collaboration and sharing**: Azure Databricks supports collaboration and sharing of notebooks, allowing multiple users to work together on the same project. It provides version control, revision history, and the ability to share notebooks with others for review or execution.

- **Machine learning and data science**: Azure Databricks provides an environment for building and deploying machine learning models at scale. It offers MLflow for experiment tracking and model management, automated ML for simplified model development, and integration with popular libraries like sci-kit-learn, TensorFlow, and PyTorch.

- **Data engineering**: Azure Databricks enables data engineering workflows, allowing users to build data pipelines, perform ETL operations, and process large volumes of data. It supports data ingestion from various sources, data cleansing, transformations, and data orchestration using Apache Spark.

- **Security and compliance**: Azure Databricks integrates with Azure Active Directory for authentication and role-based access control. It provides data encryption at rest and in transit, network isolation, and compliance with industry standards like SOC 2 Type 2, ISO 27001, HIPAA, and GDPR.

- **Monitoring and optimization**: Azure Databricks offers monitoring and diagnostics capabilities to track job performance, resource usage, and overall cluster health. It integrates with Azure Monitor, enabling monitoring and alerting on critical metrics.

These are some of the key components and features of Azure Databricks that make it a powerful platform for big data analytics, data engineering, and machine learning workloads on Azure.

Conclusion

In this chapter, we have discussed the most fundamental need for building an application, for example, how to store the data. We discussed different normalization forms and saw the different data types, such as structured and non-structure. We also discussed the different types of Azure services and looked at how they handle and store those data types. The following are high-level points that we have discussed so far:

- **Azure Blob Storage**: Azure Blob Storage is a scalable object storage service for storing and retrieving large amounts of unstructured data such as text, images, videos, and documents. Key features include:

- **Azure Files**: Azure Files offers fully managed file shares in the cloud, accessible via the Server Message Block protocol.

- **Azure Tables**: Azure Tables is a NoSQL key-value store for structured data. Integration with Azure Cosmos DB for global distribution and additional capabilities.

- **Azure Cosmos DB**: Azure Cosmos DB is a globally distributed, multi-model database service designed for high scalability, low latency, and global reach.

- **Azure SQL Database**: Azure SQL Database is a fully managed relational database service based on Microsoft SQL Server.

- **Azure Data Lake Storage**: Azure Data Lake Storage is a scalable and secure data lake service for big data analytics.

These are just a few of the data storage services provided by Azure. Each service is designed to address specific data storage requirements, allowing you to choose the most suitable option based on the nature of your data, performance needs, scalability requirements, and desired data models.

Data is the most essential building block of the architecture. We have gone through the type of data and discussed the storage techniques. The next chapter will cover another essential building block called containers and its orchestration techniques.

Questions

1. What are the available database storage options in Azure?
2. What are the primary use cases for each database storage type?
3. What is the underlying technology for each database storage type?
4. What data migration tools and options are available?
5. Are there any features for high availability and disaster recovery?
6. What are the different normalization techniques, and what benefits do they provide?
7. What is a NoSQL database, and what are the uses of that?
8. What is Cosmos DB in Azure?

Join our book's Discord space

Join the book's Discord Workspace for Latest updates, Offers, Tech happenings around the world, New Release and Sessions with the Authors:

https://discord.bpbonline.com

Chapter 4
Azure Kubernetes and Container Registry

Introduction

This chapter will discuss the **Azure Kubernetes** and **Azure Container Registry** in detail. Kubernetes is a potent container orchestration tool. In traditional development, developers develop the functional code by keeping a specific environment in mind. If there is any change in the environment, then that used to cause lots of code changes. It delays the development and deployment speed. Container tools like Docker solve this problem and provide speed to business.

In cloud-native development, container and container orchestration tools are essential. Containers provide a consistent and portable environment for applications, while container orchestration tools automate the management of large-scale container deployments, ensuring they run reliably, efficiently, and at scale. This is particularly important in modern, cloud-native, and microservices-based application architectures.

Structure

In this chapter, we will learn the following topics:

- Containers
- Docker

- Container orchestration
- Kubernetes
- Azure Kubernetes Service and Azure Container Registry
- Azure API Management
- Azure API Gateway

Objectives

In this chapter, we will closely examine tools like Docker, Kubernetes, Azure ACR, and AKS and see how they provide portability, reliability, and efficiency. We will also discuss the Azure API gateway used for managing API exposure to clients, API authorization, and authentication.

Containers

A container is a lightweight, standalone, and executable unit of the software that includes everything needed to run an application, including the code, runtime, dependencies, binaries, system tools, libraries, and dependencies. It is a standard package that can be run anywhere on a desktop or the cloud. Containers provide a consistent and portable environment, ensuring an application runs consistently across different computing environments, such as development machines, testing environments, and production servers. The following figure depicts the containerized applications:

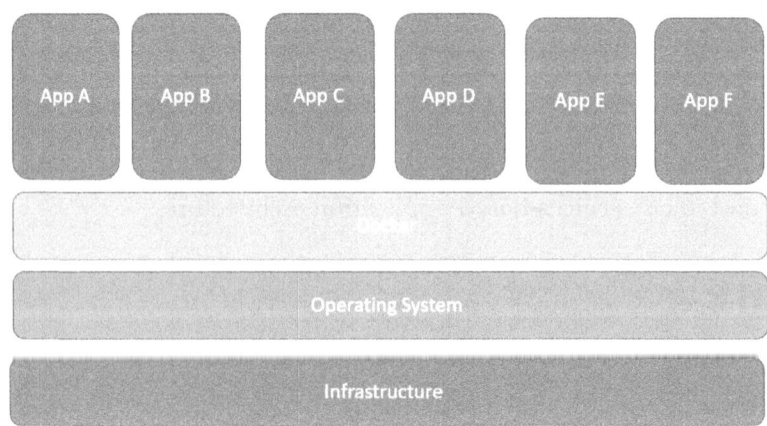

Figure 4.1: Containerized applications

Docker

Docker is an open-source platform that allows you to automate applications' deployment, packaging, and running in lightweight, isolated containers. Docker enables developers to separate application code from the infrastructure, and it provides an environment where one can run the application, and that environment is called a container. Please refer to the following figure:

Figure 4.2: Docker container

Here are some key aspects and benefits of Docker:

- **Containerization**: Docker enables you to package an application and its dependencies into a single container. This eliminates the need to install and configure dependencies on each host machine, as the container provides an isolated and consistent environment for running the application.

- **Consistency and reproducibility**: With Docker, you can create a replica of the development environment, including the operating system, libraries, and dependencies. This ensures that the application will run consistently across different machines, reducing the chances of issues arising from other environments.

- **Portability**: Docker containers can run on any machine that has Docker installed, regardless of the underlying operating system or infrastructure. This portability makes moving applications between development, testing, and production environments or even across cloud providers easier.

- **Resource efficiency**: Docker containers share the host machine's operating system kernel, making them lightweight and resource-efficient. Multiple containers can run on a single host, each with its isolated environment, without incurring the overhead of running multiple virtual machines.

- **Isolation and security**: Docker containers provide process-level isolation, ensuring that applications running in different containers do not interfere with each other. This enhances security by preventing unauthorized access or unintended interactions between applications.

- **Scalability and orchestration**: Docker makes it easy to scale applications by running multiple instances of the same container. Container orchestration platforms like Kubernetes can automatically manage Docker containers' deployment, scaling, and management across a cluster of machines, enabling efficient scaling and load balancing.

- **Fast application deployment**: Docker simplifies and speeds up the application deployment process. Containers can be created and started quickly, allowing for rapid iteration and deployment of new versions or application updates.

- **DevOps integration**: Docker enables DevOps practices by providing a standardized and portable packaging format for applications. It integrates well with **Continuous Integration/Continuous Deployment (CI/CD)** pipelines, allowing for automated application testing, building, and deployment.

- **Ecosystem and community**: Docker has a large and active community, contributing to a rich ecosystem of pre-built container images and tools. This enables developers to leverage existing containers and share their containers, making it easier to adopt and integrate with existing systems. Docker revolutionized the software packaging and deployment process by introducing a lightweight, portable containerization solution. It simplifies the management of dependencies, improves application scalability, enhances security, and promotes a consistent development and deployment environment, ultimately increasing the efficiency and reliability of the software delivery process.

Container orchestration

Container orchestration is a process of automating the deployment, management, scaling, and networking of containerized applications. Containers are lightweight, portable units that package an application and its dependencies together. Container orchestration tools are used to streamline the deployment and operation of these containers, ensuring efficient management of complex, distributed applications. Kubernetes, Docker Swarm, and OpenShift are the leading market container orchestration tools.

Container orchestration systems typically offer the following key capabilities:

- **Cluster management**: Container orchestration platforms allow you to create and manage a cluster of machines or nodes that will run your containers. They handle the cluster's setup, configuration, and coordination, abstracting away the underlying infrastructure details.

- **Container deployment**: Orchestration systems provide mechanisms for deploying containers across the cluster. They ensure that the desired number of containers are running and handle the distribution of containers on available resources.

- **Scaling and auto-scaling**: Container orchestration platforms allow you to scale your application dynamically by adding or removing containers based on workload demands. They can automatically adjust the number of containers based on defined metrics, ensuring efficient resource utilization.

- **Service discovery**: Orchestration systems provide mechanisms for service discovery, allowing containers to locate and communicate with each other. They typically offer DNS-based service discovery or internal load balancers to route traffic to containers.

- **Load balancing**: Container orchestration platforms offer load-balancing capabilities to distribute incoming traffic across containers within a service. This ensures that the workload is evenly distributed and helps with scaling and fault tolerance.

- **Health monitoring and self-healing**: Orchestration systems continuously monitor the health of containers and services. They can detect and respond to failures by automatically restarting containers, replacing failed containers with new ones, or rescheduling containers on healthy nodes.

- **Rolling updates and rollbacks**: Container orchestration platforms facilitate rolling updates of containerized applications, allowing you to update containers without downtime. They can also handle rollbacks in case of issues during the update process.

- **Security and resource isolation**: Orchestration systems provide mechanisms to isolate containers from each other and the underlying host environment, ensuring security and preventing interference between containers.

Popular container orchestration systems include Kubernetes, Docker Swarm, and Apache Mesos. These platforms offer robust container management and orchestration capabilities, allowing organizations to manage and scale containerized applications in production environments effectively.

Kubernetes

Kubernetes, often abbreviated as K8s, is an open-source container orchestration platform initially developed by Google. It is one of today's most popular and widely adopted container orchestration systems. Kubernetes provides a highly scalable, resilient, and flexible framework for managing containerized applications.

Key concepts and features of Kubernetes include:

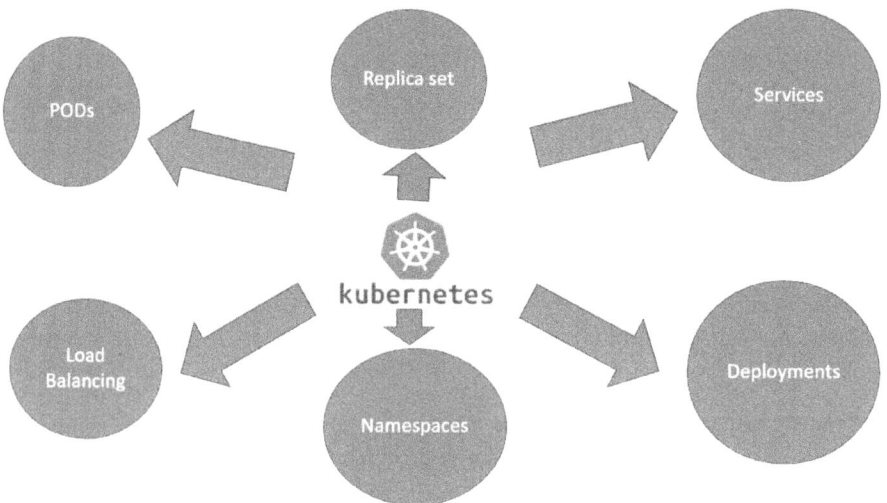

Figure 4.3: Main features of Kubernetes

- **Pods**: A Pod is the smallest unit in Kubernetes and represents a single instance of a running process or container. Pods are used to encapsulate one or more containers that are tightly coupled and share resources, such as storage and network.

- **ReplicaSets**: A ReplicaSet maintains a specified number of identical Pod replicas, ensuring that the desired number of Pods are always running. It helps with scaling, self-healing, and fault tolerance by creating or terminating Pods as needed.

- **Services**: Services define a stable network endpoint to access a set of Pods. They enable load balancing and provide a consistent way for other services or external clients to access containerized applications within the cluster.

- **Deployments**: Deployments provide declarative updates and rollbacks for applications. They allow you to define the desired state of your application, such as the number of replicas, Pod template, and update strategy. Kubernetes will automatically manage the deployment and handle rolling updates or rollbacks.

- **Namespaces**: Namespaces provide a way to divide and isolate resources within a cluster logically. They allow multiple teams or projects to share the same cluster while maintaining separation and resource quotas.

- **Labels and selectors**: Labels are key-value pairs attached to Kubernetes resources, such as Pods, Services, or Deployments. Selectors are used to identify and group resources based on labels, enabling flexible querying and targeting of resources.

- **Persistent storage**: Kubernetes supports different mechanisms for persistent storage, such as **Persistent Volumes (PVs)** and **Persistent Volume Claims (PVCs)**.

These provide a way to manage and mount storage volumes to Pods, allowing data to persist even if Pods are restarted or rescheduled.

- **Scaling and autoscaling**: Kubernetes allows you to scale applications by adjusting the number of replicas. It supports manual scaling, where you specify the desired number of replicas, and autoscaling, where Kubernetes automatically scales the number of replicas based on resource utilization metrics.

- **Service discovery and load balancing**: Kubernetes provides built-in service discovery and load balancing capabilities. Services allow Pods to be accessed by other Pods or external clients through a consistent DNS name or IP address, distributing traffic across multiple replicas.

- **Configurations and secrets**: Kubernetes provides mechanisms for managing application configurations and sensitive information like passwords or API keys. ConfigMaps and Secrets store and inject environment variables, configuration files, or sensitive data into containers.

Kubernetes has a rich ecosystem and supports integration with various tools, including logging frameworks, monitoring solutions, and CI/CD pipelines. It enables organizations to efficiently manage containerized applications, improve scalability, and enhance operational efficiency by automating many application deployment, scaling, and management aspects.

Azure Kubernetes Service and Azure Container Registry

Azure Kubernetes Service (**AKS**) and **Azure Container Registry** (**ACR**) are two services offered by Microsoft Azure that provide a comprehensive solution for deploying and managing containerized applications.

AKS is a fully managed Kubernetes service that simplifies the deployment and management of containerized applications. It allows developers to quickly deploy and scale containerized applications on a managed Kubernetes cluster without addressing the underlying infrastructure. AKS also integrates with other Azure services like Azure Active Directory for authentication and authorization, Azure Storage for persistent storage, and Azure Load Balancer for load balancing.

ACR is a private container registry that enables developers to store and manage Docker images for containerized applications. ACR allows developers to store and share container images securely across their organization and also integrates with AKS for seamless deployment of containerized applications. ACR supports Docker- and **Open Container Initiative** (**OCI**) compliant images and provides features like geo-replication, webhook triggers, and image scanning for security vulnerabilities.

Azure API Management provides a rich set of tools and features for managing APIs, including analytics, which offers insights into API usage and performance, and developer engagement, which allows developers to interact with APIs and provides a way to monitor and troubleshoot API issues.

Azure API Management provides a secure gateway for APIs, allowing developers to publish APIs for external access while enforcing authentication, authorization, and throttling policies.

When used with AKS and ACR, Azure API Management provides a complete solution for building, deploying, and managing containerized applications with APIs securely and scalable. Developers can use ACR to store and manage their Docker images and then deploy them on AKS to run their containerized applications in a controlled Kubernetes environment. At the same time, API management will help drive the APIs.

Azure Kubernetes Service

Azure Kubernetes Service (AKS) is a managed container orchestration service provided by Microsoft Azure. It simplifies containerized applications' deployment, management, and scaling using Kubernetes. AKS offers a fully managed Kubernetes cluster, eliminating the need for you to control the underlying infrastructure. Following is the figure of AKS service, and we can see that it is showing the multiple containers:

Figure 4.4: Azure Kubernetes Service

Key features of Azure Kubernetes Service include:

- **Ease of deployment**: AKS makes deploying and managing Kubernetes clusters in Azure easy. You can create a cluster with a few clicks or automate the process using Azure Resource Manager templates, Azure CLI, or Azure PowerShell.
- **Scalability and high availability**: AKS allows you to scale your applications horizontally by adjusting the number of nodes in the cluster. It also provides built-in high-availability features, such as automatic node repair and cluster upgrades, ensuring your applications are always available.

- **Integration with Azure services**: AKS integrates seamlessly with other Azure services, such as Azure Container Registry for private container image storage, Azure Monitor for cluster and application monitoring, Azure Active Directory for authentication and access control, and more.

- **Security and compliance**: AKS provides features to secure your containerized applications, including integration with Azure Policy for governance, Azure Virtual Network for network isolation, Azure Key Vault for secrets management, and Azure Security Center for threat detection and monitoring.

- **DevOps integration**: AKS integrates well with popular DevOps tools and practices. You can use Azure DevOps, GitHub Actions, or any other CI/CD tool of your choice to automate the deployment and management of your applications on AKS.

- **Cost optimization**: AKS offers features to help optimize costs, such as automatic scaling based on workload demands, virtual node integration to leverage serverless computing, and support for Azure Spot Instances to take advantage of low-cost virtual machines.

Azure Kubernetes Service simplifies the deployment and management of Kubernetes clusters, allowing developers to focus on their applications rather than the underlying infrastructure. It provides a scalable, secure, and reliable platform for running containerized workloads in the Azure cloud environment.

Azure Container Registry

Azure Container Registry (ACR) is a managed private registry service provided by Microsoft Azure. It enables you to securely store, manage, and deploy your container images. ACR integrates seamlessly with other Azure services and tools, making it a convenient choice for container image management in Azure. Please refer to the following figure:

Figure 4.5: Azure Container Registry

Here are some key features and capabilities of Azure Container Registry:

- **Private registry**: ACR allows you to create a private container registry to store your container images securely. You have complete control over who can access and download the images stored in your registry.

- **High availability and scalability**: ACR provides a highly available and scalable platform for storing and serving container images. It automatically replicates images across multiple Azure regions for redundancy and performance.

- **Authentication and access control**: ACR integrates with **Azure Active Directory (Azure AD)** to provide authentication and access control for your container images. You can configure fine-grained access policies and roles to control who can push, pull, and manage images in your registry.

- **Image vulnerability scanning**: ACR includes built-in vulnerability scanning capabilities. It can scan container images for known vulnerabilities and provide security recommendations. This helps you identify and address security risks before deploying your pictures.

- **Geo-replication**: ACR allows you to replicate your container images to different Azure regions for improved performance and data locality. This feature is useful when you have deployments in multiple areas and want to minimize network latency during image pulls.

- **Integration with Azure services**: ACR integrates seamlessly with other Azure services and tools. You can quickly deploy container images from ACR to **Azure Kubernetes Service (AKS)** or other orchestrators. ACR also integrates with Azure DevOps for streamlined CI/CD pipelines and Azure Monitor for monitoring and logging.

- **Webhooks and event-based workflows**: ACR supports webhooks, which allow you to trigger custom workflows or notifications when specific events occur in your registry. For example, you can set up a webhook to trigger a deployment pipeline whenever a new image is pushed to your registry.

- **Content trust and image signing**: ACR supports content trust and image signing, enabling you to verify container images' authenticity and integrity. You can sign your pictures with digital signatures, and ACR enforces verification during image pulls.

We have seen from the above features that Azure Container Registry provides a reliable and highly available environment for managing container images. It also offers integration with Azure services, robust access controls, vulnerability scanning, and other features that simplify the container image management workflow in Azure environments.

Azure API Management

Azure API Management is a fully managed service provided by Microsoft Azure that enables organizations to create, publish, secure, and manage **application programming interfaces** (**APIs**) for their applications. It acts as a gateway between API providers (backend services) and API consumers (developers, partners, or internal teams), offering a range of features to streamline API management processes; refer to the following figure:

Figure 4.6: Azure API Management

Here are some key features and capabilities of Azure API Management:

- **API publishing and management**: Azure API Management allows you to publish APIs and expose them to developers and consumers easily. It provides a unified platform for managing APIs, enabling you to define APIs, versioning, and create product catalogs.

- **API Gateway**: API Management acts as an API gateway, enabling you to control traffic to your APIs. It handles API requests and performs authentication, authorization, rate limiting, caching, and other gateway functionalities to ensure reliable and secure API access.

- **Developer portal**: API Management includes a developer portal that serves as a self-service platform for developers and consumers to discover, explore, and consume your APIs. It provides documentation, interactive API testing, and code samples, allowing developers to register and manage their API subscriptions.

- **Security and access control**: API Management offers various security features to protect your APIs. You can implement authentication mechanisms such as API keys, OAuth, Azure Active Directory, or custom authentication. Additionally, you can enforce authorization policies and IP restrictions and apply SSL/TLS encryption for secure data transmission.

- **API analytics and monitoring**: API Management provides rich analytics and monitoring capabilities to gain insights into API usage and performance. You can track key metrics, such as API calls, response times, errors, and user activity. This data helps you understand API usage patterns and make informed decisions.

- **Developer engagement and monetization**: With API Management, you can monetize your APIs by creating different pricing plans and subscription tiers. It offers billing, metering, and usage tracking features, allowing you to engage with developers and partners and generate revenue from your APIs.

- **Integration with backend services**: API Management integrates various backend services and technologies. It supports RESTful APIs, SOAP-based services, serverless functions, and microservices. It can act as a gateway to your existing APIs or transform and expose your backend services as APIs.

- **DevOps integration**: API Management integrates with Azure DevOps and other DevOps tools for seamless CI/CD pipelines. You can automate API deployments, versioning, and configuration changes using deployment slots and Git-based workflows.

Azure API Management simplifies the management and governance of APIs by providing a comprehensive platform with features like API publishing, security, developer portal, analytics, and monetization capabilities. It helps organizations streamline exposing, securing, and managing APIs, enabling them to drive innovation and build scalable applications quickly.

Azure API Gateway

An API Gateway is a software component between clients (such as mobile applications, web applications, or other services) and backend services or APIs. It acts as an entry point for API requests, providing a centralized interface for managing, routing, and securing API traffic. API Gateways offer several key functionalities that simplify the development, deployment, and management of APIs:

- **Request routing and load balancing**: API Gateways handle incoming API requests and route them to the appropriate backend service based on predefined rules or configurations. They can distribute traffic across multiple instances of a service to ensure scalability and high availability.

- **API versioning and lifecycle management**: Gateways often support API versioning, allowing different versions of an API to coexist and be accessed by clients. They also provide capabilities for managing the lifecycle of APIs, including deprecation, retirement, and version retirement.

- **Request and response transformation**: Gateways can modify or transform API requests and responses to ensure compatibility between clients and backend services. This includes data format conversion, content negotiation, header modification, and response caching.

- **Authentication and authorization**: API Gateways provide security features to control access to APIs. They can enforce authentication mechanisms, such as API keys, tokens, or OAuth, and handle authorization checks to ensure that only authorized clients can access protected resources.

- **Rate limiting and throttling**: Gateways help protect backend services from excessive or abusive API requests by enforcing rate-defining and throttling policies. They can control client requests within a specific period, preventing service overload or unauthorized access.

- **Logging and monitoring**: API Gateways often include logging and monitoring capabilities to track and analyze API traffic. They can generate logs for auditing purposes and collect metrics on request/response times, error rates, and overall API usage, providing insights into performance, usage patterns, and potential issues.

- **Caching**: API Gateways can cache responses from backend services to improve performance and reduce the load on those services. They store and serve cached responses for subsequent identical requests, reducing the need for backend processing and enhancing API response times.

- **Service composition and aggregation**: Gateways can aggregate or compose data from multiple backend services into a single API response. This allows clients to retrieve related data from different services through a single API call, simplifying client-side logic and reducing roundtrips.

API Gateways are commonly used in microservices architectures, where multiple services are exposed as APIs and must be managed centrally. They help streamline API development, enhance security, improve performance, and provide a consistent interface for clients, making them an essential component in modern API-driven architectures.

Conclusion

We have seen that AKS is a fully managed container orchestration service provided by Microsoft Azure. It simplifies deploying, managing, and scaling containerized applications using Kubernetes. ACR is a managed container registry service provided by Microsoft Azure. It allows storing and managing container images for Docker and other container platforms.

AKS and ACR are part of Microsoft's broader Azure ecosystem, designed to facilitate containerized applications' development, deployment, and management in a cloud-native environment. AKS primarily focuses on orchestrating containerized applications, while ACR focuses on storing and managing container images. Together, they provide a comprehensive solution for building and running containerized applications in Azure.

In the next chapter, we will review the foundational concepts around Azure, which we use for development.

Questions

Here are the commonly asked questions about Azure AKS and ACR:

1. How does AKS compare to self-managed Kubernetes Clusters?
2. What are AKS's key security features?
3. How does AKS handle scaling and autoscaling?
4. What integrations does AKS have with Azure Services?
5. What are the cost considerations for AKS?
6. How does ACR ensure the security of container images?
7. What are the options for replicating images in ACR?
8. Can ACR be integrated with CI/CD pipelines?
9. What are the best practices for managing and organizing images in ACR?
10. How does ACR handle authentication and authorization?

These questions cover various topics, from security and integration capabilities to cost considerations and best practices, providing a well-rounded understanding of Azure AKS and ACR.

Chapter 5
Developing Application on Azure

Introduction

This chapter will cover best practices and concepts around cloud native and microservices development. We will discuss how we can develop more resilient, secure, and scalable services. We containerize the application, which makes management and deployment easier.

Developers can create APIs/microservices by defining endpoints, operations, and data models using a variety of protocols, such as REST and SOAP. Once an API is designed, it can be published to the developer portal, where other developers can discover, test, and consume the API.

Developers can use **Azure Container Registry (ACR)** to store and manage their Docker images and then deploy them on AKS to run their containerized applications in a controlled Kubernetes environment.

Cloud-native technologies like Kubernetes, Istio, and Envoy are designed to support microservices and make it easier to manage them at scale. Use these technologies to simplify management and improve the performance of your microservices.

Automation is a vital and central piece of modern development. We will cover how automation tools like Azure GitHub Actions make the cloud-native development process faster and more successful.

Microsoft Azure provides two serverless options, Azure Functions, and Logic Apps, that enable developers to build event-driven, scalable, and cost-effective applications. Developers can use Azure Functions to execute small code in response to events and then use Azure Logic Apps to create workflows that orchestrate these functions and integrate with various services and applications. This allows developers to create robust, scalable, cost-effective applications that automate complex business processes.

Structure

In this chapter, the following topics will be discussed.

- Best cloud-native design practices and challenges
- Microservices architecture and patterns
- Twelve factors applications
- Containerization and deployment strategies
- Building Microservices with AKS
- Serverless development with Azure Functions
- Using Cosmos DB for NoSQL databases
- Building event-driven applications
- Building workflows with Azure Logic Apps
- Developing applications using Java and .Net

Objectives

In this chapter, we will learn hands-on development of cloud-native applications using Azure services. We will learn about cloud-native practices and also go through the microservices concept. We will also learn about 12-factor application principles and their role in microservices development. We will also discuss developing applications using a serverless approach where we do not need to worry about infrastructure provisioning and see why it is getting popular.

Event-driven architecture is one of the most popular architectures in modern engineering and application development. It is used to develop digitally decoupled applications because autonomy is significant nowadays in developing microservices. We will see what Azure Cloud Services are used to build event-driven architectures.

Best cloud-native design practices and challenges

Best cloud-native practices include microservices architecture, containerization with Docker technologies, Kubernetes orchestration, **continuous integration/continuous deployment (CI/CD)**, serverless computing, and automation. These practices enhance scalability, agility, and efficiency, allowing applications to leverage cloud environments' benefits fully. When designing cloud-native applications, there are several best practices to follow to ensure scalability, resilience, and efficient utilization of cloud resources. Here are some essential guidelines:

Microservices architecture: Design your application as a collection of small, loosely coupled services that can be developed, deployed, and scaled independently. This approach allows for better agility, fault isolation, and scalability.

Containers and orchestration: Utilize containerization technologies like Docker to package your application and its dependencies into portable and consistent units. Orchestration platforms like Kubernetes enable efficient management of containers, automated scaling, and fault tolerance.

Stateless design: Aim for stateless services whenever possible. Storing application state in a centralized and scalable data store, such as a database or object storage, allows services to be easily replaced or scaled without impacting the overall system.

API-first approach: Define clear and well-documented APIs that enable loose coupling between services. This facilitates interoperability, promotes reusability, and allows different teams to work independently.

Resilience and fault tolerance: Design applications with failure in mind. Implement fault-tolerant mechanisms such as retries, circuit breakers, and bulkheads to handle transient errors and prevent cascading failures.

Scalability and elasticity: Leverage cloud-native services like auto-scaling, load balancing, and serverless computing to handle varying workloads and optimize resource utilization. Design your application to scale horizontally by adding more instances rather than vertically by increasing the size of individual cases.

Infrastructure as Code: Use infrastructure automation tools like Terraform or CloudFormation to define and provision cloud resources. This approach allows for versioning, reproducibility, and scalability of infrastructure deployments.

Observability and monitoring: Implement comprehensive monitoring, logging, and tracing mechanisms within your application. Use tools like Prometheus, Grafana, or Elasticsearch to gain insights into your services' performance, availability, and behavior.

Security and compliance: Apply security best practices throughout the entire development lifecycle. Utilize encryption, authentication, and authorization mechanisms, and regularly update and patch software components to mitigate vulnerabilities.

Continuous integration and deployment: Embrace DevOps practices by automating your application's build, testing, and deployment. Implement CI/CD pipelines to ensure rapid and reliable delivery of new features and updates.

Remember that these best practices are general guidelines, and their applicability may vary depending on your specific requirements and the cloud platform you are using.

While microservices offer numerous benefits, their development introduces specific challenges that require careful consideration. Here are key issues and cautions associated with microservices development:

Service-to-service communication: Service calls between microservices can lead to increased network latency and potential points of failure. Developers must implement robust communication patterns and handle potential issues like timeouts and retries.

Data consistency and transaction management: Maintaining data consistency across microservices can be challenging. Developers must carefully design strategies for distributed transactions or leverage eventual consistency, depending on the application's requirements.

Increased complexity in deployment and operations: With multiple microservices to deploy and manage, operational complexity rises. Proper tooling, automation, and DevOps practices are crucial to streamline deployment, monitoring, and maintenance processes.

Data sharing and team coordination: Decoupling microservices often results in separate databases for each service. Coordinating data sharing among teams and ensuring a unified understanding of data models become critical to avoid inconsistencies.

Service discovery and load balancing: As the number of microservices grows, managing service discovery and load balancing becomes complex. Developers need effective solutions to discover dynamically and route requests to available services.

Security challenges: Securing microservices involves addressing challenges such as authentication and authorization and ensuring communication between services. Developers must implement robust security measures to safeguard the entire system.

Versioning and API compatibility: Changes to APIs and versioning require careful management to ensure backward compatibility and avoid breaking dependent services. Proper versioning strategies must be in place to handle evolving microservices.

Monitoring and debugging: With distributed systems, monitoring, and debugging become more challenging. Developers need comprehensive tools and practices to trace and troubleshoot issues across microservices.

Eventual consistency trade-offs: Eventual consistency means that in a distributed system, different parts of the system might not show the same result immediately after making changes to data. However, given some time and without new changes, they will eventually become consistent or offer the same information. It is like sending a message to friends; some might read it sooner than others due to network delays, but eventually, everyone will see the same message. This approach helps maintain system availability and performance, even if there is a brief period when things look slightly different across different parts of the system. Eventual consistency is commonly employed in distributed databases and microservices architectures to balance performance and reliability.

Adopting eventual consistency may be necessary for some microservices. Developers must carefully weigh the trade-offs and choose the appropriate consistency model for each service.

Team autonomy versus system consistency: Balancing team autonomy with the need for system-wide consistency is crucial. Teams must collaborate on shared APIs and standards while maintaining the independence to innovate within their microservices.

Addressing these challenges requires a combination of thoughtful architectural design, robust development practices, and the adoption of appropriate tools and technologies. Regular communication and collaboration among development teams are also essential to ensure the successful implementation of a microservices architecture.

Microservices architecture and patterns

Designing microservices demands a holistic approach to ensure a resilient and scalable architecture. Emphasizing service independence, each microservice should encapsulate its business logic and database, fostering agility and reducing dependencies. Adopting decentralized data management prevents tight coupling between services, enhancing scalability.

Well-defined APIs are crucial for communication, adhering to standards like RESTful principles. Using technologies such as Docker, containerization ensures consistent environments throughout the development stages. CI/CD practices automate testing, deployment, and monitoring, facilitating reliable production delivery.

Microservices must be fault-tolerant, integrating strategies like circuit breakers and retries. Robust monitoring and logging mechanisms are essential for tracking service health and performance. Scalability is optimized by designing microservices to scale independently based on specific needs.

Security measures should be implemented at each layer, including authentication and authorization. Embracing event-driven architecture enables real-time data flow and loose coupling between microservices. Organizing development teams around microservices enhances autonomy and responsibility.

Versioning practices for APIs facilitate smooth upgrades without disrupting existing services. These considerations collectively empower developers to build modular, resilient, and adaptable microservices architectures, addressing the complexities of modern application development efficiently.

Microservices architecture is an architectural style that structures an application as a collection of small, independent services that can be developed, deployed and scaled independently. Each service focuses on a specific business capability and communicates with other services through well-defined APIs.

Here are some common patterns and principles associated with microservices architecture:

Single responsibility principle: Each microservice should have a single responsibility or business capability. This helps to keep the services small, cohesive, and manageable.

Service independence: Microservices should be independent and autonomous, with their own codebase, database, and deployment pipeline. This enables teams to develop, test, and deploy services independently without impacting other services.

API gateway: An API gateway acts as a single entry point for clients to access the microservices. It handles authentication, routing, request aggregation, and other cross-cutting concerns, providing a unified interface for clients.

Service discovery: Services need a way to locate and communicate with each other dynamically. Service discovery mechanisms, such as service registries or DNS-based discovery, help services discover and maintain knowledge of other services within the ecosystem.

Event-driven architecture: Services can communicate through asynchronous messaging using events. Event-driven architectures allow loose coupling and scalability by enabling services to react to events and emit events to notify other services.

Database per service: Each microservice should have its dedicated database. This supports loose coupling, data isolation, and independent scalability. Different databases, such as relational, NoSQL, or event sourcing, can be chosen based on specific service requirements.

Circuit breaker pattern: The circuit breaker pattern helps to handle faults and prevent cascading failures in a distributed system. It provides a mechanism to detect and respond to failures in remote service dependencies, thereby improving system resilience.

Continuous integration and deployment: Embrace automation and DevOps practices to enable frequent and reliable deployment of microservices. Use CI/CD pipelines to automate building, testing, and deploying microservices.

Monitoring and observability: Implement robust monitoring and observability solutions to gain insights into microservices' health, performance, and behavior. This includes logging, metrics collection, distributed tracing, and error tracking.

Resilience and fault tolerance: Design microservices to be resilient in the face of failures. Implement fault-tolerant mechanisms like retries, timeouts, and circuit breakers to handle transient errors and ensure graceful degradation.

It is important to note that while microservices can provide many benefits, they also introduce complexity and require careful consideration of trade-offs. The suitability of microservices architecture depends on the specific requirements, team dynamics, and the nature of the application being developed.

Twelve-factors applications

The twelve-factor applications methodology is a set of best practices for building cloud-native applications that are scalable, maintainable, and portable. Heroku co-founder Adam Wiggins formulated these principles, which have been widely adopted as a guide for modern application development. Here are the twelve factors:

- **Codebase**: Maintain a single codebase under version control. This promotes code visibility, collaboration, and reproducibility.

- **Dependencies**: Explicitly declare and isolate dependencies. Use a dependency management system to ensure consistent and reproducible builds.

- **Config**: Store configuration in the environment. Keep configuration separate from code to allow easy customization and portability across different environments.

- **Backing services**: Treat backing services, such as databases, queues, and caches, as attached resources. Access them via well-defined interfaces and connect to them through configuration.

- **Build, release, run**: Strictly separate the application's build, release, and run stages. This separation ensures consistency and reproducibility across different deployment environments.

- **Processes**: Execute the application as one or more stateless processes. This allows for better scalability, resilience, and ease of management.

- **Port binding**: Expose services via a port binding mechanism. Applications should be self-contained and not rely on specific network configurations or hard-coded service locations.

- **Concurrency**: Scale out via the process model. Applications should be designed to scale horizontally by adding more instances rather than vertically by increasing the size of individual cases.

- **Disposability**: Maximize robustness with fast startup and graceful shutdown. Applications should be able to start and stop quickly without losing a vital state or causing disruption.

- **Development/production parity**: Keep development, staging, and production environments as similar as possible. Reduce divergence between environments to minimize issues and improve testing and troubleshooting.

- **Logs**: Treat logs as event streams. The log output should be treated as a continuous stream of events that can be collected, analyzed, and aggregated for troubleshooting and monitoring.

- **Admin processes**: Run administrative tasks as one-off processes. Administrative tasks, such as database migrations or data imports, should be run in an isolated and controlled environment.

By adhering to these twelve factors, developers can create scalable, resilient, and easily deployable applications across different environments. These principles promote good practices for cloud-native application design and help organizations leverage the full potential of cloud computing.

Containerization and deployment strategies

Containerization is a method of packaging software applications with their dependencies, configurations, and runtime environments into standardized units called containers. These containers are isolated and portable, allowing applications to run consistently across different environments.

When it comes to deploying containerized applications, there are several strategies you can consider:

- **Single-host deployment**:
  - **Docker compose**: Docker compose defines and manages multi-container applications on a single host. It simplifies the orchestration of multiple containers, their networking, and dependencies.

- **Orchestration platforms**:
  - **Kubernetes**: Deploy and manage containerized applications across a cluster of machines using Kubernetes. It provides features like automated scaling, load balancing, service discovery, and self-healing capabilities.
  - **Docker Swarm**: Utilize Docker Swarm to create and manage a cluster of Docker nodes, allowing you to deploy and scale containers across multiple hosts.

- **Serverless deployment**:
  - **Function as a Service (FaaS)**: Adopt serverless computing platforms like AWS Lambda, Azure Functions, or Google Cloud Functions to deploy code in response to events without worrying about the underlying infrastructure.

- **Continuous deployment**:
    - **CI/CD pipelines**: Integrate containerized applications into your CI/CD pipelines. Automate the build, testing, and deployment processes to ensure rapid and reliable delivery of new features and updates.

- **Infrastructure as Code (IaC)**:

    Tools like Terraform or Azure ARM allow you to define and provision the necessary infrastructure resources, including container runtimes, networking, load balancers, and storage, in a declarative manner.

    Terraform: Terraform is an open-source IaC software tool created by HashiCorp. It enables users to define and provision a data center infrastructure using a declarative configuration language. With Terraform, you can describe the entire infrastructure stack, comprising servers, networks, storage, and other resources in a configuration file, and then deploy and manage that infrastructure consistently and repeatedly.

    To use Terraform, you typically define your infrastructure in a configuration file (usually with a `.tf` extension), run the terraform `init` command to initialize the working directory, use Terraform plan to see what changes will be made, and finally, apply those changes using terraform apply. This process ensures the infrastructure is created or updated according to the specified configuration.

    Azure Resource Manager (ARM): Just like Terraform templates, ARM templates are used to define and deploy Azure IaC. They provide a way to describe and provision all the resources needed for an application or solution within Azure.

- **Hybrid and multi-cloud deployments**:

    Manage container deployments across multiple cloud providers or on-premises infrastructure. Tools like Kubernetes can facilitate hybrid and multi-cloud deployments, enabling portability and flexibility.

- **Blue/green deployment**: Use a blue/green deployment strategy to minimize downtime and reduce the risk of releasing new versions. In this approach, you have two identical environments (blue and green) and switch traffic from one environment to another after a successful deployment.

- **Canary deployment**: Gradually roll out new versions of containerized applications to a subset of users or traffic. This allows for testing and validation of new releases in a controlled manner before fully deploying to all users.

- **Service mesh**: Implement a service mesh, such as Istio or Linkerd, to manage network traffic, secure communication, and enable observability and control over microservices deployed in containers.

- **Auto-scaling and load balancing**: Leverage container orchestration platforms or cloud provider services to automatically scale the number of containers based on resource usage or traffic demands. Load balancers distribute traffic across container instances for optimal performance.

Remember that the choice of containerization and deployment strategy depends on your specific requirements, infrastructure, team expertise, and the complexity of your application. Evaluating and selecting the strategy that best fits your needs is essential while considering factors like scalability, resilience, ease of management, and cost efficiency.

Building Microservices with AKS

Building Microservices with **Azure Kubernetes Service (AKS)** involves the following steps:

1. **Define microservices**: Identify the individual business capabilities and boundaries for your microservices. Decompose your application into smaller, loosely coupled services that can be developed and deployed independently.

2. **Containerize microservices**: Package each microservice into a container using Docker. Create a Dockerfile that defines the container image, including dependencies and runtime configurations. Build and push the container images to a registry such as **Azure Container Registry (ACR)**.

3. **Provision an AKS Cluster**: Create an AKS cluster in Azure to host your microservices. AKS is a fully managed Kubernetes service that simplifies containerized applications' deployment, management, and scaling.

4. **Deploy microservices to AKS**: Use Kubernetes manifests, such as YAML files, to define the desired state of your microservices in the cluster. Declare the containers, replica counts, networking, and other necessary configurations for each microservice. Apply these manifests to the AKS cluster, and Kubernetes will deploy and manage the microservices.

5. **Service discovery and load balancing**: Use Kubernetes' built-in service discovery and load balancing mechanisms to expose and route traffic to your microservices. Define Kubernetes services that act as stable endpoints for accessing the microservices within the cluster.

6. **Scaling and autoscaling**: Configure scaling rules for your microservices in AKS. You can manually scale the number of replicas for each microservice based on demand or utilize Kubernetes' autoscaling capabilities, such as **Horizontal Pod Autoscaler (HPA)**, to automatically adjust the number of instances based on resource utilization metrics.

7. **Monitoring and observability**: Implement monitoring and observability solutions to gain insights into your microservices' health, performance, and behavior. Leverage Azure Monitor, Azure Log Analytics, or third-party tools to collect and analyse your AKS cluster's metrics, logs, and traces.

8. **CI/CD**: Set up CI/CD pipelines to automate your microservices' build, test, and deployment to AKS. Utilize Azure DevOps, Jenkins, or other CI/CD tools to enable seamless and reliable delivery of new features and updates.

9. **Security and access control**: Ensure the security of your microservices and AKS cluster. Apply network policies, secure communication with TLS certificates, and implement authentication and authorization mechanisms, such as Azure Active Directory integration or Kubernetes RBAC, to control access to your microservices and cluster resources.

10. **Resilience and fault tolerance**: Design your microservices to be resilient in the face of failures. Implement retry mechanisms, circuit breakers, and distributed tracing to handle transient errors and prevent cascading failures. Leverage Azure Availability Zones for high availability and disaster recovery.

Remember to consult the official Azure documentation and AKS guides for detailed instructions on setting up and managing microservices with AKS.

Here is an example of a **"Hello World"** microservice implemented in Node.js that you can deploy to AKS:

Creating a simple **"HelloWorld"** microservice in Node.js involves setting up a primary web server and defining a route that responds with the **"Hello, World!"** message. Below is an example using the Express.js framework, a popular choice for building web applications and microservices in Node.js.

First, make sure you have Node.js and **npm** (Node Package Manager) installed. You can then initialize a new Node.js project and install Express by running the following commands in your terminal:

```
npm init -y
npm install express
Javascript :helloworld.js

const express = require('express');
const app = express();
const port = 3000; // You can use any port you prefer

// Define a route for the HelloWorld microservice
app.get('/hello', (req, res) => {
  res.send('Hello, World!');
});

// Start the server
```

```
app.listen(port, () => {
  console.log(`HelloWorld microservice is running at http://local-
host:${port}`);
});
```

To deploy this microservice to AKS, follow these steps:

1. Create a new directory and navigate to it in your terminal.
2. Initialize a new Node.js project by running the command: **npm init**. Follow the prompts to generate a **package.json** file.
3. Install the required dependencies (in this case, Express) by running: **npm install express**.
4. Create a file named **app.js** in the same directory and paste the above code into it.
5. Build a Docker image for your microservice by creating a **Dockerfile** in the same directory with the following contents:

Dockerfile: A Dockerfile is a script to create a Docker image. Docker is a platform for developing, shipping, and running container applications. Containers allow you to package an application and its dependencies into a single unit, ensuring it runs consistently across different environments.

Following is a sample of a Dockerfile.

A Dockerfile starts with a base image, which serves as the foundation for your application. The base image contains the operating system and a minimal set of software needed to run your application. Here, we can see that we use **nodeJS** as the base image. In the following line, we set up the working directory and copy the **nodeJs** package JSON files.

Here is a breakdown of the Dockerfile:

- It starts with Docker Hub's official Node.js base image (specifically version 14).
- Sets the working directory inside the container.
- Copies **package.json** and **package-lock.json** to the working directory.
- Runs **npm** install to install the application dependencies.
- Copies the rest of the application code into the container.
- Exposes port 3000 (you can modify this based on your application's needs).
- Specifies the default command to run your Node.js application (assumes your **package.json** has a **start** script).

You need to customize the docker file based on your needs:

```
# Use an official Node.js runtime as a parent image
FROM node:14

# Set the working directory to /app
WORKDIR /app

# Copy package.json and package-lock.json to the working directory
COPY package*.json ./

# Install the application dependencies
RUN npm install

# Copy the current directory contents to the container at /app
COPY . .

# Expose port 3000 to the outside world
EXPOSE 3000

# Define the command to run your application
CMD ["node", "app.js"]
```

6. Build the Docker image by running the command: **docker build -t your-image-name**. (do not forget the dot at the end).

    docker build -t your-docker-image:latest .

    Replace **your Docker image** with the desired name for your Docker image. The **.** At the end, it indicates the build context and the current directory.

    Once the build is complete, you can run the Docker container using:

    docker run -p 3000:3000 -d your-docker-image:latest

    This maps port 3000 from the container to port 3000 on your host machine and runs the container in detached mode (**-d**).

    Your Node.js **"HelloWorld"** microservice should be accessible at **http://localhost:3000** in your browser.

7. Log in to your **Azure Container Registry (ACR)** by running: **az acr login --name your-acr-name**.

8. Tag the Docker image with your ACR login server address: **docker tag your-image-name your-acr-name.azurecr.io/your-image-name**.

9. Push the Docker image to ACR: **docker push your-acr-name.azurecr.io/your-image-name**.
10. Create an AKS cluster in Azure using the Azure portal or Azure CLI.
11. Deploy the microservice to AKS using a Kubernetes manifest file **helloworld-deployment.yaml** with the following content:

```yaml
apiVersion: apps/v1
kind: Deployment
metadata:
  name: helloworld-deployment
spec:
  replicas: 3 # You can adjust the number of replicas as needed
  selector:
    matchLabels:
      app: helloworld
  template:
    metadata:
      labels:
        app: helloworld
    spec:
      containers:
      - name: helloworld-container
        image: your-docker-image:latest # Replace with your Docker image details
        ports:
        - containerPort: 3000

---
apiVersion: v1
kind: Service
metadata:
  name: helloworld-service
spec:
  selector:
    app: helloworld
```

```
    ports:
      - protocol: TCP
        port: 80
        targetPort: 3000
    type: LoadBalancer # Change to "NodePort" or "ClusterIP" based on
your setup
```

Make sure to replace **your-docker-image:latest** with the actual details of your Docker image. If you do not have a Docker image, you must build one for your Node.js application.

To deploy this YAML file, use the following command:

kubectl apply -f helloworld-deployment.yaml

This will create a deployment with three replicas and a service to expose the microservice. If you run Kubernetes locally using tools like Minikube, you should adjust the type field in the Service section to either NodePort or ClusterIP.

12. Apply the Kubernetes manifest to your AKS cluster by running the following:

kubectl apply -f microservice-deployment.yaml.

After the deployment, you can access your **"Hello World"** microservice by accessing the external IP address of the **hello-world-service** service on port 80. It should respond with **"Hello World!"** when you visit it in a web browser or send a GET request to the IP address.

After deploying, you can check the status using:

- **kubectl** get pods
- **kubectl** get services

Once your microservice is running, access it through the assigned external IP or the NodePort, depending on your setup. If you used a LoadBalancer type, it might take some time for the external IP to be assigned.

This is a basic example, and in a production environment, you would likely need to enhance it with additional configurations, such as health checks, environment variables, and more, based on your specific requirements.

Please note that you must replace **your-image-name**, **your-acr-name**, and any other placeholders with your values according to your setup.

Serverless development with Azure Functions

Serverless development with Azure Functions allows you to build event-driven, scalable, cost-effective applications without managing the underlying infrastructure. Here is a step-by-step guide to getting started with Azure Functions:

1. **Create an Azure Functions App**:

    a. Go to the Azure portal (**portal.azure.com**) and create a new Azure Functions app.

    b. Choose a unique app name, select your preferred runtime (such as Node.js, C#, Python, and so on), and choose a hosting plan (consumption plan for pay-per-use or app service plan for dedicated resources).

2. **Create a function**:

    a. Within your Azure Functions app, click on **Functions** in the left-hand menu.

    b. Click on the **New Function** button to create a new function.

    c. Choose a template based on your preferred programming language and trigger type. For example, you can select an HTTP trigger for a REST API or a Blob trigger for processing files in Azure Blob Storage.

3. **Develop the function**:

    a. Azure Functions provides a code editor within the portal, or you can choose to develop locally using your preferred IDE.

    b. Write the function code based on the selected trigger and desired functionality.

    c. The code typically resides within a function file (for example, **index.js** for JavaScript) and includes a function definition and business logic.

4. **Test the function**:

    a. Use the built-in testing capabilities in the Azure portal or test the function locally using tools like Azure Functions Core Tools or Azure Storage Emulator.

    b. Trigger the function and verify that it behaves as expected.

    c. Test various input scenarios and handle error conditions.

5. **Configure bindings and triggers**:

    a. Azure Functions offer bindings to integrate with various Azure services, such as storage, databases, message queues, and more.

b. Configure input and output bindings to enable seamless communication with external resources.

   c. Define triggers to invoke the function automatically based on specific events or schedules.

6. **Deploy and monitor**:

   a. Once your function is ready, deploy it to your Azure Functions app.

   b. Monitor your functions using Azure Application Insights or the monitoring capabilities within the Azure portal.

   c. Monitor execution logs, track performance metrics, and troubleshoot any issues.

7. **Scale and manage**:

   a. Azure Functions automatically scale based on the workload, so you do not have to worry about provisioning or managing infrastructure.

   b. Configure scaling options such as auto-scaling based on CPU utilization, message queue length, or other metrics.

   c. Manage and update your functions through the Azure portal or automate deployments using CI/CD pipelines.

8. **Integration and event-driven workflows**:

   a. Azure Functions can be integrated into larger workflows or used to build event-driven architectures.

   b. Use Azure Logic Apps or Azure Event Grid to orchestrate functions with other Azure services or external systems.

   c. Leverage triggers and bindings to enable seamless communication and data flow between functions and other services.

Azure Functions offers a serverless development experience, allowing you to focus on writing code for specific business logic or event processing without the need to manage infrastructure.

Here is an example of a serverless Azure Function using JavaScript and an HTTP trigger:

Azure Function is written in JavaScript that uses an HTTP trigger. This example assumes you are using Azure Functions with the Azure Functions Core Tools:

1. **Install Azure Functions Core Tools**: If you have not already, install the Azure Functions Core Tools by running the following command:
   ```
   npm install -g azure-functions-core-tools@3 –unsafe-perm true
   ```

2. **Create a new HTTP-triggered function**: Run the following command to create a new Azure Function with an HTTP trigger:

   ```
   func init MyFunctionApp –worker-runtime node

   cd MyFunctionApp

   func new –name HelloWorld –template "HTTP trigger"
   ```

3. **Edit the function code**: Open the **HelloWorld/index.js** file in your preferred code editor and replace its content with the following:

   ```
   module. exports = async function (context, req) {
       context.log('JavaScript HTTP trigger function processed a request.');

       const name = (req.query.name || (req.body && req.body.name));

       if (name) {
           context.res = {
               // status: 200, /* Defaults to 200 */
               body: `Hello, ${name}!`,
           };
       } else {
           context.res = {
               status: 400,
               body: "Please pass a name on the query string or in the request body,"
           };
       }
   };
   ```

4. **Run the function locally**: Run the following command to start the function locally:

   ```
   func start
   ```

   This will start a local development server, and your function will be accessible at **http://localhost:7071/api/HelloWorld?name=John** (you can adjust the name parameter in the URL).

5. **Test the function**: Open your web browser or use a tool like cURL or Postman to send a request to the function URL. For example:

   ```
   http://localhost:7071/api/HelloWorld?name=John
   ```

You should receive a response like:

`Hello, John!`

6. **Deploy the function to Azure**: Once you are satisfied with it locally, you can deploy it. Run the following command:

   `func azure functionapp publish <your-function-app-name>`

Replace `<your-function-app-name>` with the name you want to give to your Azure Function App.

That is it! You now have a serverless Azure Function that responds with a personalized greeting based on the provided name. You can customize the function further by adding additional logic, integrating with other Azure services, or using different trigger types.

Remember to check the Azure portal and Azure Functions documentation for more details on managing and monitoring your functions, configuring bindings, and exploring other capabilities provided by Azure Functions.

Using Cosmos DB for NoSQL databases

Cosmos DB is a globally distributed, multi-model NoSQL database service provided by Azure. One of its standout features is supporting multiple data models within a single database engine. It accommodates various NoSQL data models, including document, key-value, graph, column-family, and wide-column store models. This flexibility allows developers to choose the most suitable model for their specific application needs, fostering data representation and querying versatility.

Beyond multiple models, Cosmos DB offers global distribution with low-latency data access, ensuring that applications perform consistently across different regions. It provides automatic and instant scalability to adapt to changing workloads, ensuring optimal performance and cost-efficiency. Additionally, Cosmos DB incorporates comprehensive security features, including encryption at rest and in transit, role-based access control, and compliance certifications, making it suitable for handling sensitive data.

The database service also includes automatic indexing, simplifying query optimization, and integrated analytics with Azure Synapse Link, enabling real-time data exploration and insights. With its commitment to high availability and strong consistency, Azure Cosmos DB is a robust choice for applications requiring a globally distributed, multi-model database with low-latency access and advanced features.

It offers many capabilities and features for building scalable and highly available applications. Here is an overview of using Cosmos DB for NoSQL databases:

1. **Choose the appropriate API**:

   Cosmos DB supports multiple APIs, each providing a different data model and programming interface:

a. **Core (SQL) API**: Offers SQL-like query capabilities and a schema-agnostic data model.

b. **MongoDB API**: Provides a MongoDB-compatible interface for existing MongoDB applications.

c. **Cassandra API**: Offers compatibility with Apache Cassandra, allowing you to migrate existing applications.

d. **Gremlin API**: Enables graph-based data modeling and traversal using Apache TinkerPop Gremlin language.

e. **Table API**: Provides a key-value table storage model for simple and low-latency data access.

2. **Create a Cosmos DB account**:

   a. In the Azure portal, create a new Cosmos DB account.

   b. Select the appropriate API based on your application requirements.

   c. Choose the desired consistency level, throughput, and geographical replication options.

3. **Create databases and containers**:

   a. Within your Cosmos DB account, create databases and containers to organize your data.

   b. A container is similar to a table or a collection in traditional databases and holds JSON documents.

   c. Define the partition key for each container, which determines how data is distributed across physical partitions for scalability.

4. **Insert and query data**:

   a. Use the API-specific client SDK or REST API to interact with your Cosmos DB account.

   b. Insert documents into containers using the provided APIs. Documents are typically represented as JSON objects.

   c. Use the API's query capabilities to retrieve data based on different criteria.

   d. For example, with the Core (SQL) API, you can use SQL-like queries, while with the MongoDB API, you can use MongoDB query syntax.

5. **Scale and optimize performance**:

   a. Cosmos DB offers horizontal scalability with built-in automatic partitioning.

   b. Monitor and optimize your application's performance using metrics and diagnostics provided by Cosmos DB.

c. Adjust throughput settings based on your application's workload and performance requirements.

d. Enable indexing and configure indexing policies to optimize query performance.

6. **Enable global distribution**:

    a. Cosmos DB provides global distribution to replicate data across multiple regions for low-latency access and high availability.

    b. Configure the desired regions and replication options in your Cosmos DB account settings.

    c. Leverage the multi-region read capability to read data from the nearest region for improved performance.

7. **Ensure high availability and durability**:

    a. Cosmos DB automatically replicates data within and across Azure regions to ensure high availability and durability.

    b. Configure the desired consistency level to balance between consistency and performance requirements.

    c. Cosmos DB provides multiple consistency models, including solid consistency, bounded staleness, session consistency, and eventual consistency.

8. **Implement security and access control**:

    a. Secure your Cosmos DB account using Azure Active Directory authentication or **shared access signatures** (**SAS**).

    b. Configure firewall rules and virtual network service endpoints to control access to your Cosmos DB account.

    c. Use **role-based access control** (**RBAC**) to grant appropriate permissions to users or applications.

9. **Monitor and diagnose**:

    a. Utilize Cosmos DB's built-in monitoring and diagnostics capabilities to gain insights into your application's performance and health.

    b. Monitor metrics such as throughput, response time, and storage usage.

    c. Analyse diagnostic logs and enable alerts to identify and address issues proactively.

Cosmos DB simplifies the development and management of NoSQL databases, offering global scalability, high availability, and multiple data models. It provides a robust foundation for building modern, data-driven applications.

Building event-driven applications

Building event-driven applications with Azure Event Grid and Azure Service Bus allows you to create decoupled and scalable architectures. Here is an example of how you can use Azure Event Grid and Azure Service Bus together:

1. **Create an Azure Event Grid Topic**:

    a. In the Azure portal, create a new Event Grid Topic.

    b. Define a unique name for the topic and select the appropriate resource group and region.

2. **Create an Azure Service Bus namespace**:

    a. Create an Azure Service Bus namespace in the Azure portal.

    b. Provide a unique name, resource group, and region for the namespace.

3. **Create a subscription for the Event Grid Topic**:

    a. Within the Event Grid Topic, create a new subscription.

    b. Define a name for the subscription and select the endpoint type.

    c. For example, you can choose the Azure Service Bus as the endpoint type.

4. **Configure the Service Bus endpoint**:

    a. In the subscription settings, provide the connection details of your Azure Service Bus namespace.

    b. Specify the topic or queue within the Service Bus namespace to receive the events.

5. **Publish events to the Event Grid Topic**:

    a. Use an Azure Function, a custom application, or any other event source to publish events to the Event Grid Topic.

    b. Events can be in JSON format and can contain custom properties.

6. **Receive events in the Service Bus Queue or Topic**:

    a. Create an Azure Function or a custom application that acts as a consumer to receive events from the Azure Service Bus.

    b. Configure the function or application to listen to the Service Bus queue or topic.

7. **Process the events**:

    a. Implement the necessary logic to process the received events within the Azure Function or application.

b. Perform any required data transformations, business operations, or integrations.

8. **Scale and monitor**:

    a. Scale the Azure Function or application based on the event processing requirements.

    b. Monitor the performance, throughput, and latency of the event processing pipeline.

    c. Utilize Azure Monitor, Application Insights, or other monitoring tools to gain insights into the system.

Using Azure Event Grid and Azure Service Bus together, you can build event-driven architectures with loosely coupled event publishers and consumers. The event publishers can emit events to the Event Grid Topic, and the subscribers (Azure Function or application) can receive and process the events from the Service Bus queue or topic. This decoupling allows for flexibility, scalability, and extensibility in your application design.

Please note that this is a high-level overview, and the actual implementation may vary based on your specific requirements and the programming languages or tools you choose to use.

Building workflows with Azure Logic Apps

Building workflows with Azure Logic Apps allows you to automate business processes and integrate various systems and services. Here is an overview of how you can use Azure Logic Apps to build workflows:

1. **Create an Azure Logic App**:

    a. In the Azure portal, create a new Azure Logic App.

    b. Provide the Logic App's unique name, resource group, and region.

2. **Choose a trigger**:

    a. Select a trigger that initiates the workflow.

    b. Logic Apps offer many triggers, such as HTTP requests, timers, file system changes, database events, etc.

    c. For example, when a specific URL is requested, you can choose an HTTP trigger to start the workflow.

3. **Add actions and connectors**:

    a. Add actions to the Logic App that perform specific tasks or operations.

    b. Logic Apps provide a rich set of built-in connectors for popular services like Azure, Office 365, Salesforce, Twitter, etc.

c. Connectors enable seamless integration with these services and allow you to create records, send emails, post messages, and more.

4. **Configure actions and connectors**:

    a. For each action or connector, configure the necessary settings and inputs.

    b. Define the connection details, authentication credentials, and data mappings as required.

    c. Logic Apps offer visual designers and expression language to define the workflow logic and transform data between steps.

5. **Handle conditions and loops**:

    a. Use control actions like condition statements and loops to implement branching and iterative logic in your workflow.

    b. Condition actions allow you to evaluate expressions and execute different paths based on the results.

    c. Loop actions enable you to iterate over collections or repeat actions until a specific condition is met.

6. **Monitor and debug**:

    a. Use the monitoring capabilities in the Azure portal or Azure Monitor to track the execution of your Logic App.

    b. Monitor the workflow runs, view the execution history, and check for errors or issues.

    c. Enable diagnostic logging and configure alerts to detect and respond to failures proactively.

7. **Handle errors and retries**:

    a. Implement error handling and retries to handle transient failures or recover from exceptions.

    b. Use built-in retry policies or custom error-handling actions to handle failures gracefully.

    c. Configure appropriate error notifications or escalation mechanisms to ensure timely response and resolution.

8. **Secure and authenticate**:

    a. Secure your Logic App by configuring authentication and authorization mechanisms.

    b. Use managed identities, service principals, or OAuth authentication to access services securely.

c. Implement **role-based access control (RBAC)** to control access to the Logic App and its resources.

9. **Test and publish**:

    a. Test your Logic App by triggering the defined triggers and validating the workflow behavior.

    b. Ensure that the actions and connectors function as expected and produce the desired outcomes.

    c. Publish the Logic App to make it available for execution and integration with other systems.

Azure Logic Apps provide a visual and intuitive way to build workflows by connecting various services and orchestrating business processes. You can create powerful automation scenarios by leveraging the rich set of triggers, actions, and connectors offered by Logic Apps.

Developing applications using Java and .Net

We are going to develop a **Hello World** SpringBoot-based service. We will see the same service in .Net and Node JS. The idea is to give a different flavor to write the same thing in other programming languages. Here is a sample code snippet for a cloud-native application using Java, .NET, and Node.js:

Java (Spring Boot)

Following is an example of a simple **"HelloWorld"** microservice using Spring Boot. This example includes a primary controller that handles HTTP requests and responds with a **"Hello, World!"** message.

Create a file named **HelloWorldController.java** in the **src/leading/java/com/example/helloworld** directory (you may need to create the directory structure if it does not exist) with the following content:

```
package com.example.helloworld;

import org.springframework.web.bind.annotation.GetMapping;
import org.springframework.web.bind.annotation.RequestMapping;
import org.springframework.web.bind.annotation.RestController;


@RestController
@RequestMapping("/hello")
```

```
public class HelloWorldController {

    @GetMapping
    public String helloWorld() {
        return "Hello, World!";
    }
}
```

This controller defines a simple endpoint at **/hello** that responds with the **"Hello, World!"** message.

Now, create a file named **HelloWorldApplication.java** in the same package (**com.example.helloworld**) with the following content:

```
package com.example.helloworld;

import org.springframework.boot.SpringApplication;
import org.springframework.boot.autoconfigure.SpringBootApplication;

@SpringBootApplication
public class HelloWorldApplication {

    public static void main(String[] args) {
        SpringApplication.run(HelloWorldApplication.class, args);
    }
}
```

This class contains the main method that starts the Spring Boot application.

That is it for the code. Now, you can build and run your Spring Boot application. If you do not have Maven installed, you can use the Maven Wrapper included in most Spring Boot projects.

Open a terminal and navigate to the root directory of your project, then run the following commands:

```
./mvnw clean install
```

```
./mvnw spring-boot:run
```

Spring Boot application will start, and the **"Hello, World!"** microservice will be accessible at **http://localhost:8080/hello** in your browser.

This is a basic example, and you can expand upon it by adding more features, improving error handling, or connecting to databases based on your requirements.

NET (ASP.NET Core)

C# Hello World Program: The following is an example of a simple **"HelloWorld"** microservice using C# and ASP.NET Core. This example includes a basic controller that handles HTTP requests and responds with a **"Hello, World!"** message.

Create a new ASP.NET Core Web API project with the following steps:

1. Open a terminal or command prompt.

2. Run the following command to create a new ASP.NET Core Web API project:
   dotnet new webapi -n HelloWorldService

   This will create a new project named HelloWorldService.

3. Navigate to the project directory:
   cd HelloWorldService

4. Open the project in your preferred code editor.

   Now, modify the **Controllers/WeatherForecastController.cs** file to create a **HelloWorldController**. Replace its content with the following:

```
using Microsoft.AspNetCore.Mvc;
[ApiController]
[Route("[controller]")]
public class HelloWorldController : ControllerBase
{
    [HttpGet]
    public ActionResult<string> Get()
    {
        return "Hello, World!";
    }
}
```

This controller defines a simple endpoint at **/hello** that responds with the **"Hello, World!"** message.

Now, you can run the application by executing the following command in the terminal:
dotnet run

SP.NET Core application will start, and the **"Hello, World!"** microservice will be accessible at **http://localhost:5000/hello** (or **https://localhost:5001/hello** if using HTTPS) in your browser.

This is a basic example, and you can further customize and expand upon it based on your requirements.

These code snippets demonstrate a simple **"Hello, world!"** web application using popular frameworks for Java, .NET, and Node.js. These applications can be extended further to include more complex functionality, database integrations, or interactions with cloud services based on your specific requirements.

Conclusion

Developing applications on Azure involves leveraging the various services and capabilities offered by the Azure cloud platform to build scalable, reliable, and secure applications. Here is a summary of developing applications on Azure:

- **Choose the right Azure services**: Azure provides various services for different application requirements, including computing, storage, databases, AI, analytics, messaging, and more. Understand your application needs and select the appropriate Azure services to meet those requirements.

- **Scalable and reliable architecture**: Design your application architecture to be scalable and resilient. Leverage Azure Virtual Machines, Azure App Service, Azure Functions, or **Azure Kubernetes Service (AKS)** to handle varying workloads and ensure high availability.

- **Data management**: Utilize Azure's diverse data services for efficient data management. Options include Azure Cosmos DB for NoSQL databases, Azure SQL Database for relational databases, Azure Storage for object storage, Azure Data Lake Storage for big data, and Azure Cache for Redis for caching.

- **Security and identity management**: Implement security measures such as RBAC, **Azure Active Directory (Azure AD)** authentication, and encryption mechanisms to protect your application and data. Leverage Azure Key Vault for secure key management.

- **Integration and messaging**: Connect your application with other services and systems using Azure Service Bus, Azure Event Grid, Azure Logic Apps, or Azure API Management. These services enable seamless integration, event-driven architectures, and API management.

- **DevOps and CI/CD**: Implement DevOps practices using Azure DevOps, GitHub Actions, or other CI/CD tools to automate the build, test, and deployment processes—Leverage Azure DevOps pipelines, Azure Container Registry, or Azure Functions for continuous integration and delivery.

- **Monitoring and diagnostics**: Utilize Azure Monitor, Application Insights, or Azure Log Analytics to gain visibility into the performance, availability, and health of your application. Monitor metrics, set alerts, and analyze logs for proactive monitoring and troubleshooting.

- **Serverless computing**: Leverage Azure Functions, Azure Logic Apps, or Azure App Service to build serverless applications. With serverless, you pay only for the actual usage, and Azure handles the infrastructure management and scalability.

- **Hybrid and multi-cloud solutions**: Azure offers solutions for hybrid scenarios, allowing you to integrate on-premises systems with cloud services seamlessly. Additionally, Azure provides multi-cloud capabilities to integrate with other cloud providers, enabling a multi-cloud strategy.

- **Cost optimization**: Optimize costs by leveraging Azure's cost management tools, right-sizing resources, using reserved instances, and implementing auto-scaling based on demand. Azure provides cost management and cost analysis features to track and optimize usage.

Azure provides a comprehensive set of services and tools to support the development of a wide range of applications, from simple web applications to complex enterprise solutions. By utilizing Azure's services and following best practices, developers can focus on building application logic while leveraging the scalability, reliability, and security features the Azure cloud platform provides.

In the next chapter, we will learn about different Azure Monitoring services used to monitor the applications, visualize their health, and watch the metrics.

Questions

1. Which Azure Services are best suited for my application's requirements?
2. Should I use Azure Functions, Azure App Service, or Azure Virtual Machines to host my application?
3. How can I design my application for scalability in Azure?
4. What is Docker, and what are common elements used in defining Dockerfile?
5. What is container orchestration, and what is the name of the Azure Container Service?
6. What is serverless architecture, and how is it beneficial?
7. What is Terraform and IaC?

Join our book's Discord space

Join the book's Discord Workspace for Latest updates, Offers, Tech happenings around the world, New Release and Sessions with the Authors:

https://discord.bpbonline.com

CHAPTER 6
Monitoring and Logging Applications on Azure

Introduction

The Azure cloud platform provides a comprehensive monitoring solution for collecting, analyzing, and responding to telemetry from your cloud and on-premises environments. You can use Azure Monitor service to maximize the availability and performance of your applications and services.

Azure Monitor service collects and aggregates the data from every layer and component of your system into a common data platform. It correlates data across multiple Azure subscriptions and tenants and hosting data for other services. Because this data is stored together, it can be connected and analyzed using a standard set of tools. The data can then be used for analysis and visualizations to help you understand how your applications perform and respond automatically to system events.

Azure Monitor service monitors these resources in Azure, other clouds, or on-premises for applications, virtual machines, operating systems, containers, and databases.

Structure

In this chapter, we will learn the following topics:

- Understanding Azure monitoring and logging services
- High-Level Architecture

- Azure Application Insights
- Azure Log Analytics
- Common Azure Cloud problems
- Setting up monitoring with Azure Monitor
- Troubleshooting common issues with Azure applications

Objectives

This chapter aims to provide a comprehensive solution for monitoring the performance, availability, and health of applications and resources on the Azure cloud. The primary objectives include real-time performance monitoring, proactive availability tracking, and efficient scalability based on demand. These services offer tools to collect and analyze metrics, logs, and traces, delivering insights into resource utilization, response times, and system performance.

Ensuring the availability and reliability of applications is crucial, with monitoring services providing alerts and notifications to address potential incidents promptly. Resource optimization is facilitated through metrics and performance data, supporting effective capacity planning and scaling strategies. Troubleshooting and diagnostics are streamlined with logging, tracing, and diagnostic tools, aiding in root cause analysis and issue resolution.

In this chapter, we will cover all these aspects of Azure Monitoring services and see how these services help provide reliability and availability to applications.

Understanding Azure monitoring and logging services

Azure provides several monitoring and logging services to help you gain insights into the performance, availability, and health of your applications and infrastructure. Here is a summary of crucial Azure monitoring and logging services:

Azure Monitor is a central monitoring service that provides a comprehensive solution for collecting, analysing, and acting on telemetry data from Azure resources. It monitors the following Azure services and provides insights:

- Applications
- Virtual machines
- Guest operating systems
- Containers, including Prometheus metrics
- Databases
- Security events in combination with Azure Sentinel

- Networking events and health in combination with Network Watcher
- Custom sources that use the APIs to get data into Azure Monitor

High-Level Architecture

Azure monitor has four layers of architecture. It starts with collecting and storing the metrics data from the different services. At the next layer, visual services provide the representation view of the data to provide insights. At the next layer, it provides the services to analyze the deep dive for particular topics and insights. The last layer is Respond, which provides the services in case of any issue.

There are four layers of Azure Monitoring services.

- **Metrics**: At this layer, data are collected from the different services for performance analysis.
- **Visualize**: Azure monitoring provides the services to visualize the data for better analysis. Users can see different perspectives of the data and conclude.
- **Analyze**: Azure provides different services to dive deep into the data and discover insights and meaning.
- **Respond**: At this layer, Azure provides services to respond in case of issues. Using AIOps and Logic Apps, we can build automated processes to execute the standard operating procedure to solve the problems.

The following figure provides a High-Level Architecture view of Azure Monitor:

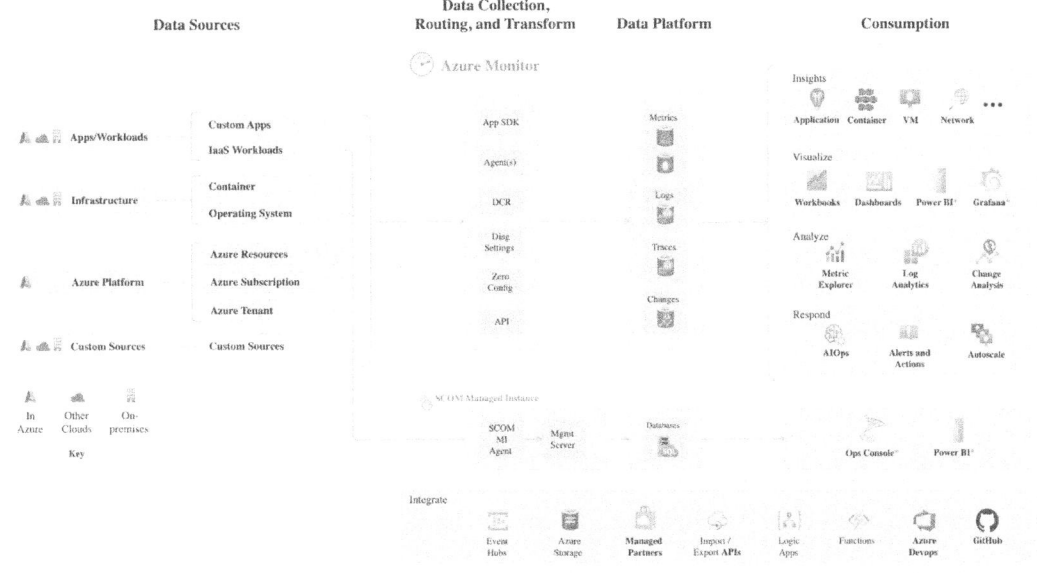

Figure 6.1: High-Level Architecture of Azure Monitoring Services

Here is the detail of different parts of the Azure Monitor system:

- The data types gathered from each monitored resource are called the data sources. The information is collected and sent to the data platform.
- The data stores for the data that has been collected make up the data platform. Metrics, logs, traces, and changes can all be stored in the data platform of Azure Monitor.
- Analysis, visualizations, insights, and responses are the functions and components that consume data.

Azure Monitor offers the following features:

Metrics: Azure Monitor collects metrics from various Azure services, allowing you to monitor performance and track resource utilization. It provides pre-defined metrics as well as the ability to create custom metrics.

Logs: Azure Monitor collects log data from Azure services, applications, and virtual machines. It supports structured logging and integrates with popular logging frameworks. You can query and analyse log data using Azure Monitor Logs.

Traces: It allows you to see the path of a request as it travels through different services and components. Azure Monitor gets distributed trace data from instrumented applications. The trace data is stored in a separate workspace in Azure Monitor Logs.

Alerts: Azure Monitor enables you to set up alerts based on metrics or log data. You can define alert rules and trigger actions like sending notifications or invoking automated actions when specific conditions are met.

Dashboards: Azure Monitor provides customizable dashboards to visualize and monitor your applications and infrastructure. You can create and share dashboards to track essential metrics and monitor the health of your resources.

Azure Application Insights

Azure Application Insights is a comprehensive **application performance monitoring (APM)** service. It is an extension of Azure Monitor service and provides application insights. It helps you detect and diagnose application performance issues by providing deep insights into application behavior.

- Learn about an application's performance in advance.
- Reactively examine application execution data to identify the incident's root cause.

Other features offered by Application Insights include, but are not limited to:

- **Live measures**: Your deployed application's activity can be observed in real-time without affecting the host environment.

- **Availability**: Synthetic transaction monitoring is another name for it. Test your applications' overall availability and responsiveness over time by probing their external endpoints.

- **Integration with Azure or GitHub DevOps**: Utilize Application Insights data and create work items for GitHub or Azure DevOps.

- **Usage**: Learn how users interact with your application and which features are most popular.

- **Advanced detection**: Through proactive telemetry analysis, automatically identify failures and anomalies.

Application Insights supports distributed tracing, also known as distributed component correlation. A specific execution or transaction's end-to-end flow can be searched for and visualized with this feature. Applications built with distributed components or microservices need to be able to track activity from start to finish.

A top-down, high-level view of the application architecture and quick visual references to component health and responsiveness are provided by the **Application map**.

Check out the Application Insights deployment planning guide to learn how many Application Insights resources are needed to cover your application or components across environments.

Application Insight's key features include the following:

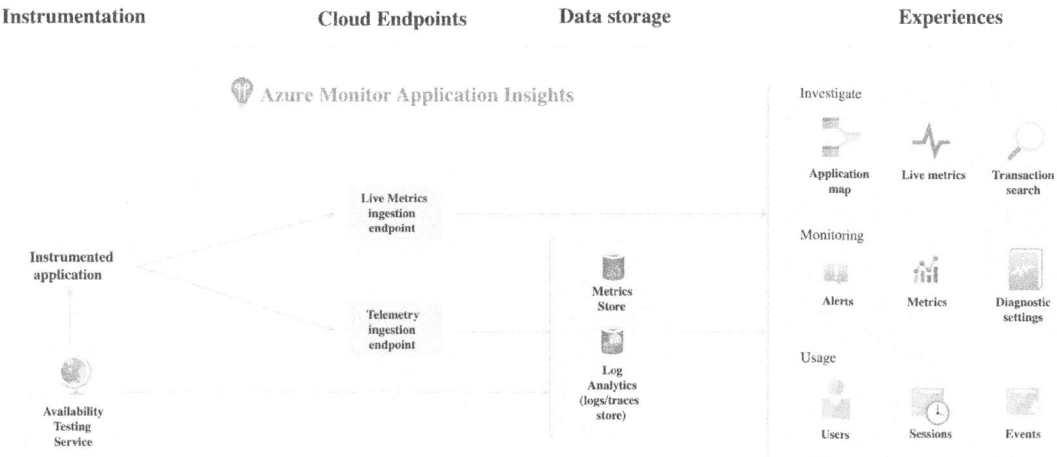

Figure 6.2: *Azure Application Insights*

Performance monitoring: Application Insights tracks application performance metrics, such as response times, request rates, and dependency calls. It provides end-to-end transaction monitoring and helps identify bottlenecks.

Exception tracking: Application Insights captures exceptions and logs detailed exception data. It allows you to analyse and diagnose application errors and provides insights into their impact on users.

Dependency tracking: Application Insights monitors dependencies, such as database calls and external services. It helps you identify slow or failing dependencies affecting application performance.

Availability testing: Application Insights allows you to set up availability tests to monitor your application's availability from multiple locations. You can configure alerts for when availability falls below specified thresholds.

How to use Application Insights

Auto instrumentation (agent) or the Application Insights SDK or Azure Monitor OpenTelemetry Distro can be added to your application code to enable Application Insights. There are many supported languages. Another cloud, on-premises, or Azure could host the applications.

Before sending the data to Azure, the Application Insights agent or SDK preprocesses telemetry and metrics. After that, it is taken in and further processed before being saved in Azure Monitor Logs (Log Analytics). Application Insights requires an Azure account because of this.

Utilizing the built-in visual experiences and the Azure portal is the easiest way to consume Application Insights. Through Azure Monitor dashboards and workbooks, advanced users can directly query the underlying data to create custom visualizations.

Consider beginning with the Application Guide for a significant-level view. You can quickly narrow down telemetry and data by type and date/time using the search experience. Alternately, you can filter down to a specific correlated operation of interest by searching within the data, such as with log traces.

Two perspectives are instrumental:

- **View of performance**: Learn how well your application, API, and downstream dependencies work. Additionally, a representative sample can be obtained for exhaustive research.

- **View of failure**: Recognize which actions or components are causing failures and prioritize errors and exceptions. The built-in views are helpful for both proactive and reactive root-cause analysis of application health.

If your application or parts deviate from the baseline, create Azure Monitor alerts to alert you to potential issues.

Application Bits of knowledge estimating depend on utilization. Only what you use is charged to you.

The preferred instrumentation technique is **auto instrumentation**. It eliminates future costs associated with updating the SDK and does not require developer investment. Additionally, it is the only method for instrumenting an application without access to the source code.

The Application Insights SDK need not be installed if:

- It would be best if you had custom metrics and events.
- Telemetry flow control is what you need.
- Language or platform restrictions typically prevent auto instrumentation from being used.
- Installing a small instrumentation package in your app and instrumenting the web app, any background components and JavaScript on the web pages are required to use the SDK. It is optional for the app and its components to be hosted in Azure.

The instrumentation monitors your app and uses a unique token to send telemetry data to an Application Insights resource. The impact on the performance of your app is minimal. Tracking calls are scheduled to be sent in a separate thread and not blocked.

Azure Log Analytics

Azure Log Analytics is a cloud-based service in Microsoft Azure that facilitates the collection, analysis, and visualization of log and performance data from diverse sources in an organization's infrastructure. It utilizes agents to gather data, and the Log Analytics workspace provides a centralized platform for querying, analyzing, and acting upon the collected information. It offers powerful query capabilities and visualization options. Key features include:

Log collection: Azure Log Analytics facilitates comprehensive log collection across diverse sources in an organization's infrastructure. It employs agents to collect and forward log data from various platforms, including Windows and Linux-based systems, virtual machines, and applications. These agents capture data on system performance, security events, application logs, and custom log sources. Azure Log Analytics also supports data ingestion from Azure services and resources, ensuring a centralized and unified approach to log collection.

The Log Analytics workspace is a repository for ingested data, enabling efficient querying, analysis, and visualization. Users can configure data collection rules, specify which logs to gather, and define custom log queries. Additionally, the service integrates with Azure Monitor, providing a seamless experience for monitoring and managing logs in the Azure environment. This centralized log collection and analysis contribute to enhanced visibility, troubleshooting capabilities, and proactive monitoring of an organization's IT infrastructure.

Log search and analysis: Azure Log Analytics is a cloud-based service in the Microsoft Azure ecosystem designed for collecting, analyzing, and visualizing log data from various sources across an organization's infrastructure. It offers a centralized platform to gain insights into system performance, detect issues, and troubleshoot problems. Users can ingest and query diverse log data from virtual machines, applications, and network resources.

With its powerful query language, **Kusto Query Language (KQL)**, users can perform advanced analytics, create custom dashboards, and set up alerts based on specific conditions. Azure Log Analytics integrates seamlessly with other Azure services, enabling comprehensive monitoring and management of resources. This tool is pivotal for organizations seeking to enhance their operational intelligence, optimize performance, and ensure the reliability of their Azure-based environments. You can search logs, correlate events, and perform advanced analytics to gain insights into application behavior and system health.

Visualization and dashboards: Log Analytics offers interactive data visualization capabilities. You can create custom dashboards to monitor specific metrics, visualize trends, and share insights with your team. Azure Log Analytics provides a robust visualization dashboard, known as Azure Monitor, that enables users to create interactive, customizable dashboards for log data analysis. This dashboard provides a unified view of collected log data, allowing users to gain insights into system health, performance, and operational trends.

Users can leverage a variety of pre-built visualizations, including line charts, bar graphs, tables, and more, to represent log data in a meaningful and actionable format. Additionally, Azure Monitor supports incorporating custom visualizations and widgets, allowing users to tailor the dashboard to their specific monitoring needs.

The dashboard enables the correlation of data from different sources, facilitating a holistic understanding of system behavior. Users can drill down into specific data points, filter information based on parameters, and set up alerts for proactive issue detection. With time-based exploration and dynamic scaling, users can effectively analyze historical trends and respond to real-time events.

Azure Monitor seamlessly integrates with other Azure services, such as Azure Application Insights and Azure Security Center, providing a comprehensive monitoring solution. This visualization dashboard enhances operational efficiency, aids in troubleshooting, and supports data-driven decision-making by offering a clear and intuitive representation of log analytics data in the Azure environment.

Based on the insights provided, Azure monitoring logs can be categorized into three high-level categories.

The following table lists the most important types of logs available in Azure:

Log category	Log type	Usage	Integration
Activity logs	Control-plane events on Azure Resource Manager resources	Provides insight into the operations that were performed on resources in your subscription.	REST API, Azure Monitor
Azure resource logs	Frequent data about the operation of Azure Resource Manager resources in subscription	Provides insight into operations that your resource itself performed.	Azure Monitor
Microsoft Entra ID reporting	Logs and reports	Reports user sign-in activities and system activity information about users and group management.	Microsoft Graph
Virtual machines and cloud services	Windows Event Log service and Linux Syslog	Captures system data and logging data on the virtual machines and transfers that data into a storage account of your choice.	Windows (using Azure Diagnostics] storage) and Linux in Azure Monitor
Azure Storage Analytics	Storage logging, provides metrics data for a storage account	Provides insight into trace requests, analyzes usage trends, and diagnoses issues with your storage account.	REST API or the client library
Network security group (NSG) flow logs	JSON format, shows outbound and inbound flows on a per-rule basis	Displays information about ingress and egress IP traffic through a network security group.	Azure Network Watcher
Application insight	Logs, exceptions, and custom diagnostics	Provides an **application performance monitoring (APM)** service for web developers on multiple platforms.	REST API, Power BI
Process data / security alerts	Microsoft Defender for Cloud Alerts, Azure Monitor logs alerts	Provides security information and alerts.	REST APIs, JSON

Table 6.1: Different types of logs in Azure

These logs can be integrated with Azure Monitor or routed to external logging systems.

These monitoring and logging services provided by Azure offer a comprehensive set of tools for monitoring, troubleshooting, and gaining insights into the performance and health of your applications and infrastructure. They allow you to proactively identify issues, optimize performance, and ensure the smooth operation of your Azure resources.

Common Azure Cloud problems

While Azure provides reliable cloud services, there can be occasional issues that users may encounter.

Here are some common Azure cloud services issues:

- **Service outages**: Azure services may experience occasional outages or disruptions due to infrastructure issues, software bugs, or planned maintenance. These outages can result in temporary unavailability or degraded performance of the affected services.

- **Connectivity issues**: Connectivity problems between Azure resources, on-premises systems, and Azure services can occur. This could be due to network misconfigurations, firewall rules, or issues with virtual network configurations.

- **Performance degradation**: Under certain circumstances, Azure services might experience performance degradation, resulting in slower response times or reduced throughput. Factors such as increased load, resource contention, or configuration issues can contribute to performance problems.

- **Authentication and authorization problems**: Issues related to authentication and authorization can arise when users encounter difficulties in authenticating Azure services, managing access control, or configuring RBAC permissions.

- **Data loss or corruption**: Although rare, data loss or corruption can occur due to software bugs, hardware failures, or human errors. It is essential to have proper backup and disaster recovery strategies to mitigate the impact of such incidents.

- **Scaling challenges**: Scaling Azure resources, such as virtual machines or Azure Functions, may encounter challenges regarding proper configuration, auto-scaling rules, or handling sudden spikes in traffic. Inefficient scaling can result in performance issues or increased costs.

- **Service integration and compatibility**: Integrating Azure services with third-party systems or ensuring compatibility between different Azure services can sometimes be challenging. Issues may arise due to version compatibility, configuration mismatches, or API changes.

- **Billing and cost management**: Understanding and managing Azure billing can be complex, particularly in environments with multiple resources and users. Users may need help with cost tracking, budgeting, resource tagging, or understanding the cost implications of different services.

- **Security and compliance**: Maintaining security and compliance in Azure environments requires proper configurations, access controls, and monitoring. Issues can arise from misconfigurations, unauthorized access attempts, or compliance gaps.

When encountering issues with Azure services, it is recommended to refer to Azure Service Health for any known incidents, review service-specific documentation and troubleshooting guides, engage with the Azure community forums, or contact Azure support for assistance in resolving the issues.

Setting up monitoring with Azure Monitor

Azure Monitor is a comprehensive cloud monitoring service provided by Microsoft Azure. It enables users to collect, analyze, and act on telemetry data from various Azure resources, applications, and infrastructure components. Azure Monitor includes features like Application Insights for performance monitoring, Log Analytics for collecting and analyzing log data, and Azure Metrics Explorer for visualizing and querying metrics. It allows users to set up alerts, create dashboards, and gain insights into their applications and resources' health, performance, and availability. Azure Monitor helps organizations ensure optimal performance, troubleshoot issues, and proactively manage the health of their Azure-based environments.

To set up monitoring with Azure Monitor, you can follow these general steps:

1. **Create an Azure Monitor resource**:

    a. Sign in to the Azure portal (**https://portal.azure.com**).

    b. Click on **+ Create a resource** and search for Azure Monitor.

    c. Select **Azure Monitor** from the search results and click **Create**.

    d. Provide the required details, such as resource group, name, and region.

    e. Click **Review + Create** and then **Create** to create the Azure Monitor resource.

2. **Enable monitoring for Azure resources**:

    a. Within the Azure Monitor resource, go to the **Monitoring** section.

    b. Click on **Add Monitoring** to add Azure resources to monitor.

    c. Select the desired Azure resources, such as virtual machines, Azure App Service, or Azure Storage accounts.

    d. Follow the prompts to enable monitoring for the selected resources.

3. **Configure diagnostic settings**:

   a. Within the Azure Monitor resource, go to the **Diagnostic settings** section.

   b. Click on **Add diagnostic setting** to configure diagnostic settings for the resources.

   c. Select the target resource or group you want to configure diagnostics.

   d. Choose the desired logs and metrics to collect, such as activity logs, diagnostic logs, or performance counters.

   e. Configure the destination for the logs, such as a storage account or Azure Event Hubs.

   f. Click **Save** to save the diagnostic settings.

4. **Set up alerts**:

   a. Within the Azure Monitor resource, go to the **Alerts** section.

   b. Click on the **New Alert Rule** to create a new alert rule.

   c. Define the conditions for triggering the alert based on metrics or log data.

   d. Configure the action groups to define the actions to take when the alert is triggered, such as sending an email, SMS, or webhook notification.

   e. Set the alert rule severity and threshold values.

   f. Save the alert rule.

5. **Visualize data and create dashboards**:

   a. Within the Azure Monitor resource, go to the **Workbooks** section.

   b. Click on **New** to create a new workbook.

   c. Select the desired visualization type, such as a chart, table, or map.

   d. Configure the data source for the workbook, selecting the appropriate metrics, logs, or other data sources.

   e. Customize the visualization, add filters, and define the layout.

   f. Save the workbook and publish it for others to view.

These steps provide a general overview of setting up monitoring with Azure Monitor. The specific configuration and options may vary depending on the Azure resources you want to watch and the particular requirements of your application or infrastructure. It would be best to refer to the Azure Monitor documentation for detailed instructions and best practices based on your specific use case.

Troubleshooting common issues with Azure applications

Troubleshooting common issues with Azure applications involves systematically identifying and resolving problems. Here are some general steps to help you troubleshoot Azure application issues:

1. **Understand the problem**:

    a. Gather information about the issue, such as error messages, symptoms, and any recent changes made to the application or infrastructure.

    b. Consult logs, metrics, and monitoring data from Azure Monitor, Azure Application Insights, or other logging services to get insights into the problem.

2. **Validate connectivity and dependencies**:

    a. Check if the Azure resources and services your application depends on are available and properly configured.

    b. Ensure that network connectivity is established between different components and services.

    c. Verify the authentication and access control settings for accessing Azure resources.

3. **Review application code and configuration**:

    a. Inspect your application code and configuration files for any errors or misconfigurations that could be causing the issue.

    b. Check for compatibility issues with Azure services or SDK versions.

    c. Validate environment-specific configuration settings, such as connection strings or environment variables.

4. **Check for service disruptions or outages**:

    a. Check the Azure Service Health dashboard for any ongoing service disruptions or outages in the Azure region where your resources are located.

    b. Monitor the Azure status page (**https://status.azure.com**) for any reported issues with specific Azure services or regions.

5. **Analyze error messages and logs**:

    a. Examine error messages, exceptions, and stack traces to understand the root cause of the problem.

b. Look for relevant logs in Azure Monitor, Application Insights, or other logging services to identify patterns or anomalies.

c. Utilize frameworks and structured logging to provide detailed and contextual information in your application logs.

6. **Leverage diagnostic tools and debugging**:

   a. Use debugging tools and techniques to inspect the application code and identify potential issues, such as breakpoints, step-through debugging, or remote debugging in Azure App Service.

   b. Utilize Azure Diagnostics Extension or Azure Diagnostics Toolkit to capture detailed diagnostic information from your application and infrastructure.

7. **Engage Azure support**: If you cannot resolve the issue through troubleshooting, consider contacting Azure support for assistance. They can provide guidance and escalate the problem if necessary.

Azure offers different support models to meet the varying needs of customers. Here are the main support models available:

8. **Basic support**: Basic support is the default support level provided to all Azure customers at no additional cost. It includes general account and billing assistance, service health notifications, access to documentation, knowledge base articles, and community forums.

9. **Developer support**: Developer support is a paid support offering that provides technical assistance to developers and IT professionals. It includes benefits such as response time guarantees, online chat support, and help with Azure development and deployment issues.

10. **Standard support**: Standard support is a comprehensive paid support offering that provides technical support for Azure services. It includes benefits such as 24/7 access to Azure support engineers, faster response times, phone support, and assistance with service outages or critical issues.

11. **Professional direct support**: Professional direct support is a higher-tier support offering for organizations that require dedicated and personalized support. It provides access to a designated **technical account manager** (**TAM**) who acts as a single point of contact for support inquiries and provides proactive guidance and assistance.

12. **Premier support**: Premier support is the highest support available for Azure customers. It offers a strategic partnership with Microsoft and provides many benefits, including access to a team of technical account managers, proactive services, architectural guidance, and personalized support plans. Here is the compare chart for all Azure support pricing plans:

	Basic	DEVELOPER	STANDARD	PROFESSIONAL DIRECT
	Request Support	Purchase Support	Purchase Support	Purchase Support
PRICE	Included for all Azure customers	$29 per month	$100 per month	$1,000 per month
SCOPE	Included for all Azure customers	Trial and non-production environments	Production workload environments	Business-critical dependence
BILLING AND SUBSCRIPTION MANAGEMENT SUPPORT	✓	✓	✓	✓
24/7 SELF-HELP RESOURCES, INCLUDING MICROSOFT LEARN, AZURE PORTAL HOW-TO VIDEOS, DOCUMENTATION, AND COMMUNITY SUPPORT	✓	✓	✓	✓
ABILITY TO SUBMIT AS MANY SUPPORT TICKETS AS YOU NEED	✓	✓	✓	✓
AZURE ADVISOR—YOUR FREE, PERSONALIZED GUIDE TO AZURE BEST PRACTICES	✓	✓	✓	✓
AZURE HEALTH STATUS AND NOTIFICATIONS	✓	✓	✓	✓
THIRD-PARTY SOFTWARE SUPPORT WITH INTEROPERABILITY AND CONFIGURATION GUIDANCE AND TROUBLESHOOTING		✓	✓	✓

Figure 6.3: Azure pricing plans

It is important to note that these support models' availability and specific features may vary depending on your location and subscription type. It is recommended to visit the Azure Support website (**https://azure.microsoft.com/support/**) for detailed information on the available support options and to choose the one that best fits your organization's needs.

Remember to document your troubleshooting steps and any changes made during the process. This helps track progress and can be helpful for future reference or sharing with support teams.

It is important to note that troubleshooting Azure application issues can vary depending on the application, architecture, and technologies used. Always refer to the relevant documentation, support resources, and community forums for detailed troubleshooting guidance specific to your scenario.

Conclusion

Azure offers a comprehensive suite of monitoring and logging services designed to provide insights into applications and infrastructure performance, availability, and health. Key components include Azure Monitor, Azure Log Analytics, and Azure Application Insights.

Azure Monitor is a central monitoring hub that collects and analyzes telemetry data from Azure resources. It encompasses Metrics for tracking performance and resource utilization with alert capabilities, logs for centralized log collection from Azure services and applications, and Application Insights for detailed application performance monitoring, including response times, request rates, dependency calls, and exception tracking.

Azure Log Analytics is a versatile service focusing on log and performance data analysis. It centralizes log data from various sources, supporting Windows and Linux environments. The service provides a robust query language for exploring and analyzing log data, enabling users to search logs, correlate events, and perform advanced analytics. Visualization and dashboard features allow the creation of custom dashboards for monitoring specific metrics, visualizing trends, and sharing insights with teams.

Azure Application Insights is an APM service embedded within Azure Monitor. It offers comprehensive insights into application performance and usage. The service monitors performance metrics, tracks dependencies, captures exceptions, and facilitates end-to-end transaction monitoring. Users can set up availability tests to monitor application availability from multiple locations, configure alerts for threshold breaches, and gain deep insights into application errors and their impact on users.

Collectively, these services provide users with the tools to proactively identify issues, optimize performance, and ensure the smooth operation of Azure resources. The capabilities offered by Azure's monitoring and logging services empower organizations to troubleshoot efficiently, gain valuable insights, and maintain the health and performance of their applications and infrastructure on the Azure cloud platform.

In the next chapter, we will learn about Azure Security and Data Governance services.

Questions

1. How does Azure Monitor help in performance monitoring?
2. What is the role of Azure Log Analytics in troubleshooting?
3. How does Azure Application Insights contribute to Application Performance Monitoring?
4. What alerting capabilities does Azure Monitor offer?
5. How can Log Analytics dashboards be customized for visualization?

Join our book's Discord space

Join the book's Discord Workspace for Latest updates, Offers, Tech happenings around the world, New Release and Sessions with the Authors:

https://discord.bpbonline.com

CHAPTER 7
Security and Governance in Azure

Introduction

Security is the crucial aspect and architecture building block that every customer does not want to compromise on. We call it the security-first approach while building any application and follow the zero-trust approach. Azure Cloud has multiple features that help security architects design and build systems that are more secure of the cloud and secure from the cloud. Finding out the attack surfaces is the key objective of any security architect.

We will learn how Azure Cloud helps build the right strategy to identify the surface of attacks, threat modeling to discover possible vulnerabilities, and the remediation plans to mitigate those. We will go through the mechanism of penetration testing, commonly known as **PEN testing,** and why it is essential today.

We will also go through the different encryption mechanisms provided by Microsoft Azure and the scenarios to use it. We will also learn what comes under the purview of customers and what goes under the purview of cloud providers regarding security responsibilities.

We will also discuss Azure Cloud's different services, like Azure Key Vault for storing secrets, Azure IAM, and AD services for user onboarding and role provisioning. We will go through Microsoft Sentinel and Microsoft Defender to monitor the infrastructure for any attacks.

Data governance is the collection of processes, policies, roles, metrics, and standards that ensure an effective and efficient use of information. This also helps establish data management processes that keep your data secured, private, accurate, and usable throughout the data life cycle.

Today, every company wants to make data-driven decisions. They want to utilize all the data available within the organization to achieve that. Organizations are building data lakes and enabling all the departments to write all their data to the lakes. That data is used for different analytics engines to find insights that help build the right strategies for organizations.

Azure Databricks, which we covered in *Chapter 3, Data Services on Azure Cloud*, provides centralized data governance using solutions like **Unity Catalog** and **Delta Sharing**. Unity Catalog is a fine-grained governance solution for data and AI, while Delta Sharing is an open protocol developed by Databricks for secure data sharing with other organizations.

Structure

In this chapter, we will learn the following topics:

- Understanding Azure security and governance features
- Best practices for securing Azure applications
- Identifying surface attacks
- Threat modeling
- Understanding Azure governance policies
- Access controls and identity management on Azure
- Data governance

Objectives

In this chapter, we will learn that security is a paramount requirement of every organization and is a fundamental part of software development. Most companies use the security-first approach in their software development. It ensures that for every business feature, we need to consider the possible surface attacks during the designing process and prepare a plan to mitigate those. We will also go through, as a cloud service provider, what services Azure provides to secure the infrastructure and services. Threat modeling is the key, so we will use different techniques to identify the threat surfaces. We will learn about various governance features and policies Azure provides to help protect data and services.

Understanding Azure security and governance features

Azure provides comprehensive security and governance features to help protect your cloud resources, data, and applications. Here are some key features and services:

- **Azure Active Directory (Azure AD)**: Azure AD is a cloud-based identity and access management service. It provides features like **multi-factor authentication (MFA)**, conditional access policies, **role-based access control (RBAC)**, and **single sign-on (SSO)** to protect user identities and control access to resources.

- **Azure Security Center**: Azure Security Center is a unified security management and monitoring service. It provides threat protection across hybrid cloud workloads and offers features such as security policy management, continuous security assessments, threat intelligence, and advanced threat detection.

- **Azure Sentinel**: Azure Sentinel is a cloud-native **security information and event management (SIEM)** service. It collects and analyzes security data from various sources, including Azure Services, third-party solutions, and on-premises systems. Azure Sentinel uses advanced analytics and machine learning to detect and respond to threats.

- **Azure Firewall**: Azure Firewall is a managed network security service that provides inbound and outbound filtering for virtual network resources. It helps protect your applications and data by inspecting and filtering network traffic based on user-defined rules.

- **Azure DDoS Protection**: Azure DDoS Protection helps safeguard your applications against **distributed denial of service (DDoS)** attacks. It automatically detects and mitigates volumetric, state-exhaustion, and application-layer attacks, protecting your Azure resources and ensuring service availability.

- **Azure Key Vault**: Azure Key Vault is a secure key and secret management service. It allows you to securely store and manage cryptographic keys, certificates, connection strings, and other sensitive information. Key Vault helps protect your secrets by providing robust access control and auditing capabilities.

- **Azure Information Protection (AIP)**: AIP helps you classify, label, and protect your sensitive data. It allows you to define data classification policies, apply labels to documents and emails, and apply encryption and access controls to protect data within and outside your organization.

- **Azure Policy**: Azure Policy is a service that allows you to enforce compliance with organizational standards and policies. It enables you to define and implement rules and controls over resources to meet security, compliance, and governance requirements.

- **Azure Resource Manager (ARM)**: ARM provides a unified management layer for deploying, managing, and organizing Azure resources. It allows you to define and enforce resource policies, apply RBAC, and implement resource tagging for improved governance and security.

- **Azure DevOps**: Azure DevOps provides development tools and services that enable organizations to build, test, and deploy applications efficiently. It includes features for version control, **continuous integration, and delivery (CI/CD)**, as well as security integration like SAST/DAST scans throughout the application lifecycle.

These are just a few examples of Azure's security and governance features. Azure continually evolves, and new features and services are regularly introduced to enhance security and compliance capabilities.

Best practices for securing Azure applications

Securing Azure applications requires following a set of best practices to protect your resources, data, and users. Here are some essential practices to consider:

- **Use strong authentication and access controls**:
  - Implement **multi-factor authentication (MFA)** for user accounts.
  - Utilize Azure AD for centralized identity and access management.
  - Implement **role-based access control (RBAC)** to grant least privilege access.

- **Secure network traffic**:
  - Use **Azure Virtual Network (VNet)** to isolate resources and control network traffic.
  - Implement **network security groups (NSGs)** to enforce access control rules.
  - Utilize Azure Firewall or Azure Application Gateway for additional network security.

- **Encrypt data**:
  - Use **Azure Storage Service Encryption (SSE)** to encrypt data at rest.
  - Utilize Azure Key Vault to manage and protect encryption keys and secrets.
  - Implement **transport layer security (TLS)** for data in transit.

- **Implement logging, monitoring, and threat detection**:
  - Enable Azure Monitor to collect and analyze resource-level and platform-level logs.

- o Utilize Azure Security Center for threat detection and continuous monitoring.
- o Implement Azure Sentinel for centralized **security information and event management (SIEM)**.

- **Apply security updates and patches**:
  - o Regularly update and patch operating systems, applications, and Azure services.
  - o Utilize Azure Security Center's recommendations for vulnerability assessments.

- **Secure DevOps practices**:
  - o Implement secure development practices, such as secure coding and code review.
  - o Utilize Azure DevOps for secure CI/CD pipelines and automated security testing.
  - o Incorporate security testing, including vulnerability scanning and penetration testing.

- **Implement data protection and privacy measures**:
  - o Classify and label sensitive data (PCI, SPI) using **Azure Information Protection (AIP)**.
  - o Apply **data loss prevention (DLP)** policies to prevent data leakage.
  - o Comply with applicable data protection regulations, such as GDPR or HIPAA.

- **Regularly backup and restore data**:
  - o Implement a backup and disaster recovery strategy for your Azure Resources.
  - o Utilize Azure Backup or Azure Site Recovery for automated backup and restore capabilities.

- **Implement security governance and compliance**:
  - o Define and enforce security policies using Azure Policy.
  - o Regularly audit and review security configurations and access controls.
  - o Monitor compliance using Azure Compliance Manager or third-party solutions.

- **Stay updated with Azure general security best practices**:
  - o Keep track of Azure security documentation, guidelines, and best practices.
  - o Follow the Azure Security Blog and attend security webinars to stay informed about the latest security updates and recommendations.

Remember that security is an ongoing process, and it is essential to regularly assess, review, and update your security measures to adapt to new threats and vulnerabilities.

Identifying surface attacks

The attack surface in security refers to all potential points where an unauthorized user or malicious entity could attempt to enter or extract data from a system. It represents the vulnerabilities and entry points that attackers could exploit to compromise the security of a system, network, or application. A larger attack surface allows attackers to find and exploit weaknesses.

There may be different elements that can contribute to the surface of attacks, and here are the details of each one:

- **Network services**: Network interfaces are highly targeted by intruders for unauthorized access. Below are a few points that can contribute to that.
- **Open ports**: Ports are virtual endpoints for network communication. Each open port represents a potential entry point for attackers. Reducing unnecessary open ports minimizes the attack surface.
- **Protocols**: Different network protocols may introduce vulnerabilities. It's crucial to secure protocols and disable any unnecessary or insecure ones.
- **Network interfaces**: Each network interface represents a potential connection point. Unneeded or insecure interfaces should be disabled or secured.
- **Software interfaces**: Software interfaces are another target for intruders to access the system unauthorizedly. Here are the common gaps that intruders try to find for unauthorized access.
- **APIs (application programming interfaces)** are interaction points between different software systems. Insecure APIs can be exploited for unauthorized access or manipulation.
- **Web services**: Similar to APIs, web services provide a means for different applications to communicate over the web. Securing web services involves implementing authentication, encryption, and proper access controls.
- **Software components**: Insecure software components, such as libraries or modules, can introduce vulnerabilities. Regularly updating and patching software is essential to address known vulnerabilities.
- **User interfaces**: User interfaces are another layer of surface attacks intruders use for unauthorized access.
- **Web interfaces**: Web applications often have user interfaces accessible over the internet. Secure coding practices, input validation, and authentication mechanisms are crucial to prevent attacks like SQL injection or cross-site scripting.

- **Applications**: Any software with a user interface should be designed with security in mind to prevent unauthorized access or manipulation.

- **Hardware interfaces**: In the era of IoT, hardware devices also provide ways to access the system.

- **External connections**: Physical connections to hardware, such as USB ports or external storage devices, can introduce security risks. Managing and securing external connections is essential to prevent unauthorized access or data leakage.

- **Devices**: Hardware devices connected to a system, including IoT devices, should be secure to prevent compromise and potential attacks on the overall system.

- **Authentication mechanisms**: Authentication is a critical aspect of the system and is one of the favorite surfaces of attacks for intruders.

- **User authentication**: Weak or compromised authentication methods can lead to unauthorized access. Secure password policies, multi-factor authentication, and proper user management are critical.

- **Access controls**: Ensuring that users have the least privilege necessary to perform their tasks reduces the risk of unauthorized access. Regularly reviewing and updating access controls is essential for security.

As we see from the above, every application layer provides attack surfaces, which intruders can use for potential attacks. Azure provides different services and mechanisms to secure the application and avoid possible attacks if it is appropriately implemented.

Securing Azure applications requires following best practices to protect your resources, data, and users. Here are some essential practices to consider:

- **Azure Security Center (ASC)**: Utilize Azure Security Center to monitor your Azure resources' security continuously. ASC provides security recommendations, threat protection, and advanced threat detection across your Azure subscriptions.

- **Log Analytics and Azure Monitor**: Enable Azure Monitor and Log Analytics to collect and analyze logs from various Azure services. Create custom queries and alerts to identify suspicious activities.

- **Azure Active Directory (AAD) Logs**: Monitor Azure AD logs for unusual sign-in activities, such as multiple failed login attempts, sign-ins from unique locations, or extraordinary times.

- **Azure Network Security Groups (NSG) and Firewalls**: Review NSG logs and traffic flow to identify unauthorized access attempts or unusual network traffic patterns. Monitor Azure Firewall logs for suspicious traffic patterns, such as repeated attempts to access blocked resources.

- **Azure Application Gateway and Web Application Firewall (WAF)**: Analyze logs and metrics from these services to identify potential attacks targeting web applications.

- **Azure DDoS Protection**: Monitor DDoS protection metrics for any unexpected traffic spikes that could indicate a potential DDoS attack.

- **Azure Security Logs**: Enable diagnostic settings for Azure resources to stream logs to Azure Log Analytics. This provides visibility into activities across your resources.

- **Azure Key Vault Auditing**: Enable auditing on your Azure Key Vault to track access and operations on secrets, keys, and certificates.

- **Azure Sentinel Security Information and Event Management (SIEM)**: If available, use Azure Sentinel as your system to correlate events and generate alerts based on security incidents.

- **Threat Intelligence Feeds**: Integrate threat intelligence feeds into your security monitoring. These feeds can provide information about known malicious IP addresses, domains, and indicators of compromise.

- **Azure Bastion and VPN Gateway**: Monitor logs related to Azure Bastion and VPN Gateway for any unusual access patterns.

- **Azure Security Policy and Compliance Center**: Regularly review compliance reports and security policies to ensure your resources are configured according to best practices.

- **Multi-Factor Authentication (MFA) Logs**: Monitor MFA logs for unusual or failed authentication attempts.

- **User and Entity Behavior Analytics (UEBA)**: Utilize UEBA solutions to detect anomalies in user and entity behavior, helping to identify potential insider threats.

- **Incident Response Plan**: Have a well-defined incident response plan to respond effectively to identified security incidents.

Remember that a holistic approach to security involves monitoring, detection, prevention, and response. Regularly update security configurations, conduct security assessments, and stay informed about emerging threats and vulnerabilities. Additionally, consider leveraging Azure's native security services and partner solutions for enhanced protection. Remember that security is an ongoing process, and it is essential to regularly assess, review, and update your security measures to adapt to new threats and vulnerabilities.

Threat modeling

Threat modeling is a process that helps identify and mitigate potential security threats and vulnerabilities in a system or application.

When applying threat modeling in the context of Azure cloud, consider the following steps:

1. **Identify the scope**: Clearly define the scope of your threat modeling exercise, such as the Azure cloud services, applications, or specific components you want to analyze.

2. **Understand the system**: Gain a deep understanding of the Azure cloud environment, including its architecture, data flows, communication channels, and dependencies. Identify the assets, such as sensitive data, virtual machines, databases, or APIs, that need protection.

3. **Identify threats**: Brainstorm potential threats and attack vectors that could exploit vulnerabilities in your Azure cloud environment. Consider common and Azure-specific threats, such as unauthorized access, data breaches, denial-of-service attacks, misconfigurations, or insider threats.

4. **Assess vulnerabilities**: Evaluate the system and its components for vulnerabilities that could be exploited by the identified threats. Consider weak access controls, insecure configurations, lack of encryption, or outdated software.

5. **Prioritize threats**: Prioritize the identified threats based on their potential impact and likelihood of occurrence. Focus on high-impact threats that are more likely to occur and could cause significant damage to your Azure resources and data.

6. **Mitigation strategies**: Develop mitigation strategies to address the identified threats and vulnerabilities. Consider Azure's native security features and services, such as access control mechanisms, encryption, Azure Security Center recommendations, or Azure Policy. Also, follow security best practices like least privilege access, secure coding, and regular patching and updates.

7. **Validate and refine**: Test and validate your mitigation strategies to ensure their effectiveness. Use tools like Azure Security Center, Azure Advisor, or vulnerability scanners to identify any remaining vulnerabilities. Iterate and refine your mitigation strategies as necessary.

8. **Document and communicate**: Document the threat modeling process, including the identified threats, vulnerabilities, and mitigation strategies. Share the findings with relevant stakeholders, development teams, and security personnel to ensure a shared understanding and alignment.

9. **Integrate into the development lifecycle**: Incorporate threat modeling as an ongoing activity within the Azure cloud application development lifecycle. Perform regular reviews and updates to address new threats, changes in the environment, or updates to Azure services.

By incorporating threat modeling into your Azure cloud environment, you can proactively identify and address potential security risks, improving the overall security posture of your applications and data.

Understanding Azure governance policies

Azure governance policies are rules and guidelines that help enforce compliance, security, and best practices within an Azure environment. They enable organizations to define and manage standards for their Azure resources.

Here are some different types of Azure governance policies:

- **Azure Policy**: Azure Policy is a service that allows you to create, assign, and enforce policies across your Azure subscriptions. It helps ensure compliance with organizational standards and regulatory requirements. Azure Policy enables you to define rules that control resource properties, configurations, and access controls.

- **Azure Blueprints**: Azure Blueprints provide a way to package and automate the deployment of cloud environments that adhere to organizational standards and best practices. Blueprints consist of artifacts, including Azure Policy definitions, role assignments, resource groups, and resource templates. They enable the consistent and repeatable deployment of compliant Azure environments.

- **Azure management groups**: Azure management groups allow you to organize and manage access, policies, and compliance across multiple Azure subscriptions. They provide a hierarchical structure for applying governance controls, enabling centralized management and policy enforcement at scale.

- **Azure RBAC (role-based access control)**: Azure RBAC allows you to manage access to Azure resources based on predefined roles and permissions. It provides fine-grained control over who can perform specific actions on resources. RBAC policies can be used to enforce consistent access controls across Azure subscriptions and resources.

- **Azure cost management + billing**: Azure cost management + billing offers policy capabilities to control and optimize cloud costs. It lets you define spending limits, budget alerts, and cost thresholds. Policies can be applied to manage resource tagging, enforce resource usage quotas, or optimize cost allocation and billing.

- **Azure Resource Manager (ARM) templates**: ARM templates provide a way to define and deploy Azure resources using a declarative syntax. Templates can include policy definitions that enforce specific configuration requirements during resource deployment. By embedding policies in templates, you can ensure that resources are provisioned consistently and according to defined governance standards.

- **Azure Compliance Center**: Azure Compliance Center offers a set of built-in and customizable policies for achieving compliance with various regulatory frameworks, such as GDPR, HIPAA, ISO, and NIST. These policies help monitor and report on compliance-related activities within Azure.

- **Azure Security Center**: Azure Security Center provides security policies and recommendations to help protect Azure resources. It offers predefined security policies aligned with industry best practices and regulatory standards. These policies help identify and address security vulnerabilities, misconfigurations, and potential threats.

Some key Azure governance policies and tools are available to help organizations maintain control, enforce compliance, and adhere to best practices across their Azure environments. They provide a framework for managing and governing resources effectively while ensuring security and regulatory compliance.

Access control and identity management on Azure

Implementing access control and identity management in Azure involves leveraging **Azure Active Directory** (**Azure AD**) and other related services to manage user identities, control access to Azure resources, and enforce security policies. Here are the steps to implement access control and identity management in Azure:

1. **Set up Azure Active Directory (Azure AD)**:

    a. Create an Azure AD tenant if you do not have one.

    b. Configure user accounts, groups, and roles in Azure AD.

2. **Integrate Azure AD with your applications**:

    a. Register your applications in Azure AD to enable **single sign-on** (**SSO**) and user authentication.

    b. Configure authentication methods like password-based sign-in, **multi-factor authentication** (**MFA**), or social identity providers.

3. **Define RBAC**:

    a. Assign users and groups to predefined or custom roles controlling access to Azure resources.

    b. Use Azure RBAC to grant permissions at different levels, such as subscription, resource group, or individual resources.

4. **Implement conditional access policies**:

    a. Configure conditional access policies in Azure AD to enforce additional security controls based on user, device, location, or other conditions.

    b. Enable features like MFA, device registration, or session controls based on policy requirements.

5. **Utilize Azure AD Privileged Identity Management (PIM)**:

    a. Enable PIM to manage privileged access to Azure resources.

    b. Assign time-bound, **just-in-time** (**JIT**) access to administrative roles and enforce approval workflows.

    c. Monitor and audit elite role assignments and access activities.

6. **Implement Azure AD Identity Protection**:

    a. Enable Azure AD Identity Protection to detect and respond to risky sign-in behaviors or potential identity threats.

    b. Configure risk-based policies to enforce additional security measures, such as requiring MFA for suspicious activities.

7. **Implement Azure AD Connect for hybrid environments**:

    a. Use Azure AD Connect to synchronize on-premises Active Directory with Azure AD for seamless user authentication and identity management.

    b. Enable password hash synchronization or pass-through authentication to provide a unified login experience.

8. **Leverage Azure AD B2B and B2C**:

    a. Use Azure AD B2B to invite external users to collaborate securely on Azure resources.

    b. Implement Azure AD B2C for managing customer identities and enabling external user sign-up and sign-in experiences.

9. **Monitor and analyze user and access activities**:

    a. Azure AD logs and reporting capabilities are utilized to monitor user sign-in activities, audit access attempts, and detect potential security threats.

    b. Integrate Azure AD with Azure Monitor or Azure Sentinel for advanced security monitoring and threat detection.

10. **Regularly review and update access control:**

    a. Perform periodic reviews of access controls, roles, and permissions to ensure they align with your organization's requirements.

    b. Implement access reviews to validate and recertify user access to Azure resources periodically.

By following these steps and leveraging Azure AD's features and services, you can implement robust access control and identity management practices in your Azure environment, ensuring secure and controlled access to your resources.

Data governance

Azure provides several data governance methodologies and tools to help organizations manage and govern their data effectively.

Here are some critical Azure data governance methodologies:

- **Data classification and labeling**:
    - **Azure Information Protection (AIP)**: AIP allows you to classify and label sensitive data based on content, context, and user-defined policies. It enables consistent data protection across Azure services and helps enforce data handling and access policies.

- **Data cataloging and discovery**:
    - **Azure Data Catalog**: Azure Data Catalog is a service that provides a unified view of your data assets across various sources. It enables data discovery, classification, and lineage tracking to enhance data governance and management practices.

- **Data lineage and traceability**:
    - **Azure Purview**: Azure Purview can be considered the next generation of Azure Data Catalog, which helps capture and visualize data lineage, allowing you to track the origin, transformations, and movement of your data. It provides insights into data dependencies and facilitates compliance and regulatory requirements.

- **Data quality management**:
    - **Azure Data Factory**: Azure Data Factory offers integration and transformation capabilities, including data cleansing and validation. It allows you to build data pipelines that ensure data quality and consistency.

- **Data encryption and protection**:
    - **Azure Storage Service Encryption (SSE)**: SSE automatically encrypts data at rest within Azure Storage services, providing an additional layer of data protection.
    - **Azure Key Vault**: Azure Key Vault enables secure key management and provides encryption keys for Azure services and applications. It helps protect sensitive data by safeguarding encryption keys and secrets.

- **Data masking and anonymization**:
    - **Azure Data Masking**: Azure Data Masking helps protect sensitive data in non-production environments by dynamically masking sensitive data elements.

It enables controlled access to masked data for development and testing purposes.

- **Data access control**:

    o **Azure RBAC**: Azure RBAC allows you to manage access to Azure resources based on predefined roles and permissions. It helps enforce fine-grained access controls to safeguard data.

    o **Azure AD (Azure Active Directory)**: Azure AD provides identity and access management capabilities, enabling you to control user access to data and applications in Azure.

- **Data retention and archiving**:

    o **Azure Blob Storage Lifecycle Management**: Blob Storage Lifecycle Management allows you to define policies for data retention and automatic archiving or deletion based on specified criteria.

    o **Azure Archive Storage**: Azure Archive Storage offers a cost-effective solution for long-term data archiving. It enables you to store rarely accessed data at a lower cost while ensuring data durability.

- **Data compliance and privacy**:

    o **Azure Policy and Azure Blueprints**: Azure Policy and Azure Blueprints help enforce compliance controls and best practices across Azure resources and deployments. They assist in aligning with regulatory requirements, such as GDPR or HIPAA.

    o **Azure Compliance Manager**: Azure Compliance Manager provides a central dashboard to assess, track, and monitor compliance with various regulatory standards and frameworks.

These methodologies and tools provide a comprehensive approach to data governance in Azure, ensuring data security, compliance, and effective management throughout the data lifecycle. Organizations can leverage these capabilities to implement robust data governance practices and maintain control over their data assets.

Conclusion

Microsoft's cloud platform, Azure, champions a security-first approach, urging organizations to assess potential attack surfaces proactively. Azure offers a comprehensive suite of security and governance features to fortify cloud resources, applications, and data. Azure AD, a cloud-based identity and access management service, integrates multi-factor authentication, conditional access policies, RBAC, and SSO. The Azure Security Center unifies security management, incorporating threat protection, policy management, assessments, and advanced threat detection. Azure Sentinel, a cloud-native SIEM service, employs advanced analytics and machine learning to identify and respond to threats.

Azure Firewall ensures network security with managed inbound and outbound filtering, while Azure DDoS Protection safeguards against DDoS attacks. For sensitive information, Azure Key Vault manages secure keys and secrets, and Azure Information Protection classifies, labels, and protects data with encryption and access controls. Azure Policy enforces governance by defining rules and controls for security and compliance.

Implementing access control involves configuring Azure AD, defining RBAC, and using Azure AD PIM. Data governance in Azure spans data classification, cataloging, lineage, encryption, masking, access control, retention, and compliance. Azure provides a robust ecosystem to fortify cloud environments, ensuring security, governance, and effective data management throughout the application lifecycle.

The next chapter will discuss the **continuous integration/continuous deployment (CI/CD)** process and pipeline development. We will see how CI/CD provides agility and speed to the development process.

Questions

1. How does the security-first approach influence the software development process, and why is it a fundamental part of development?

2. Can you briefly list and briefly explain the three key security features Azure provides to protect cloud resources, applications, and data?

3. What are the essential steps in the threat modeling process for securing Azure applications, and why is it considered a critical practice?

4. Describe the steps involved in implementing access control and identity management in Azure, emphasizing the role of Azure Active Directory.

5. Explain how Azure supports data governance, covering methodologies and tools for data classification, cataloging, encryption, access control, and compliance.

6. What are the essential best practices for securing Azure applications, covering authentication, network security, data encryption, and continuous security integration in DevOps?

7. Name two Azure services designed explicitly for threat detection and monitoring and explain how they enhance the overall security posture.

8. Why is threat modeling considered a crucial step in the development lifecycle, and how does it contribute to building secure applications in Azure?

9. Discuss Azure services and features related to data protection, including encryption, key management, and tools for safeguarding sensitive information.

Join our book's Discord space

Join the book's Discord Workspace for Latest updates, Offers, Tech happenings around the world, New Release and Sessions with the Authors:

https://discord.bpbonline.com

CHAPTER 8
Deploying Applications on Azure

Introduction

Azure offers several services for implementing **continuous integration and continuous delivery (CI/CD)** pipelines for building, testing, and deploying applications.

Azure DevOps is a comprehensive set of services for managing the entire application lifecycle. It includes version control, build and release management, testing, and project management features.

Azure Pipelines is a fully managed CI/CD service that enables building, testing, and deploying code to any platform or cloud. It supports CI and delivery for various programming languages and platforms, including .NET, Java, Python, and Node.js.

Azure Container Registry is a fully managed service for storing and managing container images. **Azure Kubernetes Service (AKS)** is a managed Kubernetes service that simplifies containerized applications' deployment, management, and scaling.

Azure GitHub Actions is a powerful tool for automating the deployment and management of applications on Azure, as it provides a seamless integration between GitHub Actions and Azure services. Developers can use Azure GitHub Actions to deploy and manage their applications quickly without leaving the GitHub ecosystem.

Azure Serverless services Azure Functions and Logic Apps can be deployed using various methods depending on the application's specific requirements. It can be deployed by Azure portal, CLI, and Visual Studio.

Regardless of the method used, developers should always follow best practices for deployment, such as using source control, testing the code before deployment, and monitoring the application once it is deployed.

Structure

In this chapter, we will learn the following topics:

- Introduction to DevOps and CI/CD
- Key principles of DevOps
- Understanding DevOps CI/CD in Azure cloud
- Setting up DevOps pipeline with Azure DevOps
- Implementing automated QA
- Azure DevOps and GitHub Actions
- Using Azure Kubernetes Service
- Azure Functions and Logic Apps
- Best practices for deploying applications on Azure

Objectives

By the end of this chapter, we will learn how Azure CI/CD and DevOps services enhance and automate the software development lifecycle. CI involves automating the building and testing of code changes, ensuring consistency and reliability. CD extends this automation to the deployment phase, allowing for swift and frequent releases of software updates. The overarching goal is to deliver high-quality software to end-users quickly and efficiently. Emphasizing automation for a standardized, error-free process, CI/CD fosters collaboration between development and operations, accelerating time to market. **Infrastructure as Code (IaC)** ensures consistency, embedded security reduces vulnerabilities, and continuous monitoring adapts to dynamic changes for prompt issue resolution in production.

In summary, learning Azure CI/CD and DevOps empowers professionals to automate, collaborate, and accelerate software development, resulting in efficient, reliable, and customer-centric applications. This skill set is essential for staying competitive and responsive in the ever-evolving IT industry.

Introduction to DevOps and CI/CD

DevOps and **continuous integration/continuous deployment (CI/CD)** are two closely related practices in software development that aim to improve collaboration, speed, and efficiency in delivering high-quality software. Let us start with an introduction to DevOps and then delve into CI/CD.

DevOps

DevOps is a cultural and organizational approach that promotes collaboration between **development (Dev)** and **operations (Ops)** teams throughout the entire software development lifecycle. It breaks down the traditional barriers between these teams, fostering better communication, cooperation, and shared responsibilities. DevOps aims to streamline processes, enhance automation, and improve software delivery. The following figure details the Azure DevOps services and how they help in each part of the process, such as building, planning, integration, and deployment.

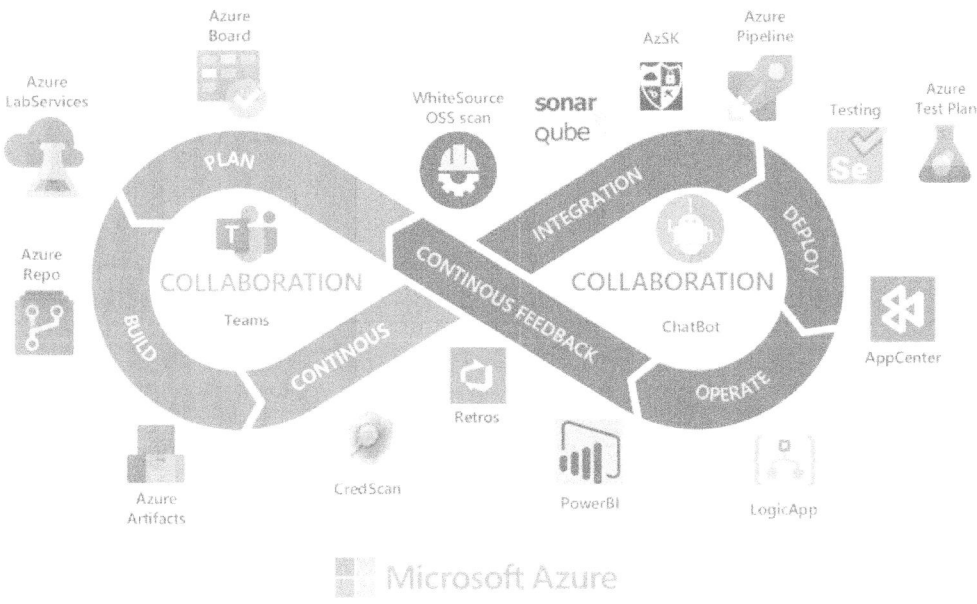

Figure 8.1: Azure DevOps process

Continuous integration and continuous deployment

CI/CD stands for **continuous integration and continuous deployment**. It is a set of modern software development practices aimed at improving software applications' efficiency, quality, and speed. CI/CD involves automating and streamlining various stages of the software development lifecycle, from code writing to deployment and beyond. Here is a breakdown of what CI/CD entails:

Continuous integration

Continuous integration (CI) focuses on regularly integrating code changes from multiple developers into a shared code repository. The main goal is to catch integration issues early by automatically building and testing the codebase whenever new changes are pushed. CI aims to ensure that the integrated code remains stable and functional throughout development.

Key practices of CI include:

- Frequent code commits to the version control system.
- Automated building and compilation of the codebase.
- Automated testing, including unit tests and integration tests.
- Early detection of integration issues and bugs.

Continuous deployment/continuous delivery

Continuous delivery involves automated build, test, and preparation of code changes for release but requires manual intervention for deployment to production. In contrast, continuous deployment automates the entire release process, including deployment to production, without human intervention. Continuous deployment and continuous delivery CD are both practices in software development aimed at automating and streamlining the release process.

Continuous deployment: CD automatically deploys every code change that passes through the CI process to the nonproduction and production environments, making new features and bug fixes available to users immediately. This means that new features, bug fixes, and updates are rapidly pushed to users as soon as they are ready. Once the changes are validated in staging or pre-production environments, they are automatically deployed to production environments without requiring manual approval or intervention. This results in a continuous flow of updates to production, allowing organizations to deliver new features and bug fixes rapidly.

Continuous delivery: Continuous delivery is a practice where code changes are automatically built, tested, and prepared for release to production environments. However, the actual deployment to production needs to be automated and requires human intervention. Continuous delivery aims to ensure that software is always in a releasable state, allowing teams to release updates to production at any time with minimal manual effort. Instead, changes that pass automated tests are automatically prepared and packaged for deployment. The deployment to the production environment is then triggered manually or as part of an automated process. As you can see in the following figure, CI/CD is a continuous process:

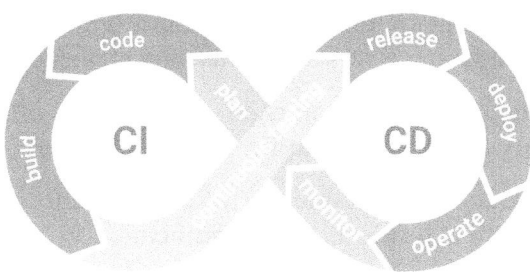

Figure 8.2: CI/CD process

Benefits of CI/CD:

The following are the benefits of CI/CD:

- **Faster releases**: CI/CD enables quicker release cycles by automating many manual processes, reducing human error, and improving efficiency.

- **Higher quality**: Automated testing and continuous monitoring help catch and fix issues early, leading to higher-quality software.

- **Reduced risk**: Frequent and automated testing reduces the risk of introducing bugs into production environments.

- **Efficient collaboration**: Developers can work concurrently on different features without causing integration conflicts.

- **Feedback loop**: Rapid feedback from automated tests helps developers address issues promptly.

- **Deployment consistency**: Automation ensures consistent deployment processes across environments.

Tools and practices:

CI/CD is supported by various tools and practices, such as version control systems (for example, Git), CI servers (for example, Jenkins, Travis CI), automated testing frameworks, containerization technologies (for example, Docker), configuration management tools (for example, Ansible, Puppet), and cloud platforms (for example, Azure DevOps, AWS CodePipeline).

Key principles of DevOps

The following are the fundamental principles of DevOps:

- **Collaboration**: Promoting open communication and collaboration between development, operations, and other stakeholders involved in the software delivery process.

- **Automation**: Utilizing automation tools and processes to eliminate manual, repetitive tasks, reducing errors and increasing efficiency.

- **Continuous integration**: Merging code changes from multiple developers into a shared repository frequently, ensuring early detection of integration issues.

- **Continuous deployment**: Automating the deployment process to release software rapidly and reliably to production environments.

- **Monitoring and feedback**: Continuously monitor the application and gather user feedback to drive further improvements and enhancements.

- **CI/CD**: CI/CD is a set of practices that automate integrating code changes and deploying applications to production environments. It is an essential component of the DevOps philosophy.

Understanding DevOps and CI/CD in Azure

DevOps and CI/CD are widely practiced in cloud environments, and Microsoft Azure provides a comprehensive set of tools and services to support these practices. Let us explore how DevOps and CI/CD work in Azure:

Azure DevOps Services: Azure DevOps Services is a cloud-based platform that provides various tools to support the entire DevOps lifecycle. It includes features for source code management, project planning and tracking, continuous integration, continuous delivery, and more. Teams can collaborate, manage their code repositories, track work items, and automate their CI/CD pipelines using Azure DevOps Services.

Azure Repos: Azure Repos is a version control system provided by Azure DevOps Services. It supports both Git and **Team Foundation Version Control (TFVC)**, allowing teams to host and manage their source code repositories in the cloud. Developers can use Azure Repos to manage code changes, collaborate with others, and maintain version history.

Azure Pipelines: Azure Pipelines is a robust CI/CD platform within Azure DevOps Services. It enables teams to define and automate their build, test, and deployment pipelines. Azure Pipelines supports building applications for various platforms, including .NET, Java, Node.js, Python, and more. It integrates with popular source control systems, including Azure Repos, GitHub, and Bitbucket.

Azure Artifacts: Azure Artifacts is a package management system in Azure DevOps Services. It allows teams to create, host, and share various packages, such as NuGet, npm, Maven, and Python. With Azure Artifacts, you can store and manage your packages and build outputs in a centralized repository, making managing software dependencies across projects easier.

Azure Boards: Azure Boards is a project management and work tracking tool within Azure DevOps Services. It provides features for agile planning, backlog management, work item tracking, and team collaboration. Teams can use Azure Boards to create and track user stories, tasks, bugs, and other work items, ensuring visibility and traceability throughout development.

Azure Test Plans: Azure Test Plans is a testing tool integrated with Azure DevOps Services. It enables teams to plan, track, and coordinate their testing efforts. With Azure Test Plans, you can create test plans, define test cases, execute manual or automated tests, and track test results. It also integrates with popular testing frameworks and tools for automated testing.

Azure Container Registry and AKS: Azure provides services for containerization and orchestration, which are integral to modern application deployment. Azure Container Registry allows you to store and manage your container images securely. AKS simplifies the deployment and management of containerized applications using Kubernetes. These services can be integrated into your CI/CD pipelines to enable seamless container-based deployments.

Azure Monitor and Azure Application Insights: Azure Monitor and Azure Application Insights are monitoring and telemetry services in Azure. They help you gain insights into the performance, availability, and usage of your applications and infrastructure. By integrating monitoring and logging into your CI/CD pipelines, you can proactively detect and address issues, ensuring the smooth operation of your applications in production.

By leveraging Azure DevOps Services and the various tools and services within Azure, you can implement robust DevOps practices and establish efficient CI/CD pipelines for your software projects. These Azure offerings enable collaboration, automation, scalability, and seamless deployment of applications in the cloud environment.

Setting up a DevOps pipeline with Azure DevOps

Setting up a DevOps pipeline with Azure DevOps involves several key steps. Let us walk through the process:

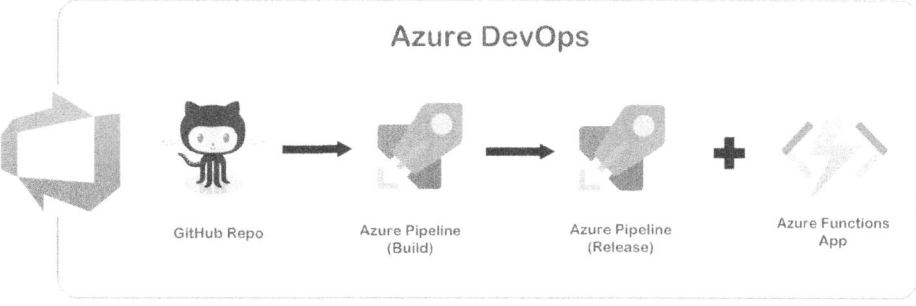

Figure 8.3: Azure DevOps pipeline components

1. **Create an Azure DevOps organization and project**

    a. Sign in to Azure DevOps at **https://dev.azure.com** with your Azure credentials.

    b. Create a new organization or choose an existing one.

    c. Create a new project within the organization. This project will serve as the container for your DevOps pipeline and related artifacts.

2. **Set up source control**

    a. Connect your source code repository to Azure DevOps. You can choose Azure Repos, GitHub, or other supported version control systems.

    b. Create a repository within Azure DevOps or link to an existing repository.

3. **Define your build pipeline**

    a. Navigate to your Azure DevOps project and select **Pipelines | Builds | New pipeline**.

    b. Choose your source control repository and select the appropriate branch.

    c. Select a template or configure your pipeline manually.

    d. Define the steps for building your application, including compiling code, running tests, and generating artifacts.

    e. Configure any additional build-related tasks, such as code analysis or packaging.

4. **Configure CI**

    a. Set up triggers for your build pipeline to automatically run on every code commit or at specific intervals.

    b. Configure branch filters or include/exclude rules per your project's requirements.

    c. Save and validate your CI pipeline.

5. **Set up release pipeline**

    a. Navigate to your Azure DevOps project and select **Pipelines | Releases | New pipeline**.

    b. Choose the appropriate template or create a new release pipeline from scratch.

    c. Define your deployment stages, such as Dev, QA, and production.

    d. Configure the appropriate deployment tasks for each stage, such as deploying to Azure App Service, AKS, or virtual machines.

e. Set up release triggers to automatically deploy when a new build is available or manually trigger deployments.

6. **Configure CD**

   a. Link your release pipeline to the appropriate artifact source, such as the build pipeline or container registry.

   b. Configure deployment conditions, approvals, and other settings for each deployment stage.

   c. Define any necessary configuration or environment variables for your application.

   d. Save and validate your CD pipeline.

7. **Monitor and improve**

   a. Set up monitoring and logging using Azure Monitor and Application Insights.

   b. Configure alerts and notifications for monitoring events or performance thresholds.

   c. Continuously monitor and analyze metrics to identify areas for improvement in your pipeline and application.

8. **Test and iterate**

   a. Implement automated testing using Azure Test Plans or other testing frameworks.

   b. Include testing tasks in your build or release pipeline to ensure quality and reliability.

   c. Continuously iterate on your pipeline by incorporating feedback, improving automation, and enhancing deployment processes.

By following these steps, you can establish a robust DevOps pipeline with Azure DevOps, automating and streamlining your software development, testing, and deployment processes.

Implementing an automated QA process

Implementing automated testing and quality assurance in Azure involves leveraging various Azure services and tools to set up a comprehensive testing and quality assurance workflow. Here is a step-by-step guide to implementing automated testing and quality assurance in Azure:

1. **Define testing strategy and frameworks**:
   a. Determine the types of tests required for your application, such as unit, integration, functional, performance, and security tests.
   b. Choose appropriate testing frameworks and tools that align with your application's technology stack and requirements. Azure supports many testing frameworks, including NUnit, MSTest, Selenium, and more.
2. **Azure DevOps services integration**:
   a. Set up your application's source control repository in Azure Repos or integrate with an external repository like GitHub.
   b. Create a new Azure DevOps pipeline to automate the build and deployment process using Azure Pipelines.
   c. Configure the pipeline to fetch code, compile, and build the application.
3. **Incorporate automated testing**:
   a. Integrate your testing frameworks and tools into the Azure DevOps pipeline.
   b. Add test execution tasks to the pipeline to run automated tests as part of the build process.
   c. Use tasks specific to your chosen testing frameworks, such as VSTest, MSTest, or NUnit, to execute unit and other tests.
4. **Code quality and static analysis**:
   a. Include static code analysis tasks in the pipeline to ensure code quality and adherence to coding standards.
   b. Use SonarQube or other static code analysis tools in the Azure marketplace to analyze your codebase for issues and vulnerabilities.
   c. Configure gates in the pipeline to enforce code quality thresholds and prevent the deployment of code that fails to meet those thresholds.
5. **Performance testing**:
   a. Utilize Azure Application Insights to monitor the performance of your application in real time.
   b. Incorporate load testing tools like Apache JMeter or Azure DevOps Load Testing to simulate high user loads and analyze the application's performance under stress conditions.
6. **Security testing**:
   a. Integrate security testing tools like OWASP ZAP or SonarQube security scanner to identify vulnerabilities in your application's code and dependencies.

b. Configure automated security scans as part of the Azure DevOps pipeline to catch security flaws early in development.

7. **Test reporting and analysis**:

   a. Leverage Azure Test Plans to track and manage test cases, suites, and results.

   b. Generate test reports and metrics using Azure Test Plans, Azure Pipelines, or other reporting tools to gain insights into your application's test coverage and quality.

8. **Continuous monitoring and feedback loop**:

   a. Set up monitoring and logging using Azure Monitor and Azure Application Insights to gather telemetry data from your application in production.

   b. Configure alerts and notifications based on predefined thresholds to proactively identify and address issues.

   c. Collect user feedback through feedback mechanisms like Azure feedback or integration with external feedback systems.

By following these steps, you can establish an automated testing and quality assurance workflow in Azure that enhances your applications' quality, reliability, and security.

Azure DevOps and GitHub Actions

Deploying an application on Azure using Azure DevOps and GitHub Actions is a powerful combination that allows for seamless CI/CD workflows. Here is a step-by-step guide on how to deploy an application on Azure using these tools:

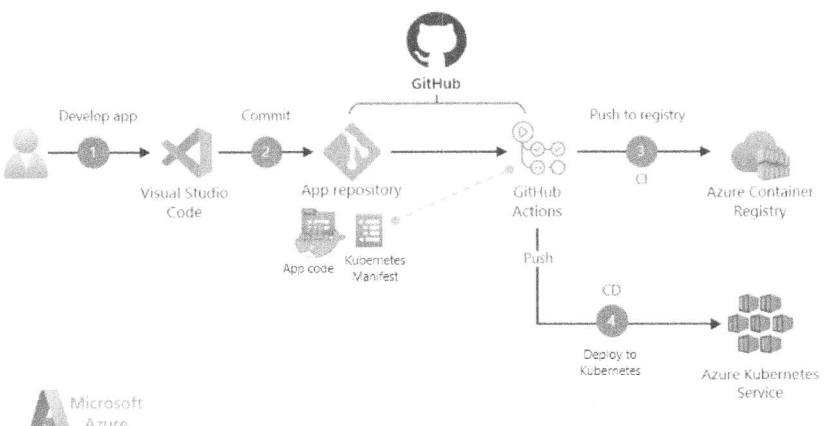

Figure 8.4: *Azure DevOps Arch with GitHub actions*

The preceding figure illustrates how GitHub Action helps streamline the CI/CD process.

Components

This section will show how GitHub Action works by integrating different components. We will discuss each component and its role:

GitHub Actions is an automation solution that can integrate with Azure services for CI. In this scenario, GitHub Actions orchestrates the creation of new container images based on commits to source control, pushes those images to Azure Container Registry, and then updates the Kubernetes manifest files in the GitHub repository.

Azure Kubernetes Service (AKS) is a managed Kubernetes platform that lets you deploy and manage containerized applications without container orchestration expertise. As a hosted Kubernetes Service, Azure handles critical tasks like health monitoring and maintenance for you.

Azure Container Registry stores and manages container images used by the AKS cluster. Images are securely stored and can be replicated to other regions by the Azure platform to speed up deployment times.

GitHub is a web-based source control system that runs on Git and is used by developers to store and version their application code. In this scenario, GitHub holds the source code in a Git repository. In the push-based approach, GitHub Actions is used to build and push the container image to Azure Container Registry.

Argo CD is an open-source GitOps operator that integrates with GitHub and AKS. Argo CD supports continuous deployment. Flux could have been used for this purpose. Still, Argo CD showcases how an app team might choose a separate tool for their specific application lifecycle concerns, compared with using the same tool the cluster operators use for cluster management.

Azure Monitor helps you track performance, maintain security, and identify trends. Other resources and tools, such as Grafana, can use metrics obtained by Azure Monitor.

Process

Now, we will set up the CI/CD process by integrating Azure resources.

1. **Set up Azure resources**:

    a. Create the necessary Azure resources such as Azure Web App, Azure Functions, AKS, or other services based on your application requirements.

2. **Azure DevOps configuration**:

    a. Create an Azure DevOps organization and project if you have not already.

    b. Connect your GitHub repository to Azure DevOps by creating a new pipeline in Azure DevOps.

c. Choose the appropriate template for your application (for example, .NET, Node.js, Python).

d. Configure the pipeline to fetch code from the connected GitHub repository.

3. **Define build pipeline**:

   a. Define the build pipeline in Azure DevOps to compile, build, and package your application.

   b. Specify the necessary build tasks such as restoring dependencies, building the code, running tests, and generating artifacts.

4. **Configure CI**:

   a. Set up CI triggers in Azure DevOps to automatically start the build pipeline whenever a new commit or pull request is on the connected GitHub repository.

   b. Define branch filters or include/exclude rules to control when the pipeline runs.

5. **GitHub Actions configuration**:

   a. Configure GitHub Actions in your GitHub repository to automate the deployment process.

   b. Create workflow files (for example, YAML files) that define the steps and actions required for deployment.

6. **Define deployment workflow**:

   a. Define a deployment workflow in GitHub Actions that triggers when a new build artifact is available.

   b. Specify the necessary steps for deploying the application to Azure. This includes provisioning infrastructure, deploying containers, or deploying Azure App Service.

7. **Configure deployment credentials**:

   a. Set up deployment credentials or service principals to securely authenticate and authorize the deployment process.

   b. Store the necessary secrets or credentials as GitHub repository or Azure DevOps pipeline variables.

8. **Test and validate**:

   a. Include automated tests as part of your deployment workflow to ensure the correctness and quality of the deployed application.

b. Run functional tests, integration tests, or any other relevant tests against the deployed environment.

9. **Monitor and troubleshoot**:

    a. Utilize Azure Monitor, Azure Application Insights, or other monitoring tools to track the performance and health of your deployed application.

    b. Set up alerts and notifications to proactively detect and address any issues.

10. **Continuous deployment**:

    a. Extend your deployment workflow to include multiple deployment stages, such as development, staging, and production, with appropriate testing and validation steps.

    b. Configure deployment triggers and approvals to control the promotion of deployments across stages.

By following these steps, you can establish an end-to-end CI/CD pipeline with Azure DevOps and GitHub Actions, enabling you to automate the deployment of your applications to Azure while ensuring quality and reliability.

Using Azure Kubernetes Service

Azure Kubernetes Service (AKS) is a managed container orchestration service provided by Microsoft Azure. It simplifies containerized applications' deployment, management, and scaling using Kubernetes.

Here is an overview of how to use Azure Kubernetes Service for container orchestration:

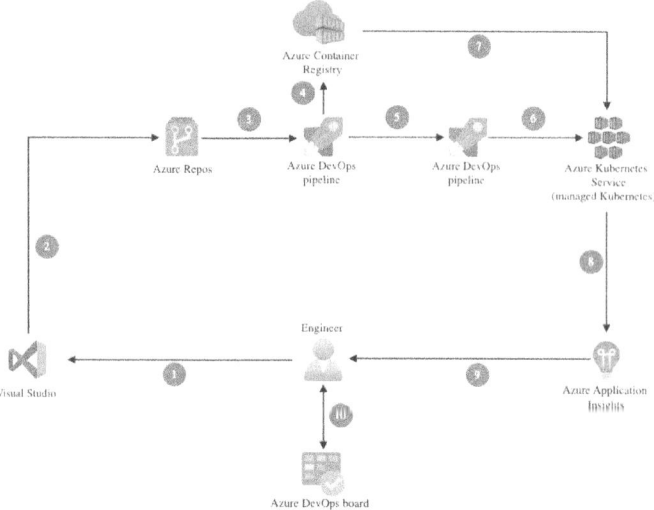

Figure 8.5: *Azure DevOps with AKS*

Here, we will go through the process of provisioning AKS service, an orchestration tool provided by Azure Cloud:

1. **Provision an AKS cluster**:

    a. Create an AKS cluster in the Azure portal or using Azure CLI, Azure PowerShell, or Azure Resource Manager templates.

    b. Configure the cluster specifications such as node count, virtual machine size, networking, and authentication.

2. **Connect to the AKS cluster**:

    a. Obtain the necessary credentials and configure your local development environment to connect to the AKS cluster.

    b. Use the Azure CLI or Azure portal to download the Kubernetes configuration file (**kubeconfig**) required to authenticate and interact with the cluster.

3. **Containerize your application**:

    a. Package your application into container images using tools like Docker.

    b. Define a Dockerfile to specify your application's build steps, dependencies, and runtime configuration.

4. **Push container images to a registry**:

    a. Use **Azure Container Registry** (**ACR**) or other container registries to store and manage your images.

    b. Push your container images to the registry, ensuring they are tagged appropriately for versioning and tracking.

5. **Define Kubernetes manifests**:

    a. Write Kubernetes manifest files (YAML or JSON) that describe the desired state of your application, including deployments, services, ingress, and other resources.

    b. Specify resource requirements, environment variables, networking, and other configurations.

6. **Deploy and manage applications**:

    a. Apply the Kubernetes manifests to the AKS cluster using the **kubectl** command-line tool or other Kubernetes management interfaces.

    b. Monitor the deployment status and check for errors or issues in the application's pods, services, or other resources.

7. **Scale and manage the cluster**:

    a. Use AKS to scale your application by adjusting the number of desired replicas, horizontal pod autoscaling, or cluster node scaling.

    b. Monitor the cluster's health, performance, and resource utilization using Azure Monitor and Kubernetes native monitoring features.

8. **Implement CI/CD pipelines**:

    a. Integrate AKS into your CI/CD pipelines to automate the build, deployment, and scaling processes.

    b. Use Azure DevOps, GitHub Actions, or other CI/CD tools to orchestrate the pipeline and trigger deployments to AKS based on code changes or other defined criteria.

9. **Continuous monitoring and logging**:

    a. Enable monitoring and logging for your AKS cluster and applications using Azure Monitor, Azure Log Analytics, and other monitoring tools.

    b. Set up alerts, dashboards, and metrics to gain visibility into the cluster's performance, application health, and resource utilization.

By leveraging Azure Kubernetes Service, you can simplify the management of containerized applications, achieve efficient scaling, and automate the deployment process in a reliable and scalable manner.

Azure Functions and Logic Apps

Azure Functions and Logic Apps allow you to build and run scalable and event-driven applications without worrying about infrastructure management.

Here is an overview of how to deploy serverless applications using Azure Functions and Logic Apps:

1. **Create an Azure Functions App**:

    a. Create an Azure Functions App in the Azure portal or using Azure CLI, Azure PowerShell, or Azure Resource Manager templates.

    b. Configure the necessary settings, such as the runtime stack (.NET, Node.js, Python, and so on), hosting plan (consumption or dedicated), and other options

2. **Develop Azure Functions**:

    a. Write your serverless functions using the chosen language and framework Azure Functions supports.

b. Define each function's trigger(s) and bindings to specify how they will be invoked and interact with other Azure services and resources.

3. **Test and debug**:

    a. Test your Azure Functions locally using the Azure Functions Core Tools or your preferred development environment.

    b. Validate the functionality of your functions and ensure they are responding correctly to triggers and producing the expected outputs.

4. **Publish Azure Functions**:

    a. Publish your Azure Functions to the Azure Functions App by deploying the compiled code or scripts to the target Azure environment.

    b. Use Azure CLI, Azure PowerShell, or Visual Studio Code extensions to publish the functions.

5. **Create an Azure Logic App**:

    a. Create an Azure Logic App in the Azure portal or use Azure CLI, Azure PowerShell, or Azure Resource Manager templates.

    b. Configure the workflow and specify the triggers and actions that define the logic of your serverless application.

6. **Configure Logic App connectors**:

    a. To interact with external resources, use pre-built connectors for various Azure services, SaaS applications, and on-premises systems.

    b. Configure the connectors and authenticate with the necessary credentials or access keys.

7. **Design Logic App workflow**:

    a. Design the Logic App Designer workflow by arranging triggers, actions, conditions, loops, and error handling.

    b. Specify the inputs, outputs, and transformations required to achieve the desired application logic and functionality.

8. **Test and validate Logic App**:

    a. Test the Logic App by triggering the defined triggers manually or simulating events that would trigger the app.

    b. Verify that the workflow is executed correctly and produces the expected results.

9. **Deploy Logic App**:

    a. Publish and deploy the Logic App to the Azure environment using the Azure portal, Azure CLI, Azure PowerShell, or deployment templates.

    b. Ensure the Logic App is deployed in the appropriate Azure region and connected to the required resources.

10. **Monitor and manage**:

    a. Monitor the execution and performance of your Azure Functions and Logic Apps using Azure Monitor and Azure Application Insights.

    b. Set up logging, metrics, and alerts to gain visibility into the application's behavior and troubleshoot any issues.

By leveraging Azure Functions and Logic Apps, you can build highly scalable and event-driven serverless applications that respond to triggers, integrate various services, and automate workflows without managing infrastructure.

Best practices for deploying applications on Azure

When deploying an application on Azure, there are several best practices to ensure a secure, reliable, and efficient deployment.

Here are some essential best practices for deploying applications on Azure:

- **Infrastructure as Code (IaC)**:
    - Use Infrastructure as Code tools such as Azure Resource Manager templates, Azure Bicep, or Terraform to define and manage your infrastructure in a declarative and version-controlled manner.
    - Automate the provisioning and configuration of Azure resources to ensure consistency and reproducibility.
- **Secure access**:
    - Follow the principle of least privilege and provide appropriate access control to Azure resources using **Azure Active Directory** (**Azure AD**) for identity management.
    - Implement **multi-factor authentication** (**MFA**) and RBAC to restrict access to sensitive resources.
    - Utilize Azure Managed Identity or Azure Key Vault to securely store and manage secrets and connection strings.

- **Networking**:
  - Utilize Azure **Virtual Network** (**VNet**) to isolate and secure your resources.
  - Use **Network Security Groups** (**NSGs**) and Azure Firewall to control inbound and outbound traffic.
  - Consider implementing Azure Application Gateway or Front Door for load balancing and application delivery.

- **High availability and scalability**:
  - Design your application for high availability by leveraging Azure Availability Sets or Availability Zones to distribute resources across fault domains and update domains.
  - Use Azure Load Balancer or Azure Traffic Manager to distribute traffic across multiple instances or regions.
  - Consider auto-scaling your resources based on demand using Azure Autoscale or Azure Virtual Machine Scale Sets.

- **Data management**:
  - Leverage Azure Storage options such as Azure Blob Storage, Azure Files, or Azure Managed Disks to store and manage your application data.
  - Implement data redundancy and backups using Azure Backup, Azure Site Recovery, or Azure Database services.
  - Ensure data encryption at rest and in transit using Azure Storage Service Encryption, Azure Disk Encryption, or Azure SQL Database Transparent Data Encryption.

- **Monitoring and logging**:
  - Implement comprehensive monitoring and logging using Azure Monitor, Azure Application Insights, or third-party tools.
  - Set up alerts, dashboards, and metrics to track your application and infrastructure's health, performance, and usage.
  - Enable diagnostic logs for Azure resources and configure log retention and analytics for effective troubleshooting and auditing.

- **Continuous CI/CD**:
  - Automate your build and deployment processes using Azure DevOps, GitHub Actions, or other CI/CD tools.
  - Implement a pipeline that includes build, testing, deployment, and validation stages.

- o   Use deployment slots or blue-green deployment strategies for seamless updates and rollbacks.

- **Security and compliance**:
    - o   Implement Azure Security Center to monitor and manage security threats and vulnerabilities.
    - o   Regularly apply security updates and patches to your Azure resources.
    - o   Ensure compliance with industry and regulatory standards such as GDPR, HIPAA, or ISO 27001 by following Azure's compliance offerings.

- **Cost optimization**:
    - o   Use Azure Cost Management and Azure Advisor to monitor and optimize your Azure resource usage and costs.
    - o   Right-size your resources based on actual usage and implement cost-saving measures like reserved instances, spot instances, or serverless options where applicable.

- **Disaster recovery and business continuity**:
    - o   Implement a disaster recovery plan using Azure Site Recovery or Azure Backup for critical workloads.
    - o   Perform regular backups and test the restore process to ensure data recovery and business continuity in the event of a failure.

By following these best practices, you can ensure a secure, scalable, and efficient deployment of your applications on Azure while maximizing the benefits of the Azure cloud platform.

Conclusion

Azure DevOps Services is a cloud-based platform that supports modern software development practices and methodologies. It provides tools and services covering the entire software development lifecycle, enabling teams to plan, build, test, deliver, and monitor applications effectively.

DevOps is supported by various tools and practices, such as version control systems (for example, Git), CI servers (for example, Jenkins, Travis CI), automated testing frameworks, containerization technologies (for example, Docker), configuration management tools (for example, Ansible, Puppet), and cloud platforms (for example, Azure DevOps, Azure Pipeline).

In summary, DevOps is a crucial methodology in modern software development, emphasizing automation, collaboration, and continuous improvement. It enables teams to deliver high-quality software more frequently and reliably, contributing to a faster and more responsive development lifecycle.

Until now, we have covered significant building blocks of Azure Cloud Services and discussed their features and how they support the agility and scale of software development and operations.

In the next chapter, we will discuss Azure's advanced services that help execute complex integrations and extensibility to integrate the services into the enterprise ecosystem seamlessly.

Questions

1. What is Azure DevOps, and how does it fit into the DevOps methodology?
2. What are the core services/components within Azure DevOps?
3. How can I use Azure DevOps to implement **continuous application integration and deployment (CI/CD)**?
4. What are the benefits of using Azure DevOps for CI/CD compared to other tools?
5. Can you explain how Azure Repos (Git) works and how it differs from other version control systems?
6. What are Azure Boards, and how can they assist in managing Agile projects?
7. How do Azure Test Plans help with automated testing and quality assurance?

Join our book's Discord space

Join the book's Discord Workspace for Latest updates, Offers, Tech happenings around the world, New Release and Sessions with the Authors:

https://discord.bpbonline.com

CHAPTER 9
Advanced Azure Services

Introduction

Azure offers various innovative services, such as Machine Learning, Artificial Intelligence, and **Internet of Things (IoT)** capabilities, to help organizations leverage emerging technologies and stay ahead of the curve.

Azure Machine Learning empowers data scientists to build various Machine Learning models faster and more accurately. Azure Cognitive Services helps developers understand the complexities of AI and helps build AI models in unsophisticated ways.

Azure IoT Hub is a fully managed cloud service that provides a scalable and secure platform for connecting, monitoring, and managing millions of IoT devices. It enables organizations to securely connect and manage their IoT devices, collect and analyze data in real time, and integrate with other Azure services to build IoT solutions.

Structure

In this chapter, we will learn the following topics:

- Introduction to data analysis
- Azure Machine Learning
- Azure Cognitive Services

- Azure Synapse Analytics
- Azure IoT Hub

Objectives

Every organization has lots of data; after digitization, data growth has reached a new level. Every day, petabytes of data are being created by enterprises. Organizations want to leverage this data to gain more insights so that it can help make the right decisions for the enterprise. In this chapter, we will go through the details of the data analysis process and levels of data processing. We will see how wisdom gets extracted from data.

We will also cover what services Azure Cloud provides to analyze that data, which helps organizations make meaningful decisions. We will go through the Azure Machine Learning process to analyze the data. We will also learn about Azure Cognitive Services, see the use cases, and learn how it helps in real life. Finally, we will learn about Azure Synspese Analytics and how it helps process large-scale data.

Introduction to data analysis

Data analysis inspects, cleans, transforms, and models data to discover useful information, draw conclusions, and support decision-making. It involves various techniques and methods from different fields, including statistics, mathematics, computer science, and domain-specific knowledge. The primary goal of data analysis is to extract meaningful insights from raw data, allowing businesses, researchers, and individuals to make informed decisions and predictions.

In data analysis, the **Data-Information-Knowledge-Wisdom (DIKW)** framework helps illustrate the progression from raw data to actionable insights. Data analysts use statistical, mathematical, and computational techniques to move through these stages and extract meaningful information and knowledge from the data. The DIKW Continuum is a concept of synthesizing data to have meaningful information to produce the knowledge necessary to have the right wisdom to make informed clinical decisions.

Following is the DIKW Pyramid, where we can see the journey of data to wisdom. At the bottom, we have lots of data in structured and unstructured formats, and from then, we go to the next level, where we extract the information after the first level of processing. We further process the data, get the knowledge, and then get the wisdom.

Level 1 (Data): At this level, we get raw and unprocessed facts without context.

40	20	Red
40	30	Blue

Table 9.1: Level 1(Data)

Level 2 (Information): Now, at this level, we labeled the data and organized it to get some contextual information. From the table, when we added the label to the data, we can say that there are two cars (red and blue) covering 40 minutes in 20 and 30 minutes, respectively.

40 Km	20 Min	Red car
40 Km	30 Min	Blue car

Table 9.2: Level 2(Information)

Level 3 (Knowledge): In this level, we need to perform some data analytics and find insights using mathematics. For example, with the following data, we can derive the speed of the cars and say that the red car travels at 120 km/hr while the blue car travels at 80 km/hr. The speed we calculated could have been more present in levels 1 and 2, so we have put some extra effort into retrieving that knowledge.

40 Km	20 Min	Red car
40 Km	30 Min	Blue car

Table 9.3: Level 3 (Knowledge)

Level 4: At this stage, we need to go beyond and make a well-informed decision backed by the data and analytics. These decisions will give the enterprise a new direction. With the above example, we can say that one car is overspeeding because driving at 120 km/hr is prohibited on highways in many countries. This information gives insurance companies insights to levy more monthly charges as the driver needs to follow the norm. Following is the DIKW Pyramid, and we can see how data is getting synthesized at the top; we gain wisdom:

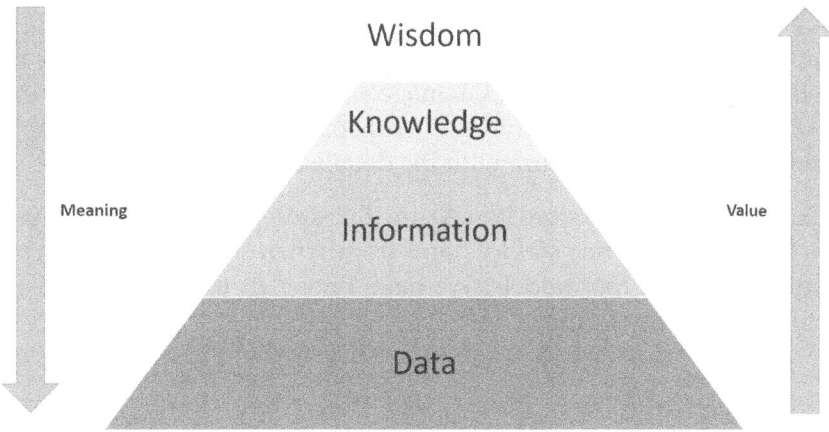

Figure 9.1: DIKW Pyramid

Azure offers various innovative services, such as Machine Learning, Artificial Intelligence, and **Internet of Things (IoT)** capabilities, to help organizations leverage emerging technologies and stay ahead of the curve.

Azure Machine Learning empowers data scientists to build various Machine Learning models faster and more accurately. Azure Cognitive Services helps developers understand the complexities of AI and helps build AI models in non-sophisticated ways.

Azure Databricks helps organizations build ETL pipelines for processing massive amounts of data and provides seamless integrations with open-source libraries and Spark capabilities.

Azure IoT Hub is a fully managed cloud service that provides a scalable and secure platform for connecting, monitoring, and managing millions of IoT devices. It enables organizations to securely connect and manage their IoT devices, collect and analyze data in real time, and integrate with other Azure services to build IoT solutions.

We will cover different services under the umbrella of advanced services provided by Azure Cloud.

Azure Machine Learning

Azure Machine Learning is a cloud-based service Microsoft provides as part of the Azure cloud computing platform. It is designed to enable developers and data scientists to build, deploy, and manage **Machine Learning (ML)** models at scale. Azure Machine Learning offers a range of tools and services to streamline the end-to-end Machine Learning workflow, from data preparation to model deployment.

Azure Machine Learning architecture

Azure Machine Learning workspace is a central hub for your Machine Learning activities. It provides an organized environment for managing datasets, experiments, models, and deployment targets. You can create and manage resources such as compute clusters, data stores, and experiment tracking within the workspace. The following figure depicts the Azure Machine Learning architecture with the details of steps.

In *step 1*, we ingest the data and store it in Azure data storage, from where data gets picked up by Azure Synapse Analytics services and from where it goes to the Azure Machine process to build and train the models. We have Power BI to visualize the results data. Please refer to the following figure:

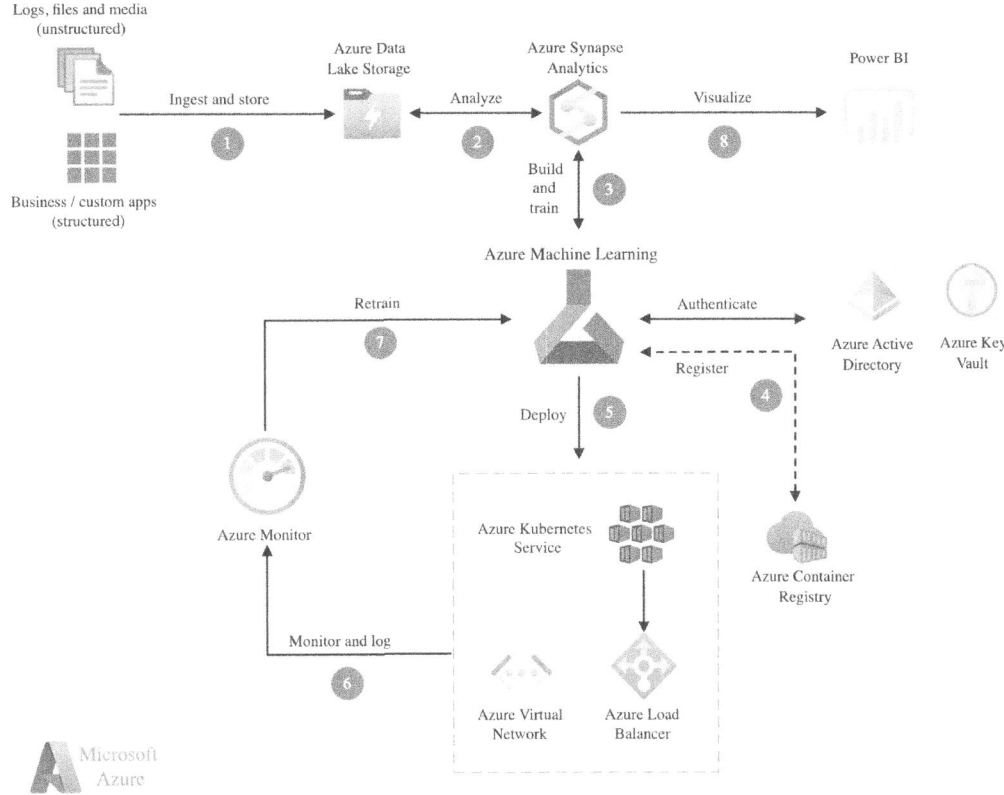

Figure 9.2: *Azure Machine Learning Architecture*
Source: Microsoft Azure

Here are the steps in detail for the Machine Learning process:

Data preparation

Preparing data is a crucial step in the Machine Learning process. Azure ML provides tools to clean, transform, and preprocess data. You can use familiar libraries like Pandas and Scikit-learn or leverage Azure's data preparation capabilities to ensure your data is in the correct format for model training.

Model training

Azure ML supports many Machine Learning algorithms and frameworks, including TensorFlow, PyTorch, and scikit-learn. You can train models using either code-based approaches or the AutoML feature, which automates the process of algorithm selection, hyperparameter tuning, and model evaluation to save time and effort.

Model deployment

After training a model, Azure ML allows you to deploy it as a web service. This service can be accessed by applications, devices, or other services for real-time predictions. Azure ML provides deployment options like **Azure Kubernetes Service** (**AKS**) for containerized deployments and Azure Container Instances for more straightforward scenarios.

Monitoring and management

Monitoring the performance of deployed models is crucial for maintaining their accuracy and effectiveness. Azure ML offers tools to track metrics, watch data drift (changes in input data distribution), and set up alerts for potential issues. This helps ensure that models remain reliable in production environments.

Azure Machine Learning (**Azure ML**): It offers comprehensive monitoring and management capabilities for Machine Learning models, including monitoring data drift. Here are key aspects:

Model Monitoring: Azure ML provides tools to monitor model performance over time. Organizations can track key metrics, such as accuracy and inference latency, to ensure models continue to meet performance expectations.

Data drift monitoring: Monitoring data drift involves tracking changes in input data distribution over time. Azure ML helps detect shifts in data patterns, enabling proactive adjustments to maintain model accuracy. This is crucial for ensuring models perform well with evolving real-world data.

Explainability and fairness monitoring: Azure ML includes features for model interpretability and fairness monitoring. Explainability tools help understand model predictions, while fairness monitoring detects and addresses biases in models, promoting ethical and unbiased AI.

Endpoint monitoring: Monitoring model endpoints ensures their availability and responsiveness. Azure ML provides insights into endpoint health, allowing organizations to address issues promptly and maintain reliable model deployments.

Alerting and notifications: Azure ML supports alerting mechanisms, notifying stakeholders when predefined thresholds or anomalies are detected in model performance, data drift, or other monitored parameters. This facilitates timely responses to potential issues.

Model retraining: Automatic or triggered retraining capabilities in Azure ML enable models to adapt to changing data patterns. When significant data drift is detected, organizations can retrain models to ensure continued accuracy and relevance.

Integration with Azure Monitor: Azure ML seamlessly integrates with Azure Monitor, providing a unified platform for monitoring and managing various Azure resources, including Machine Learning models. This simplifies the overall monitoring and management workflow.

By combining these monitoring features, Azure ML enables organizations to maintain the effectiveness and fairness of their Machine Learning models in production. Continuous monitoring and automated alerting and retraining ensure that models remain accurate, reliable, and aligned with evolving data patterns and business requirements.

Experimentation and version control

Azure ML facilitates iterative experimentation by allowing you to track and manage different versions of your code, data, and models. This is essential for reproducing results, comparing approaches, and collaborating effectively within teams.

Collaboration

Azure ML enables collaboration among data scientists, analysts, and developers. You can share Jupyter Notebooks, datasets, and experiments within the workspace, promoting knowledge sharing and teamwork. This collaborative environment enhances productivity and fosters innovation.

Integration

Azure ML integrates seamlessly with popular data science tools and libraries. You can use Jupyter Notebooks for coding, Git for version control, and other Azure services like Azure Databricks for advanced data analysis and preprocessing.

Security and Compliance

Azure ML provides security features such as **role-based access control (RBAC)** and data encryption to protect sensitive data. It also supports compliance with regulatory standards like HIPAA and GDPR, making it suitable for industries with strict data handling requirements. Operating on Microsoft Azure, Azure ML ensures a secure infrastructure, encrypting data in transit and at rest to safeguard sensitive patient information. **Role-based access control (RBAC)** is implemented, enabling organizations to manage user permissions and restrict access to authorized personnel, aligning with HIPAA requirements.

Comprehensive audit logging in Azure ML allows organizations to monitor user activities, providing an essential audit trail for compliance verification and incident investigation. Azure holds certifications and undergoes regular third-party audits, including those for HIPAA compliance, demonstrating its commitment to industry standards.

Additionally, Azure ML offers a **HIPAA Business Associate Agreement (BAA)**, formalizing Microsoft's commitment to handling **protected health information (PHI)** in a HIPAA-compliant manner. Organizations can leverage Azure ML's data residency options, choosing the geographical region for storing healthcare data to comply with regulatory expectations. While Azure provides a secure foundation, organizations must implement proper configurations and practices within Azure ML to ensure end-to-end HIPAA compliance for their Machine Learning workflows and healthcare applications.

Use cases

Azure ML is helping many industries to process their data and find insights. Azure ML finds applications in a wide range of industries and scenarios. Some of the industries and their use cases are as follows:

- **Healthcare**: The healthcare industry uses ML at scale and tries to understand the patient data to diagnose better. For example, retinal photographs are being used to predict health.

- **Finance**: The finance industry uses the data to perform fraud detection, credit risk assessment, and algorithmic trading.

- **Retail**: The retail industry uses the data for customer segmentation, demand forecasting, and recommendation systems.

- **Manufacturing**: The manufacturing industry is the data for lowering operational costs through predictive machinery maintenance, quality control, and supply chain optimization.

In summary, Azure Machine Learning offers a comprehensive suite of tools and services that cater to the entire Machine Learning lifecycle. Its integration with the Azure ecosystem, framework and language flexibility, and collaboration focus make it a powerful platform for building, deploying, and managing Machine Learning solutions at scale.

Azure Cognitive Services

Azure Cognitive Services is a suite of cloud-based **Artificial Intelligence (AI)** services and APIs provided by Microsoft. These services enable developers to integrate advanced AI capabilities into their applications without requiring deep AI or Machine Learning expertise. Azure Cognitive Services cover many functionalities, from vision and speech recognition to language understanding and decision-making. Let us explore the key components in detail:

Figure 9.3: *Azure cognitive services*

The following are the key components and their practical use cases:

- **Vision services**: Vision services are used for image analytics and classification.
  - **Computer vision**: Analyzes images and extracts information, such as object detection, text extraction, image classification, and content moderation.
  - **Face**: Detects and recognizes faces in images, providing attributes like age, gender, emotions, and facial landmarks.
  - **Custom vision**: Allows you to build and deploy custom image classifiers tailored to your specific use cases.

     The medical industry uses these services for image analysis to diagnose diseases properly and provide patient feedback. The retail industry uses image-based inventory management by using these services. The manufacturing sector uses computer vision for quality improvements.

- **Speech** services are used for language processing and translation from speech to text.
  - **Speech to text**: Converts spoken language into written text, enabling transcription of audio content.
  - **Text to speech**: Converts text into natural-sounding speech, facilitating applications like voice assistants and accessibility tools.
  - **Speaker recognition**: Identifies and verifies individuals based on their unique voice characteristics.

     The care industry uses speech-to-text for medical records, text-to-speech for accessible content, and language translation in e-learning platforms, and the finance industry uses speaker recognition for fraud detection.

- **Language services**: These services help in natural language processing by interpreting and extracting relevant information.
  - **Text analytics**: Analyzes text data to extract sentiment, key phrases, entities, and language detection, aiding in understanding customer feedback and text mining.
  - **Language Understanding (LUIS)**: Enables natural language processing and understanding, empowering applications to interpret user intents and extract relevant information.
  - **Translator**: Translates text or speech across languages, supporting real-time communication and localization.

     These services are used for language translation in e-learning platforms and sentiment analysis of patient feedback.

- **Decision services**: These services help in making the right decisions.
  - **Personalizer**: Utilizes reinforcement learning to optimize content and experiences based on user behavior and preferences.
  - **Anomaly detector**: Detects anomalies in data, which is valuable for identifying unusual patterns or behavior.

    The manufacturing sector uses these services for anomaly detection in sensor data.

- **Search services**:
  - **Azure Cognitive Search**: Facilitates building powerful application search experiences by enabling full-text search, faceted navigation, and AI capabilities for content enrichment.

- **Immersive reader**: Improves reading comprehension by providing text-to-speech, font customization, and language translation features.

- **Form recognizer**: Extracts structured data from forms and documents, automating data entry and processing.

- **Azure Metrics Advisor**:
  - **Metrics Advisor**: Monitors and detects anomalies in time-series data, providing insights into data quality and performance.

- **Integration and development**: Azure Cognitive Services are accessible through REST APIs, SDKs, and client libraries, allowing developers to integrate AI capabilities into their applications across various platforms and programming languages.

- **Customization**: Many services offer customization options, allowing developers to fine-tune models to their specific needs or build custom models using their own data.

In summary, Azure Cognitive Services provides a range of pre-trained models that leverage **Artificial Intelligence (AI)** to perform various tasks without requiring extensive custom training. These pre-trained models are part of the Azure Cognitive Services offerings and cover different domains of AI capabilities. These pre-trained models enable developers to integrate sophisticated AI capabilities into their applications with minimal effort. They are designed to handle everyday use cases across various industries, such as healthcare, finance, retail, and more. Additionally, Azure Cognitive Services provides customization options for certain services, allowing developers to fine-tune models based on specific requirements if needed.

By leveraging Azure Cognitive Services' pre-trained models, developers can save time and resources, accelerating the implementation of AI functionalities in their applications without requiring extensive AI expertise or training data.

Azure Cognitive Services provides developers with powerful AI capabilities that can be easily integrated into applications to enhance user experiences, automate processes, and gain insights from data without requiring deep AI expertise. The broad range of services ensures that applications across various domains can leverage AI to solve complex problems and provide innovative solutions.

Azure Synapse Analytics

Azure Synapse Analytics, formerly known as **Azure SQL Data Warehouse**, is a cloud-based analytics service provided by Microsoft. It is designed to enable organizations to analyze large volumes of data quickly and efficiently by integrating big data and data warehousing capabilities into a single platform. The following figure depicts the Azure Synapse Analytics:

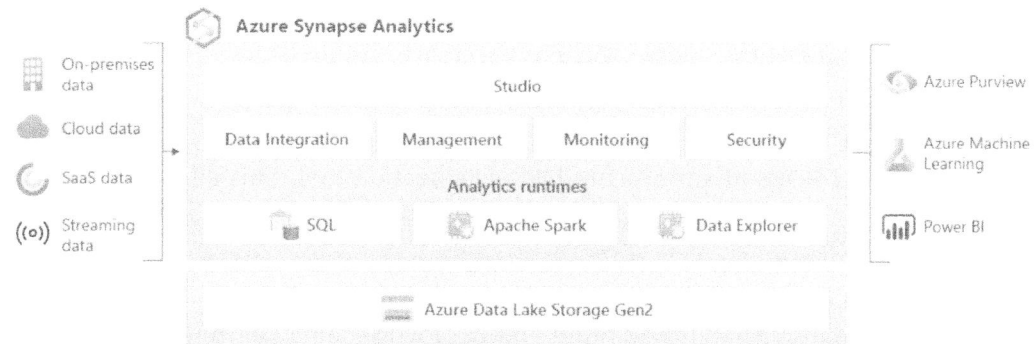

Figure 9.4: *Azure Synapse Analytics*

Azure Synapse Analytics is suitable for handling diverse workloads, including data warehousing, data integration, big data analytics, and AI-powered analytics. Let us delve into its key features and components:

- **Integrated analytics**: Azure Synapse Analytics combines two types of analytics, serving as both a data warehousing and big data analytics platform. This integration eliminates the need for separate systems, simplifying management and reducing data movement.

- **Data warehousing**: It provides enterprise-level data warehousing capabilities for storing structured data. Synapse Analytics uses a distributed architecture that enables efficient querying and processing of large datasets, making it suitable for complex analytical queries.

- **Big data analytics**: Synapse Analytics integrates with big data tools like Apache Spark. This enables you to process and analyze unstructured and semi-structured data alongside structured data, unlocking insights from various sources.

- **On-demand provisioning**: You can provision resources based on your workload requirements. Resources are separated into compute and storage, allowing you to scale each independently. This ensures cost-effectiveness by paying only for the resources you use.

- **Data integration**: Synapse Analytics offers built-in integration capabilities through features like Data Factory. This allows you to move and transform data from various sources into your data warehouse, facilitating the creation of a comprehensive analytics solution.

- **Advanced security**: It provides robust security features, including data encryption, advanced threat protection, and Azure Active Directory integration. This ensures that your data remains secure and compliant with industry standards.

- **Workload management**: Synapse Analytics supports workload management, allowing you to allocate resources to different workloads based on priority. This ensures that critical queries get the necessary resources without affecting other workloads.

- **Power BI integration**: Azure Synapse Analytics integrates seamlessly with Power BI, Microsoft's powerful data visualization tool. This allows you to create compelling reports and dashboards using data from your Synapse Analytics environment.

- **Machine Learning integration**: You can leverage Azure Machine Learning services within Synapse Analytics to build and deploy Machine Learning models directly on your data. This enables you to generate predictive insights and integrate AI into your analytics workflows.

- **Use cases**: Azure Synapse Analytics is suitable for a range of use cases:
    - **Business intelligence**: Generating insights from historical data to support decision-making.
    - **Advanced analytics**: Performing complex analytical queries on large datasets.
    - **Real-time analytics**: Combining streaming and historical data for real-time insights.
    - **Data warehousing**: Storing and querying structured data for reporting and analysis.
    - **Data integration**: Integrating and transforming data from various sources for analytics.

Azure Synapse Analytics is a robust platform that seamlessly combines data warehousing and big data analytics. Its capabilities to handle diverse workloads, integrate with various tools, and enable advanced analytics make it a valuable solution for organizations looking to harness the power of their data to drive informed decisions and innovation.

Azure IoT Hub

Azure IoT Hub is a cloud-based service provided by Microsoft that enables secure communication, management, and monitoring between **Internet of Things (IoT)** devices and back-end applications. It is a central hub for managing the bidirectional communication and data flow between IoT devices and the cloud. Azure IoT Hub supports various IoT scenarios, from remote monitoring and device management to real-time analytics and predictive maintenance. Here is a comprehensive look at its features and components:

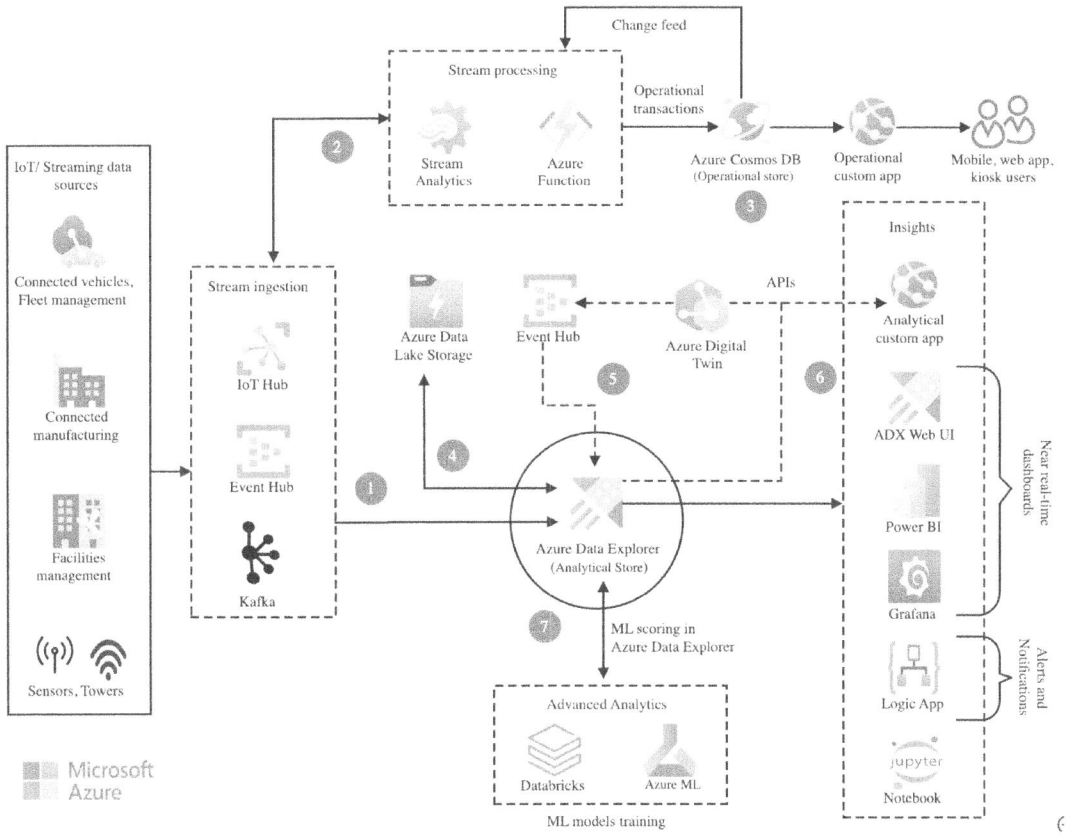

Figure 9.5: *Azure IoT Hub*
Source: Mircosoft Azure

As we can see from the preceding figure, Azure IoT Hub is a combination of components and services working together. Let us go through the details of Azure IoT hub components and features.

- **Device connectivity**: Azure IoT Hub supports various device protocols and communication patterns, including MQTT, HTTP, AMQP, and WebSocket. This enables IoT devices with diverse capabilities to connect to the cloud securely.

- **Device management**: IoT Hub provides features for managing IoT devices at scale:
    - **Device identity and security**: Each device is assigned a unique identity and credentials, ensuring secure authentication and authorization.
    - **Device twin**: A digital representation of each device that stores metadata, configurations, and reported properties. It enables synchronization and management of the device state.
    - **Direct methods**: Allows cloud applications to invoke methods on specific devices for configuration updates or remote actions.
    - **Device jobs**: Enables batch operations, such as firmware updates or configuration changes.
- **Communication and telemetry**: IoT Hub facilitates bidirectional communication between devices and the cloud.
    - **Telemetry ingestion**: Devices can send telemetry data (sensor readings, status updates) to the cloud for real-time analysis.
    - **Cloud-to-device messaging**: Cloud applications can send commands, notifications, and messages to specific devices.
- **Security**: In the IoT world, where devices are talking with each other, device security becomes a fundamental aspect of IoT Hub.
    - **Device authentication**: Devices use security tokens or X.509 certificates to authenticate with IoT Hub.
    - **Message encryption**: Data sent between devices and the cloud is encrypted to ensure confidentiality.
    - **Firewalls and virtual networks**: Devices can be protected by placing IoT Hub behind firewalls or in virtual networks.
- **Scalability and high availability**: IoT Hub is designed for high availability and scalability to accommodate IoT solutions of any size. It can handle millions of devices and messages, automatically scaling resources based on demand.
- **Device SDKs**: Microsoft provides SDKs for various programming languages and platforms, making developing IoT solutions for different devices easier.
- **Integration and analytics**: IoT Hub integrates with other Azure services to enable end-to-end IoT solutions:
    - **Azure Stream Analytics**: Allows real-time analytics on incoming device data.
    - **Azure Functions**: Trigger serverless functions based on device events.
    - **Azure Logic Apps**: Automate workflows and actions based on device events.

- **Monitoring and diagnostics**: IoT Hub offers monitoring and diagnostics capabilities to track device connectivity and troubleshoot issues.
    - **Device Explorer**: Provides a web-based interface to monitor device connections and messages.
    - **Built-in Metrics**: Collects metrics for monitoring usage and performance.
- **End-to-end security**: Azure IoT Hub provides a secure foundation for IoT solutions.
    - **Identity registry**: Manages device identities and access control.
    - **Device-to-cloud security**: Ensures encrypted communication for data sent from devices to the cloud.
    - **Cloud-to-device security**: Secures commands and messages sent from the cloud to devices.
- **Use cases**: Azure IoT Hub is used in various industries and scenarios, including:
    - **Manufacturing**: Remote monitoring and predictive maintenance of industrial equipment.
    - **Intelligent cities**: Monitoring and managing infrastructure like streetlights and waste bins.
    - **Healthcare**: Collecting and analyzing data from medical devices for patient care.
    - **Retail**: Tracking inventory levels and customer behavior for efficient operations.

Azure IoT Hub provides a robust and scalable platform for connecting, managing, and monitoring IoT devices securely and efficiently. Its comprehensive features enable organizations to build end-to-end IoT solutions, harnessing the power of data generated by IoT devices for actionable insights and innovation.

Conclusion

Azure advanced services encompass a range of specialized offerings beyond the core infrastructure provided by Microsoft Azure. These services are designed to cater to specific industries, complex scenarios, and advanced functionalities. They include Azure AI services like Cognitive Services and Azure Machine Learning, IoT services, Azure Data Services such as Azure Synapse Analytics, DevOps services, and Azure Security Center.

They might come with additional costs while suitable for various industries and businesses. Azure provides user-friendly interfaces and documentation to help users integrate these services with existing applications. Security, compliance, and industry-specific solutions are essential for Azure Advanced Services.

Modern enterprises are based on data, and advanced analytics are the architecture's core that helps enterprises make data-based decisions.

In the next chapter, we will discuss architecture's best practices and design patterns and some practical use cases.

Questions

1. What are the Azure Advance Services, and what are their uses?
2. How is Azure Advance Services helping the industry in making the right decisions?
3. What are Azure Cognitive Services, and what are their uses?
4. What is an IoT Hub, and how does it help connect devices?
5. What is Azure Synapse Analytics, and how does it help?

Join our book's Discord space

Join the book's Discord Workspace for Latest updates, Offers, Tech happenings around the world, New Release and Sessions with the Authors:

https://discord.bpbonline.com

CHAPTER 10
Case Studies and Best Practices

Introduction

Cloud-native best practices are a set of guidelines and principles for building and managing applications and services leveraging the advantages of cloud computing. These practices are designed to help organizations take full advantage of cloud platforms' flexibility, scalability, and resilience, so it is essential to follow the cloud-native standards and practices to take full advantage.

Structure

In this chapter, we will go through the following topics:

- Transforming a monolithic application
- Cloud-native best practices
- Real-world cloud-native applications

Objectives

In this chapter, we will go through the core principles of cloud-native development that everyone should keep in mind, and we will also go through the common real-world examples built using cloud-native services.

Those examples can be seen as templates and applied to other places where they fit.

Transforming a monolithic application

Legacy transformation to microservices is a complex process that requires careful planning and consideration. It is essential to prioritize incremental changes, monitor the impact of each step, and be prepared to adapt the strategy based on feedback and evolving requirements.

Transforming a monolithic application into a microservices architecture involves several key considerations and best practices. Here are some essential steps and things to consider:

Assessment and planning: This is the very step of the process where the monolithic application will be assessed to determine how complex it is and how much effort, cost, and time will be required. The assessment phase is critical in transforming a monolithic application into a microservices architecture. This phase thoroughly analyzes the existing monolithic application to understand its structure, dependencies, and business logic. The assessment phase lays the foundation for the subsequent planning and execution phases of the microservices transformation, the insights gained during this phase help develop a comprehensive strategy and roadmap for a successful migration.

Define microservices boundaries: Identify and define the limits of microservices. Consider factors such as business domains, functionalities, and dependencies between components. Microservice boundaries should align with specific business functionalities, enabling independent development, deployment, and scalability. Identify cohesive and loosely coupled domains where a microservice encapsulates a single responsibility. Consider minimizing inter-service dependencies and fostering a clear API contract for communication. Strive for autonomy and encapsulation, allowing teams to independently own and evolve their microservices. Regularly reassess and refine boundaries based on changing business needs. Successful microservice boundaries balance granularity, maintainability, and business alignment, supporting the agility and scalability inherent in a microservices architecture.

Decomposition of services: Microservice decomposition breaks down a monolithic application into more minor, independent services, each addressing a specific business capability. It involves identifying and restructuring cohesive functionalities into modular components, promoting easier development, testing, and deployment. This architectural shift enhances scalability, fosters agility, and allows teams to work on individual services autonomously. Decomposition aims to reduce complexity, enable better resource utilization, and align with microservices principles, optimizing the application for improved maintainability and responsiveness to changing business requirements.

The following figure shows how a sizeable monolithic code is getting decomposed into multiple microservices. Decomposition is also called legacy transformation, where monolithic services must be planned for how they will be decomposed into microservices. Please refer to the following figure:

Case Studies and Best Practices ■ 173

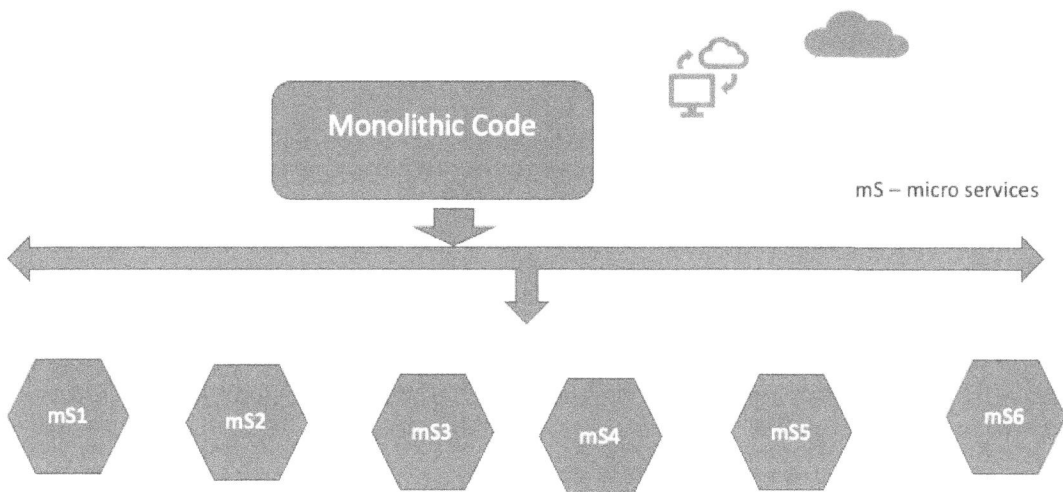

Figure 10.1: *Monolithic to microservices*

Identify services: Break down the monolithic application into more minor, manageable services. This may involve identifying cohesive business functionalities and separating them into individual services.

Data transformation and migration: Legacy applications might have years of data requiring proper planning and transformation efforts to migrate to a new platform. For example, the legacy database can use Oracle, which needs to migrate to Azure Cosmos DB. The development team must develop migration scripts to transform the data from legacy to a new cloud database. This process is called initial load, where the development team will define how much data will be changed and loaded to the new system. This decision happens with the discussion with the business and stakeholders.

Once the application goes live, initial load scripts will be executed, and legacy data will be transformed and loaded to the new system to give users a seamless experience. Initially, the application will update the old and new databases, but there will be times when the old system will shut down, and so will the database.

Along with migrating legacy data, we must determine how data will be managed in a microservices architecture. This may involve data partitioning, replication, or sharing strategies. Microservices data management involves specific principles to ensure adequate storage, retrieval, and data processing within a distributed architecture. First, adopt a decentralized data management approach, allowing each microservice to have its database. This promotes autonomy and minimizes dependencies. Embrace the concept of event-driven architecture, where microservices communicate through asynchronous events, enhancing scalability and resilience.

Implement the proper database per service, choosing databases that align with the specific needs of each microservice. Use polyglot persistence to employ various types of databases based on data requirements. Apply the principles of eventual consistency to handle data synchronization across microservices, acknowledging that consistency may not be immediate but will be achieved over time.

Utilize APIs for data access and ensure well-defined contracts to facilitate communication between microservices. Implement data versioning to manage changes in data structures gracefully. Employ event sourcing and **Command Query Responsibility Segregation (CQRS)** for complex domains, separating write and read operations.

Lastly, prioritize data security and privacy, implementing proper access controls, encryption, and compliance measures. Regularly monitor and manage data across microservices to ensure performance, reliability, and adherence to evolving business needs. These principles collectively enable effective data management in a microservices architecture, balancing flexibility, autonomy, and data integrity.

Communication and APIs: There are many ways to communicate, but Microservices communication mainly relies on RESTful APIs, emphasizing loose coupling, asynchronous messaging, and decentralized data management. Use versioning for backward compatibility, implement service discovery for dynamic interaction, and leverage load balancing for optimal resource utilization. Ensure security with authentication, authorization, and HTTPS. Employ tools like API gateways, circuit breakers, and message brokers. Embrace event-driven architecture for scalability. Prioritize monitoring, logging, and distributed tracing for visibility. Consumer-driven contracts and contract testing enhance API design and reliability. Collectively, these principles foster resilient, scalable, and adaptable microservices in a distributed system.

API design: Define clear and well-documented APIs for communication between microservices. This promotes loose coupling and allows services to evolve independently. API design principles for microservices are crucial for effective communication and service collaboration. Prioritize clarity, consistency, and simplicity in API design to enhance usability. Follow RESTful principles, ensuring statelessness, well-defined endpoints, and standardized HTTP methods. Use resource-based URLs and provide clear documentation using tools like Swagger.

Microservice architecture should also support the legacy application because there will be a period when the legacy and new systems will run. In the first stage, we will write to both systems but read from the new systems.

Implement proper versioning to support backward compatibility and enable service evolution. Design APIs to be granular, focusing on specific business functionalities, promoting loose coupling, and encouraging independent development and deployment. Consider the needs of service consumers, implementing features like pagination, filtering, and sorting. Prioritize error handling, providing meaningful responses and status codes. Security is paramount, with authentication and authorization mechanisms and HTTPS usage. Regularly review and refine API designs based on evolving business requirements, fostering adaptability and scalability in microservices architecture.

Communication protocols: Choose appropriate communication protocols, such as HTTP/REST or messaging, based on the requirements of each microservice. Microservices commonly communicate using RESTful HTTP protocols, emphasizing statelessness, standardized endpoints, and HTTP methods for interoperability. This fosters loose coupling and scalability. Asynchronous messaging, facilitated by message brokers like Kafka or RabbitMQ, is widely adopted for event-driven communication. This approach enables the decoupling of services, improving flexibility in distributed architectures. The choice of protocol aligns with the principles of microservices, promoting modularity, independence, and adaptability to dynamic business needs.

Infrastructure and containerization: Microservices leverage containerization (for example, Docker) for encapsulation and portability, ensuring consistent deployment across environments. Orchestration tools like Kubernetes automate scaling and management, enhancing high availability. **Infrastructure as Code (IaC)** principles enable automated provisioning using tools like Terraform. Dynamic resource allocation in the cloud supports scalability and resilience, while service discovery mechanisms facilitate emotional communication. Immutable infrastructure practices enhance consistency and security. Container-specific monitoring and centralized logging ensure visibility. **Continuous integration/continuous deployment (CI/CD)** pipelines automate testing and deployment, providing rapid updates. These principles collectively optimize microservices for agility, scalability, and reliability in a cloud-native environment.

DevOps and automation: DevOps and automation principles are integral to successfully implementing microservices, emphasizing collaboration, efficiency, and rapid delivery. Adopt a DevOps culture promoting cooperation between development and operations teams throughout the microservices lifecycle. Implement CI/CD pipelines to automate testing, building, and deployment, ensuring consistent and reliable releases.

IaC enables automated provisioning and management of infrastructure, enhancing scalability. Embrace configuration management tools for consistency across environments. Automatic monitoring and alerting facilitate proactive issue detection and resolution. Implement testing automation, including unit tests, integration tests, and contract tests, to ensure the reliability of microservices. These principles create an environment where microservices can be developed, tested, and deployed rapidly and consistently, meeting a microservices architecture's agility and scalability demands.

Centralized monitoring: Implement processes to monitor and troubleshoot microservices. This helps in identifying issues and understanding the flow of requests across services. Because application logs will be distributed, we need to ensure that we can correlate the sequence of calls through multiple microservices.

Distributed tracing: Use tools to trace requests as they move through various microservices. This aids in understanding performance bottlenecks. To track and trace the chain of calls in distributed microservices, adopt distributed tracing practices—instrument each microservice with a tracing library like OpenTelemetry or Zipkin. Use correlation IDs to identify and link requests across services uniquely. Implement structured logging with trace information for easy analysis. Leverage an API gateway that supports trace context propagation. Consider using a service mesh like Istio, which provides built-in tools for tracing. Choose middleware and frameworks with native tracing support. Utilize monitoring and **application performance monitoring** (**APM**) tools such as Datadog or New Relic. Ensure trace information is propagated through custom headers or standard HTTP headers. Container orchestration tools like Kubernetes often support distributed tracing. This comprehensive approach enables visibility into the entire request lifecycle, facilitating effective monitoring, troubleshooting, and optimization in a distributed microservices environment.

Secure communication: Implement secure communication between microservices using protocols like HTTPS. Ensure proper authentication and authorization mechanisms are in place. Securing microservices involves implementing robust measures to protect against various threats. Employ appropriate authentication and authorization mechanisms to control access to services. Use secure communication protocols like HTTPS and enforce encryption for data in transit.

Apply the principle of least privilege, ensuring that each microservice has only the necessary permissions. Regularly update dependencies and libraries to address known vulnerabilities. Implement secure coding practices and conduct regular security audits and code reviews. Employ container security measures, including image scanning and runtime protection. Centralize logging for monitoring and detecting security incidents. Use **identity and access management** (**IAM**) solutions for comprehensive user management. Implement measures for data privacy and compliance with regulations. Regularly conduct penetration testing to identify and address potential vulnerabilities. Adopting a defense-in-depth strategy and staying informed about evolving security best practices are crucial to maintaining a secure microservices architecture.

Data encryption: Encrypt sensitive data at rest and in transit. Implement proper access controls to protect microservices and their data. Implementing robust data encryption mechanisms in microservices design is crucial to safeguard sensitive information. Utilize **Transport Layer Security** (**TLS**) or its predecessor, **Secure Sockets Layer** (**SSL**), to encrypt data in transit, ensuring secure communication between microservices. Employ robust encryption algorithms (for example, AES) for encrypting data at rest within databases or storage systems, mitigating the risk of unauthorized access. Implement encryption and decryption logic within the microservices, ensuring that sensitive data is protected internally and during external communication.

Utilize secure critical management practices to safeguard encryption keys, preventing unauthorized access to the encrypted data. Additionally, consider using application-level encryption for specific data fields, providing an extra layer of protection for susceptible information. By incorporating these encryption mechanisms, microservices can ensure the confidentiality and integrity of data throughout its lifecycle in a distributed and scalable architecture.

Unit testing: Implement unit tests for each microservice to ensure individual components work correctly.

Integration testing: Conduct thorough integration testing to validate interactions between microservices.

Contract testing: Use contract testing to ensure that services adhere to agreed-upon APIs and fully adhere to the contract to reduce surprises at a later stage.

Horizontal scaling: Design microservices to scale horizontally based on demand. Implement auto-scaling mechanisms to handle varying workloads.

Load balancing: Use load balancers to distribute incoming traffic across multiple microservices instances. Load balancing in microservices involves distributing incoming traffic across multiple instances to optimize resource utilization, enhance scalability, and ensure high availability. Utilize load balancers to evenly distribute requests among microservices evenly, preventing overloading of individual components and facilitating horizontal scaling. Employ strategies such as round-robin, least connections, or weighted algorithms to tailor load balancing based on specific requirements. Regularly monitor and adapt load balancing configurations to accommodate changing workloads, ensuring efficient performance and responsiveness across the microservices architecture. Load balancing is critical for maintaining a balanced and reliable system in dynamic, distributed environments.

API documentation: Provide comprehensive documentation for each microservice API, including usage guidelines, data formats, and error handling.

Service discovery: Implement service discovery mechanisms to help microservices locate and communicate with each other dynamically. Service discovery in microservices is the automatic identification and registration of services within a network. It enables dynamic communication between microservices, allowing them to locate and connect without manual intervention. Service discovery mechanisms, often facilitated by tools like Consul or Eureka, maintain a registry of available services and their endpoints. This dynamic discovery ensures that microservices can adapt to changes in the environment, scale horizontally, and collaborate seamlessly in a distributed architecture, promoting agility and flexibility in deploying and managing microservices.

Ownership: Assign ownership of microservices to specific teams, fostering accountability and responsibility.

Phased rollout: Plan a phased rollout of microservices to minimize disruptions. Gradually migrate functionality from the monolith to microservices while ensuring that both coexist during the transition.

Monitoring and feedback: Monitoring and feedback in microservices involve continuous observation and analysis of the system's performance, availability, and behavior. It includes using tools like Prometheus, Grafana, or commercial **application performance monitoring (APM)** solutions to collect and visualize metrics. Feedback loops are established through centralized logging, alerting, and tracing to identify issues promptly and provide insights for optimization. Regularly assessing the collected data helps teams refine microservices for improved reliability, efficiency, and user experience. Monitoring and feedback mechanisms are integral to maintaining a responsive, scalable, and resilient microservices architecture in alignment with evolving business needs.

Cloud-native best practices

Best practices for building and maintaining cloud-native applications in Azure will be discussed in this section. Here are some critical cloud-native best practices:

Microservices architecture: This is the first and foremost principle to take the application to prepare for the cloud. We need to decompose applications into small, independently deployable services. We need to ensure that these services are independent and can be managed separately. This promotes flexibility, scalability, and ease of maintenance. We have already discussed the 12 factors we must follow when designing and developing microservices.

Containers: Containerization is the next step and building block of cloud-native architecture. Containerization helps to create a single deployable unit of the application in the form of an image. These images are portable, so use containerization technology like Docker to package your application and its dependencies. Containers are portable and provide consistency between development and production environments.

Orchestration (Azure Kubernetes Services): Cloud offers to manage the services at scale. Managing infrastructure at scale through manual efforts is cumbersome and costly, so cloud native provides orchestration frameworks to manage the services using automation. We can use container orchestration tools like Kubernetes to manage and scale containers efficiently. AKS automates deployment, scaling, and management tasks, making it easier to run complex applications. The following figure shows the features provided by Azure Kubernetes Services:

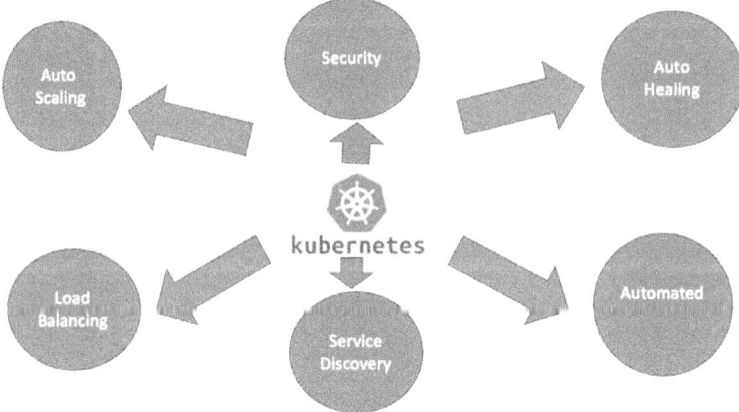

Figure 10.2: Azure Kubernetes Services

Immutable Infrastructure (Use Azure resource manage templates): In cloud-native development, along with the writing functional aspects, the development team must write the infrastructure code, with all the environment context details required to provide the run time environment for code execution. We can define our infrastructure using Azure ARM, which can be used to write infrastructure code. We can treat infrastructure as code and create immutable infrastructure templates. This ensures consistency and simplifies deployments and updates. The following figure shows four isolated infrastructures: Dev, Test, UAT, and production, which different purposes and teams in the software development life cycle will use. For example, Dev env will be used by the development team, while the QA team will use test. UAT env is where the business performs the user acceptance testing, while production is the live environment where customers will be interacting:

- **Immutable Infrastructure**

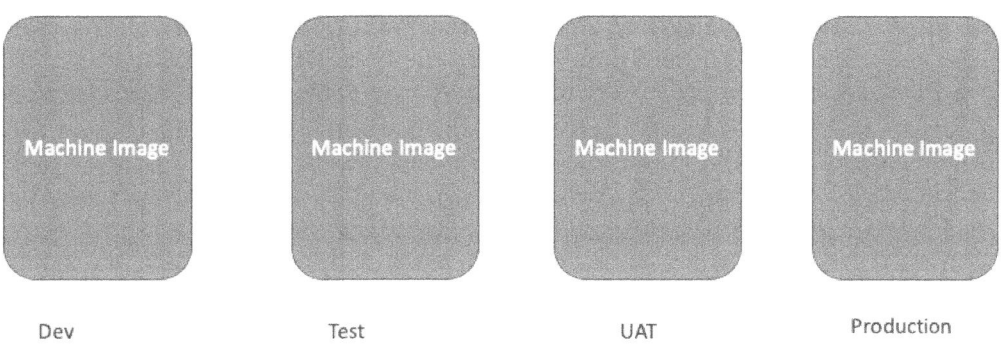

Figure 10.3: Immutable infrastructure

Continuous integration/deployment (CI/CD using Azure DevOps): Modern-day businesses want speed and agility to compete in the market. They want to deliver the changes as soon as they can. This is only possible when we have proper infrastructure in place. When we use microservices architecture and agile as a process, the third step will be delivering the changes quickly. We need to implement CI/CD pipelines to automate the testing, integration, and deployment of code changes. This enables faster development cycles and reduces the risk of errors.

We can use Azure DevOps to build applications faster and deploy them with the same speed. CI/CD is a continuous cycle that keeps on going in the cycle. As part of the CI, code will be developed, built, and tested, and as part of CD, release, deployment, and monitoring activities will continue. It is depicted in the following figure:

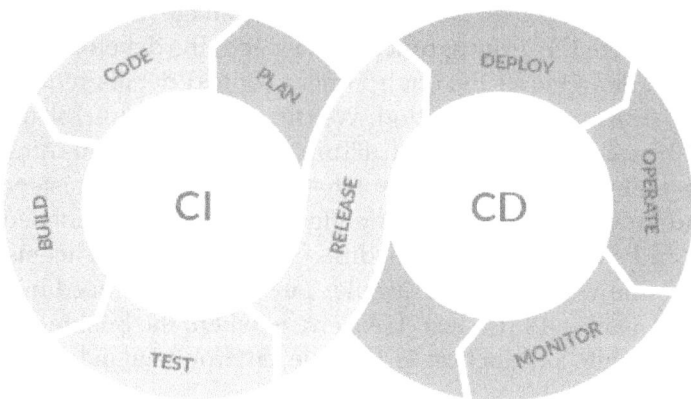

Figure 10.4: Azure DevOps (CI/CD)

DevOps culture: Foster a culture of collaboration between development and operations teams. Encourage automation, communication, and shared responsibility for application delivery and operations. DevOps culture fosters better cohesion within the development and operations team to work jointly and collaborate. Typically, every team works in silos which confuse and delays responses and also lack transparency and accountability. DevOps pushes more about fixing the proper ownership and providing better business agility and speed. It is what is shown in the following figure:

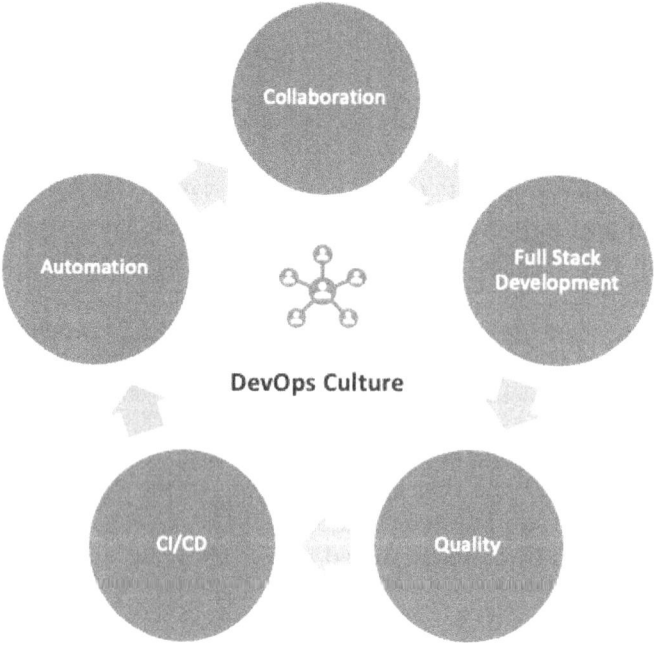

Figure 10.5: Fostering DevOps culture

Monitoring and observability (Azure Monitor and Azure Application Insights): Monitoring and observability are two different aspects for engineers. Monitoring was the reactive way to deal with the application production issues, while observability provided the proactive way to deal with the system issues. It is mainly used for site reliability engineers, giving a different approach to modern-day application operation management.

As part of that, we need to implement robust monitoring and observability solutions to gain insights into your application's performance and health and ensure that we monitor every aspect of the system. It is essential in microservices because the system is distributed, and many services work together to deliver the functionality. Implement monitoring and observability using Azure Monitor and Azure Application Insights. Collect telemetry data, monitor performance, and gain insights into your applications.

Monitoring is the systematic collection of data on the health and performance of a system. On the other hand, Observability is the capability to infer the internal state of a system based on its external outputs. Monitoring provides specific metrics and alerts, while observability focuses on understanding system behavior and troubleshooting. Together, they form a comprehensive approach for managing and improving complex operational systems' reliability, performance, and troubleshooting capabilities, providing insights into the system's internal workings and user experiences. We need to make sure that the observability index of the application is higher; more observability means better metrics and information about the system issues, which will result in less time to solve the problems, as shown in the following figure:

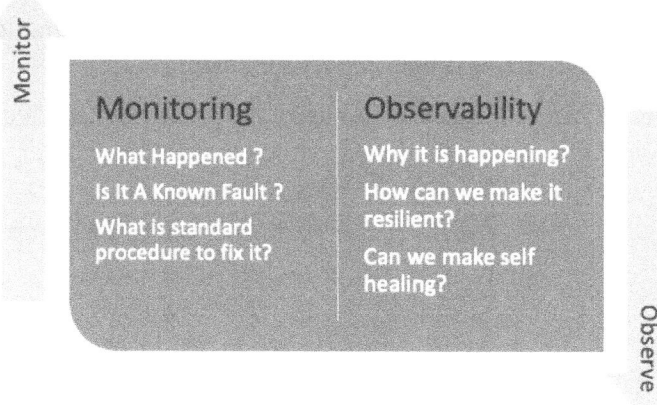

Figure 10.6: Monitoring versus observability

Security by design (Azure Security Center): Integrate security into every aspect of your cloud-native application development process. Implement security practices like least privilege access, encryption, and vulnerability scanning. We must ensure that our security measures protect all the infrastructure assets and services. The following figure shows that we are watching the load balancer, database, Kubernetes, and machines. We need to use the right tools and services available to make sure that all the resources are correctly configured and protected; refer to the following figure:

Figure 10.7: *Azure Security Center*

Leverage Azure Security Center to monitor the security aspects of the application and infrastructure in one place. It provides recommendations and threat protection capabilities.

Automated scaling and scaling horizontally: Design applications to scale horizontally by adding more service instances as needed. This helps handle increased loads and ensures high availability.

Use Azure Cloud's auto-scaling features to adjust resources automatically based on application demand. This optimizes cost and performance.

The following figure shows that Azure monitor has triggered an alert at the CPU consumption threshold, and it triggered a webhook to create another instance of the application:

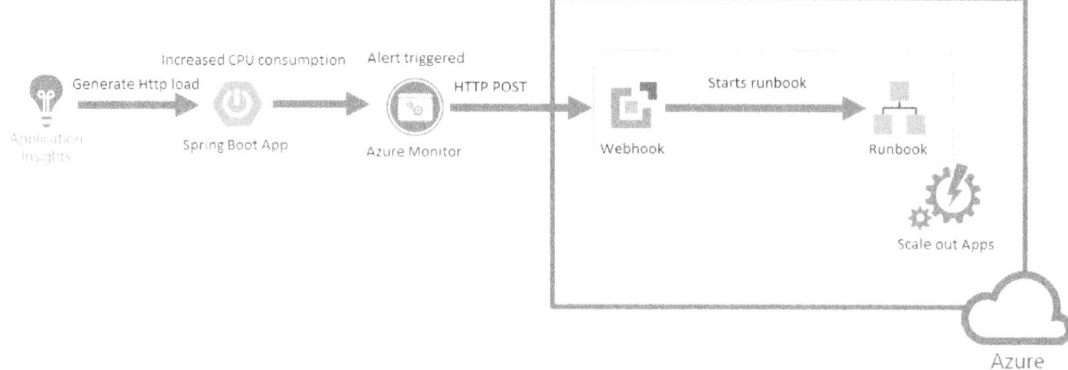

Figure 10.8: *Azure Auto Scaling*

- **Statelessness**: Strive for stateless services whenever possible. Storing a state in a central, scalable data store reduces complexity and enhances reliability.

- **Resilience and fault tolerance**: We need to have the mindset that everything fails and think about the design that if something fails, how quickly we can recover. Design for failure by building redundancy and fault tolerance. Use load balancing, distributed systems, and circuit breakers to maintain service availability.

- **Resource efficiency**: Optimize resource usage by right-sizing infrastructure components, using serverless technologies where applicable, and regularly reviewing and optimizing costs.

- **Documentation and knowledge sharing**: Document your architecture, processes, and best practices. Encourage knowledge sharing within your organization to ensure everyone is on the same page.

- **Compliance and governance (Azure Policy and Blueprints)**: Ensure your cloud-native applications comply with industry regulations and organizational governance policies. Use tools and processes to track and enforce compliance.

Enforce organizational standards and compliance by using Azure Policy and Blueprints. Define governance standards for your resources. The following figure shows how Azure Blueprints helps by providing ARM templates, policy definitions, and RBAC controls:

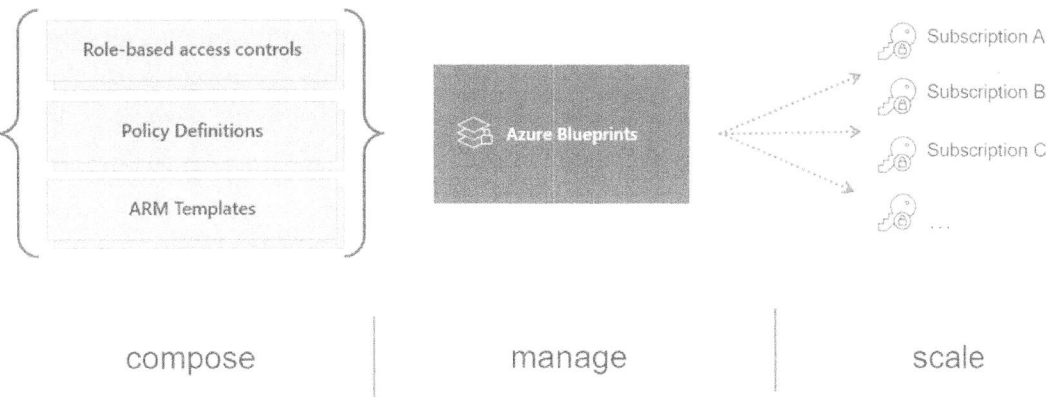

Figure 10.9: Azure Policy and Blueprints

Cost management (Azure Cost Management and Billing): Implement cost management and optimization practices to monitor and control cloud spending. Regularly review and adjust resources based on usage patterns. Putting the proper mechanism in place to observe the cost of cloud resources is the key to the cloud. There might be spills and leaks in resource utilization, which will increase the price of the cloud. Azure cost management tool helps in this regard to monitor the resources appropriately and take the corrective actions:

Figure 10.10: Azure Cost Management

We must monitor your Azure spending using Azure Cost Management and Billing tools. Also, we need to set up budgets and alerts to monitor resource utilization and take steps to control costs proactively.

Backup and disaster recovery: Implement robust backup and disaster recovery strategies to protect data and ensure business continuity.

Feedback loops: Continuously gather feedback from users and operations to improve your applications. Use this feedback to iterate and enhance your cloud-native solutions.

These best practices are partial, and their application may vary depending on your organization's and application's specific requirements. However, the above guidelines can help you build and manage cloud-native applications that are more scalable, resilient, and efficient.

This chapter will cover some case studies implemented in real life and discuss building two large-scale applications serving customers.

Real-world cloud-native applications

For the first use case, a business customer wanted to build a system to capture all the events related to the customer's order. The idea was to capture all the events associated with the order life cycle so that we can map all the journeys of the order through which it goes and find out the gaps that can be fixed to improve the customer experience.

To achieve that, we created an event hub using Azure EventHub, developed the SpringBoot-based microservices, and directed all the applications(frontend and backend) to send the data using the APIs if they have worked on the order. The idea was to capture all the events related to the customer order and build the customer journey. After that, we analyzed that data to find the gaps in the journey and asked the systems to fix them. In the following figure, we can see that there are multiple customer-facing applications like POS, online, and call centers. The customer is using all these systems for different purposes. For example, it can be used in retail for placing orders and solving customer queries.

Architecture has three main layers; the first layer is the front-end layer, which customers will use to interact, while the service layer is the microservice layer, wired up with the front end. We have an event layer using Azure Event Hub, which will capture all the events generated by customer-facing applications. The database layer is the last layer, which will be used to capture and store all the events data; refer to the following figure:

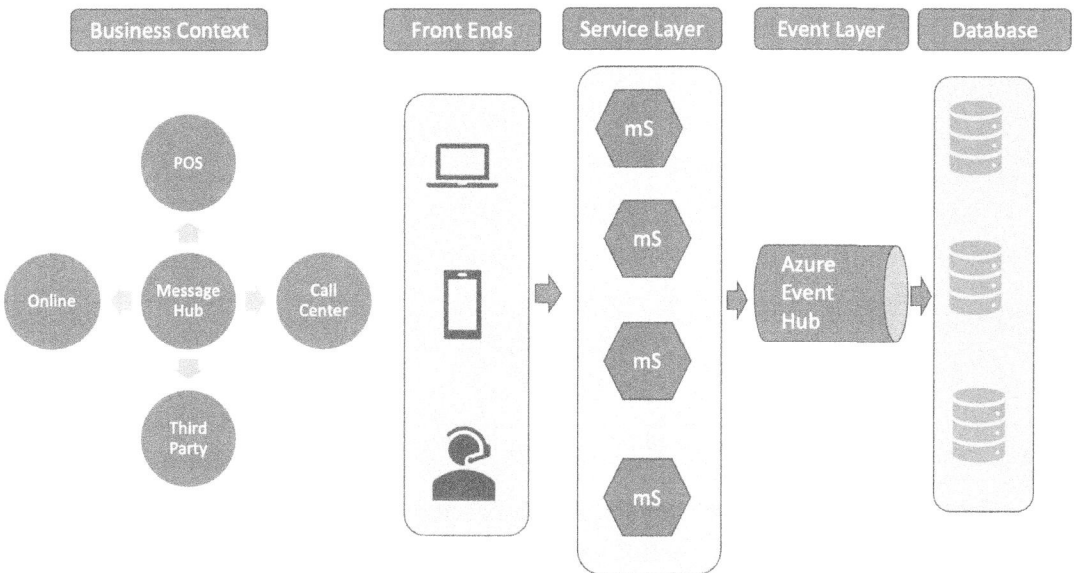

Figure 10.11: Capturing customer journey

The second case study will discuss building a real-time application that provides real-time monetizing data to the users to improve the overall throughput. The problem was that every store employee got some commission for each order they processed. Their current system was providing this commission data after three days. The management's idea was to provide this information in real time to boost the morale of the store employees. Ultimately, it will help improve the store's bottom line because real-time incentive information will motivate them to improve.

To solve this, we developed the SpringBoot-based microservices and used Azure Event Hub to capture all the events. We developed orchestration services for applying the rules on the message data and massaged the data. After refining the data, it was converted to a JSON document payload, and finally, it was stored in Azure Cosmos DB:

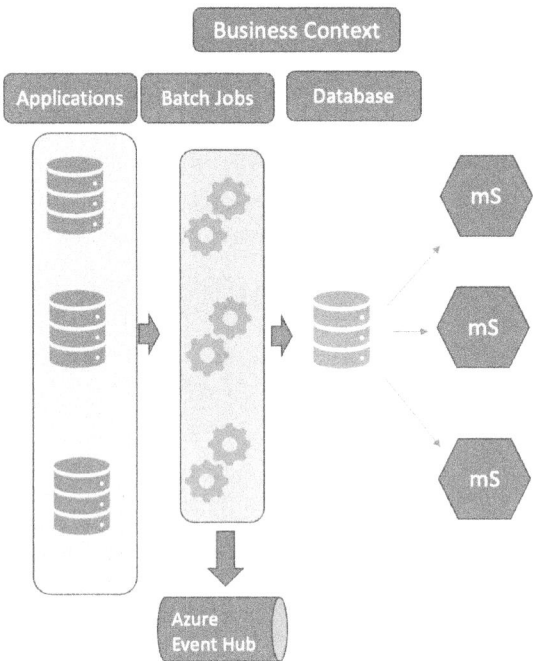

Figure 10.12: Capturing customer journey

We can see in the above image that the batch processing layer has been changed to the event capturing layer by using Azure Event Hub. Because the batch process was not the actual time, it ran on well-defined intervals, so applications were not getting real-time data. The application started getting real-time data by replacing it with event streaming infrastructure.

Here are some more real-world examples of how some of the world's largest companies have implemented microservices in their applications:

Netflix

Netflix is a pioneer in microservices. Its platform comprises numerous small, independently deployable services, handling functions like user recommendations, content delivery, and billing.

Microservices usage: Netflix has a highly distributed architecture with microservices for various functionalities such as user recommendations (personalization algorithms), content delivery (streaming servers), and billing (subscription management). In the following figure, we can see Netflix's high-level architecture. Netflix is running its services on AWS cloud:

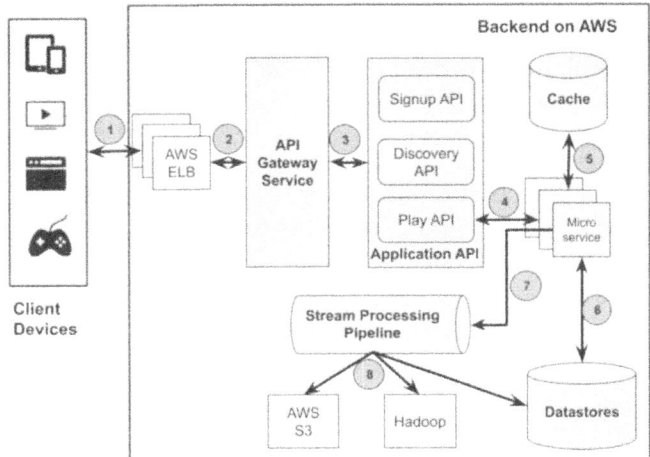

Figure 10.13: Netflix microservices architecture

Challenges: To handle large-scale traffic, Netflix employs a resilient and fault-tolerant architecture, and it often contributes to open-source projects related to microservices and cloud computing.

Spotify

Spotify utilizes microservices to manage its music streaming platform. Different services handle user authentication, playlist creation, content streaming, and recommendations, enabling agility and scalability.

Microservices usage: Spotify handles different aspects of its music streaming platform, including user authentication, playlist creation, content streaming, and personalized recommendations.

Agile development: The microservices architecture at Spotify enables independent development teams to work on specific features, promoting agility and faster release cycles.

Uber

Uber's ride-sharing platform relies on microservices to handle its operations, including user management, trip booking, and payment processing.

Microservices usage: Uber relies on microservices for various aspects, such as user authentication, ride booking, real-time GPS tracking, and payment processing.

Scalability: Microservices enable Uber to scale different components independently, handling peak demand in various cities.

Amazon

Amazon's e-commerce platform is built on microservices. Each service, such as inventory management, recommendation engine, and payment processing, operates independently for scalability and resilience.

Amazon utilizes microservices architecture to build scalable and resilient systems, enhancing agility and facilitating rapid innovation. Each service focuses on specific business functions, enabling independent development and deployment. This approach promotes fault isolation, allowing teams to manage failures without disrupting the system. Amazon's microservices leverage technologies like AWS Lambda, Docker, and Kubernetes for efficient containerization and orchestration. By decoupling components, Amazon achieves flexibility in scaling, enabling seamless updates, and improving overall system reliability, ultimately enhancing customer experience across their diverse services, from e-commerce to cloud computing.

Microservices usage

Amazon's e-commerce platform uses microservices for product catalog, recommendation engine, order processing, and payment handling. In the following figure, we can see the high-level architecture of microservices used by **Amazon.com**. It is a three-layer architecture at the first level of the user interface. Amazon uses Cloud Front along with S3, and it uses three types of databases. Aurora is Amazon's relational database, DynamoDB is the NoSQL, while elastic cache is their Cache DB:

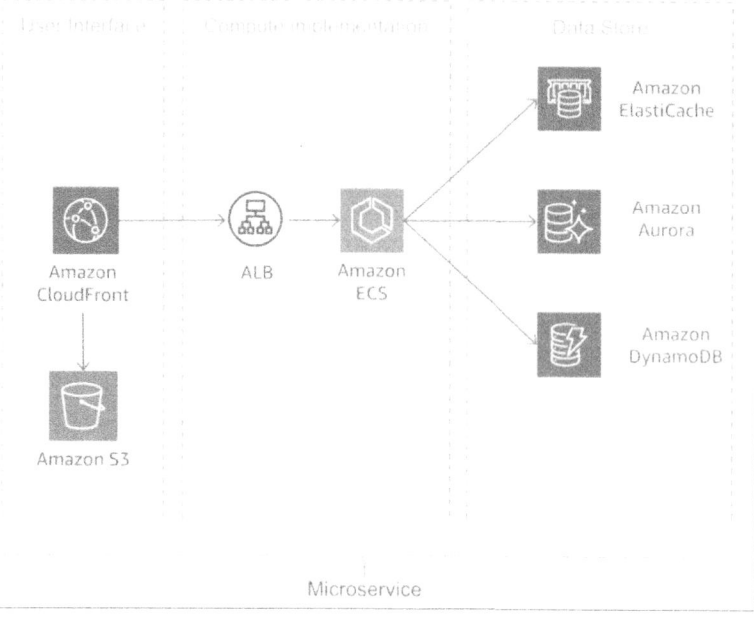

Figure 10.14: Microservice architecture used by Amazon

Airbnb

Airbnb has adopted a microservices architecture to support its online marketplace. Services manage functions like property listings, booking transactions, and user reviews.

Microservices usage: Airbnb manages different aspects of its online marketplace, including property listings, booking transactions, user reviews, and messaging.

Internationalization: Microservices allow Airbnb to quickly adapt its platform for different regions and languages.

Etsy

Etsy, an e-commerce platform for handmade and vintage items, utilizes microservices for features like product search, inventory management, and order processing.

Microservices usage: Etsy's architecture is utilized for product search, inventory management, order processing, and user feedback.

Community engagement: Microservices enable Etsy to provide a personalized experience for its users and foster a sense of community among buyers and sellers.

Twitter

Twitter transitioned to a microservices architecture to handle its large-scale social media platform. Services manage functionalities such as tweet posting, user timelines, and trending topics.

Microservices usage: Twitter transitioned to a microservices architecture to handle features like tweet posting, user timelines, notifications, and trending topics.

Scalability and performance: Microservices allow Twitter to scale different functionalities independently and optimize the platform's performance.

LinkedIn

LinkedIn employs microservices for its professional networking platform. Different services handle user profiles, connections, job recommendations, and content delivery.

Microservices usage: LinkedIn employs microservices for managing user profiles, professional connections, job recommendations, content delivery, and messaging.

Networking: Microservices facilitate LinkedIn's networking features, helping users connect with professionals and discover relevant content.

Walmart

Walmart has embraced microservices for its online retail operations. Services manage product catalogs, order processing, customer accounts, and inventory management.

Microservices usage: Walmart's online retail operations rely on microservices for managing product catalogs, order processing, customer accounts, inventory, and shipping.

Omnichannel retailing: Microservices enable Walmart to provide a seamless shopping experience across various channels, including online and in-store.

Coca-Cola

Coca-Cola adopted microservices to enhance its digital marketing and customer engagement platforms. Services manage loyalty programs, content delivery, and customer interactions.

Microservices usage: Coca-Cola adopted microservices for its digital marketing and customer engagement platforms, including services for loyalty programs, content delivery, and customer interactions.

Customer engagement: Microservices help Coca-Cola engage with customers through personalized experiences, loyalty rewards, and targeted marketing campaigns.

Conclusion

These best practices help you build and manage cloud-native applications on Azure effectively, ensuring scalability, reliability, security, and cost optimization. We have discussed the core best practices we need to follow to leverage during the cloud adoption journey.

It starts with seeding the microservices architecture strategy first and then thinking about building the CI/CD pipelines and fostering the DevOps culture.

We also need to ensure that we are using the Azure orchestration tools and that development is writing the infrastructure code, which will confirm what type of runtime will be provided to execute the code. Security should be central to whatever we do and ensure we follow the policy and governance. Adapt these practices to your specific project and organizational needs.

The next chapter will conclude with the final thoughts about the Azure cloud offering.

Questions

1. What is Azure, and why is it essential for cloud best practices?
2. What are the key benefits of following Azure best practices?
3. How do you ensure high availability in Azure?
4. What role does Azure DevOps play in cloud best practices?
5. How can you ensure data security in Azure?
6. What are some strategies for optimizing Azure costs?
7. Explain the importance of monitoring and observability in Azure.
8. What are Azure Blueprints, and why are they useful?
9. How can you implement disaster recovery in Azure, and why is it important?
10. What role does Azure IAM play in cloud best practices?

Join our book's Discord space

Join the book's Discord Workspace for Latest updates, Offers, Tech happenings around the world, New Release and Sessions with the Authors:

https://discord.bpbonline.com

Chapter 11
Cloud, Generative AI, and Future Trends

Introduction

Cloud computing is changing the IT landscape and enabling organizations to achieve new scale and speed. Organizations need not think and worry about services like networking, scalability, and availability when demand keeps changing. Cloud computing makes it easier for organizations to handle fluctuations in demand, which is particularly useful for businesses with seasonal or variable workloads.

Technologies such as Artificial Intelligence/Machine Learning, edge computing, virtual cloud desktops, serverless computing, automation, hybrid cloud, SASE, and cloud disaster recovery are shaping the future of cloud computing.

Structure

In this chapter, we will go through the following topics:

- Recap of key concepts and takeaways
- Generative AI: An overview
- Azure Cloud and generative AI
- Learning generative AI Azure services

- Writing your first generative AI program
- Future trends in cloud-native development
- Azure Cloud future trends

Objectives

The future of cloud computing and AI is marked by continued growth, innovation, and integration. Cloud computing will evolve with advancements like edge computing, enabling processing closer to data sources for reduced latency. The convergence of cloud and AI will lead to more accessible and scalable AI services, fostering widespread adoption. Emerging areas include quantum computing, which holds promise for solving complex problems, and AI-driven automation in fields like cybersecurity. Fusing AI with the **Internet of Things** (**IoT**) will drive smart infrastructure, while Blockchain integration enhances security and transparency. As technology matures, ethical considerations and responsible AI practices will gain prominence, shaping the future landscape of these transformative technologies.

In this chapter, we will go through the emerging areas of cloud computing and see how generative AI is changing the technology landscape and transforming organizations.

Recap of key concepts and takeaways

Cloud computing is a vast and complex field with many key concepts and principles. We have already discussed all the building blocks in the above chapters. Here are some of the fundamental concepts in cloud computing just for quick reference:

Virtualization

Virtualization is the technology that allows multiple **virtual machines** (**VMs**) or containers to run on a single physical server, enabling efficient resource utilization and isolation. Virtualization is a technology that enables the creation of virtual, rather than physical, versions of computing resources, such as servers, networks, or storage devices. It allows multiple virtual instances to run on a single physical system, optimizing resource utilization. Virtualization abstracts the underlying hardware, enabling greater flexibility, scalability, and efficiency in managing and deploying computing environments. This technology is fundamental to cloud computing, allowing for the efficient allocation and sharing of resources and isolating different workloads on the same physical infrastructure.

On-demand self-service

Cloud services are typically available on-demand, allowing users to provision and manage resources as needed without human intervention from the service provider. On-demand self-service in cloud computing refers to the capability of users to provide and manage computing resources autonomously without requiring human intervention. Users can access and deploy services, such as virtual machines or storage, on a pay-as-you-go basis as needed, without manual approval or assistance. This characteristic empowers users to scale resources up or down based on demand, providing flexibility and efficiency. On-demand self-service is a crucial feature of cloud computing, enabling rapid and convenient access to computing resources without the delays associated with traditional infrastructure provisioning.

Auto scalability

Cloud resources can be easily scaled up or down to accommodate changes in workload, providing elasticity and cost efficiency. Scalability in the cloud refers to the ability of a system or application to handle an increasing workload by efficiently adapting to growing demands. Cloud services offer both vertical and horizontal scalability. Vertical scalability involves increasing the capacity of existing resources, like adding more power to a single server. Horizontal scalability involves adding more instances or nodes to a system and distributing the load. Cloud platforms enable dynamic scalability, allowing organizations to scale resources up or down based on demand, ensuring optimal performance and cost-effectiveness as workloads fluctuate. This flexibility is fundamental to meeting varying performance requirements in a cloud environment.

Service models

Cloud computing offers various service models, including **Infrastructure as a Service (IaaS)**, **Platform as a Service (PaaS)**, and **Software as a Service (SaaS)**, each with different levels of control and management. If you move from left to right in the image below, you will observe that cloud providers have started taking control of everything, but it comes at a cost. Customers need to think about what level of service they need and make decisions based on that. The following figure shows each type of cloud offering services:

On Prem	IaaS	PaaS	SaaS
Application	Application	Application	Application
Data	Data	Data	Data
Runtime	Runtime	Runtime	Runtime
Middleware	Middleware	Middleware	Middleware
Operating System	Operating System	Operating System	Operating System
Virtualization	Virtualization	Virtualization	Virtualization
Servers	Servers	Servers	Servers
Storage	Storage	Storage	Storage
Networking	Networking	Networking	Networking

Figure 11.1: Cloud service models

Cloud deployment models

There are different deployment models in cloud computing, including public cloud (resources shared among multiple organizations), private cloud (dedicated to a single organization), community cloud, and hybrid cloud (a combination of public and private clouds).

In the public cloud deployment model, the service provider is still responsible for managing the infrastructure and maintaining the resources, even though multiple individuals and companies use it. As a result, all equipment is located at the service provider's premises. AWS, GCP, Azure, IBM, and Salesforce are examples of public cloud providers. Using the public cloud provides excellent convenience, reliability, and scalability, but data security and privacy remain points of concern.

While on the surface, the public and private cloud models may appear to be drastically different deployment models, the truth is that they are very similar. Their architectures are built almost identically and include similar cloud resources. While the public cloud model provides infrastructure and resources for the general public, the private cloud model is only available to one company. **Private clouds**, also known as **enterprise** or **on-premises clouds**, can be located on the premises of the company that owns them, or a third-party company can host them.

Private cloud deployment also offers convenience, scalability, and reliability, similar to what we receive in the public cloud. Still, organizations must manage the infrastructure in a private cloud, which requires lots of cost and effort.

Community cloud deployment models may be modeled after public clouds, but they are much more similar to private cloud models. Although the infrastructures are organized almost the same, one significant difference is the licensed user base.

In the private cloud model, one company owns and manages the infrastructure; in the community cloud model, the private cloud infrastructure is owned by one organization, and several companies with similar capabilities share their resources.

These shared or multi-tenant cloud models work best when each participating organization has similar security, privacy, storage, and other performance requirements. Organizations will benefit from sharing resources with the same parameters if this happens. In addition, partners can participate in joint projects, streamline project development, and share implementation and maintenance costs and tasks.

Pay-as-you-go pricing

Cloud providers typically use a pay-as-you-go or subscription-based pricing model, where users pay only for the resources they consume, reducing capital expenditure. This is one of the critical benefits cloud providers provide, and customers want to reap it.

Service Level Agreements

Public cloud companies have well-defined Service Level Agreements (SLA) for their services and meet them. SLAs define the expected performance and availability of cloud services, outlining the responsibilities of both the provider and the customer.

Resource pooling

Cloud providers pool computing resources to serve multiple customers, with each customer's data and applications isolated from others.

Network access

Cloud services are accessible over the internet from anywhere, and resources are distributed worldwide, in their term **regions**, providing ubiquitous access to resources. One can choose what areas must be selected based on customer distribution.

Security and Compliance

Cloud providers implement security measures and compliance certifications to protect data and meet regulatory requirements.

Data center locations

Cloud providers have data centers in various geographic regions, allowing users to choose the location that best suits their needs for latency, data sovereignty, and disaster recovery.

Elastic load balancing

Cloud services often include load-balancing features to distribute traffic across multiple servers or instances for improved performance and fault tolerance.

Redundancy and high availability

Cloud providers offer redundancy and high availability options to ensure applications remain accessible even during hardware or network failures.

Data storage options

Cloud computing offers various data storage options, including object storage, block storage, and databases, each suitable for different use cases.

Orchestration

Orchestration tools enable the automation and management of complex, multi-component applications in the cloud.

DevOps and CI/CD

DevOps practices and **continuous integration/continuous deployment (CI/CD)** pipelines are essential for efficiently developing, deploying, and managing cloud-based applications.

Monitoring and management tools

Cloud providers offer tools for monitoring and managing resources, helping users maintain performance and cost control.

Data transfer and bandwidth costs

Users must consider data transfer costs when moving data in and out of the cloud and bandwidth costs for network traffic.

These key concepts form the foundation of cloud computing. They are essential for understanding cloud services, leveraging them effectively, and making informed decisions when adopting cloud solutions for various business needs.

Generative AI: An overview

Generative AI is a class of artificial intelligence systems designed to generate content often indistinguishable from human-created content. Unlike traditional AI models that are task-specific, generative AI can create diverse outputs, including images, text, music, and more. A prominent subset of generative AI is **generative adversarial networks (GANs)**, where two neural networks, a generator and a discriminator, are trained in tandem.

The generator creates content, while the discriminator evaluates its authenticity. The generator improves its ability to produce increasingly realistic content through iterative training. GANs have been successful in various applications, from creating lifelike images to generating synthetic data for training other AI models.

Generative AI has transformative implications across the art, entertainment, and medicine industries. It can automate content creation, aid in data augmentation, and even generate realistic simulations for training purposes. However, ethical considerations arise, as generative AI can be misused for deepfake generation or other deceptive practices. Balancing the potential benefits with responsible use and ethical guidelines is crucial in harnessing the power of generative AI.

Large language models

A large language model (**LLM**) is an Artificial Intelligence model designed to understand and generate human-like language. Generative AI, on the other hand, is a broader concept that encompasses various models, including LLMs, which are capable of generating new content, such as text, images, or even music.

In generative AI, LLMs excel at natural language understanding and expression. They can generate text paragraphs, articles, or code snippets based on a prompt or context. LLMs leverage transformer architectures, enabling them to capture intricate patterns and dependencies in language.

The versatility of LLMs extends to various applications, including content creation, chatbots, language translation, and code generation. They can understand context, generate contextually appropriate responses, and perform language-based tasks like summarization or question-answering.

However, ethical considerations arise, as LLMs can be misused to generate misleading or harmful content. Addressing biases in training data and implementing robust moderation mechanisms are essential.

In summary, LLMs are a powerful subset of generative AI, showcasing the potential of pre-trained models in generating high-quality, context-aware, and diverse textual outputs across a wide range of applications.

LLMs are a Machine Learning model, often based on deep neural networks, trained on vast amounts of text data. These models learn language patterns, structures, and semantics, allowing them to understand context, generate coherent sentences, and perform language-related tasks. Notable examples of LLMs include OpenAI's **Generative Pre-trained Transformer** (**GPT**) series.

How LLMs help in generative AI and content creation

LLMs, such as OpenAI's GPT-3, play a pivotal role in generative AI by excelling in creating diverse and contextually rich content. LLMs are trained on massive datasets containing a broad spectrum of language patterns and demonstrate a remarkable ability to generate coherent and contextually relevant text.

LLMs generate articles, essays, creative writing, and more in content creation based on given prompts or input. Their understanding of context allows them to maintain coherence within longer pieces, adapting to different writing styles or tones. LLMs can mimic the writing style of specific genres and authors or even adapt to technical or creative contexts.

Moreover, LLMs facilitate the automation of content generation in various industries. They can assist in drafting marketing copy, generating product descriptions, and even creating personalized content for users. The adaptability and versatility of LLMs make them valuable tools for streamlining content creation processes and addressing the growing demand for diverse and engaging textual content.

However, ethical considerations, including biases in training data and the potential for generating misleading information, must be carefully addressed to ensure the responsible use of LLMs in content creation.

LLMs, like GPT, play a significant role in generative AI and content creation for several reasons:

Natural language understanding: NLP is a crucial aspect of generative models, allowing them to understand and generate human-like text. Models like OpenAI's GPT have demonstrated impressive language generation capabilities.

LLMs excel at understanding the nuances of human language, allowing them to generate contextually relevant and grammatically correct text.

Text generation: LLMs can generate coherent and contextually relevant text based on their input. This makes them valuable for content creation, including writing articles, stories, or code snippets.

Creativity and innovation: Generative AI enables machines to exhibit creativity by generating content such as images, text, or even music. This feature has applications in various fields, including art, design, and content creation.

LLMs can be fine-tuned to exhibit creative behavior. This is especially useful in creative writing, poetry generation, and other artistic applications.

Chatbots and conversational agents: LLMs power advanced chatbots and conversational agents, enabling more natural and context-aware user interactions. Generative AI is pivotal in prompt engineering and building chatbots, allowing natural language understanding and generation. Engineering models like OpenAI's GPT-3 can be fine-tuned to perform specific tasks or generate targeted responses by providing well-crafted prompts. This technique allows developers to guide the AI's behavior and tailor its output.

In chatbot development, generative AI enhances conversational experiences by generating human-like responses. Chatbots powered by generative AI can understand user inputs, respond contextually, and simulate more natural conversations. The flexibility of generative AI allows for dynamic interactions, making it suitable for diverse applications, from customer support to virtual assistants. However, ensuring ethical use, addressing biases, and refining prompts are essential considerations to optimize the performance and reliability of generative AI-powered chatbots.

Knowledge synthesis: By learning from vast amounts of text data, LLMs can synthesize information and generate content that appears knowledgeable and informed.

LLMs like GPT-3 excel in knowledge synthesis by comprehensively analyzing and understanding vast amounts of textual data. They use extensive training on diverse sources to generate coherent and contextually relevant information. LLMs can synthesize knowledge on various topics, providing nuanced and informative responses based on input prompts. This capability makes them valuable tools for content creation, language understanding, and generating detailed explanations, contributing to efficient knowledge synthesis across various domains.

Multimodal capabilities: Some LLMs, like GPT-3, have multimodal capabilities, allowing them to handle various data types, including text and images. This enhances their usefulness in tasks like image captioning or generating textual descriptions for images.

LLMs contribute to building multi-modal capabilities by integrating diverse data types seamlessly. While initially designed for text, LLMs can be extended to process and generate content across various modalities like images, code, and more. Through fine-tuning and domain-specific training, LLMs adapt to understand and develop content in multiple formats, fostering the development of comprehensive multi-modal AI systems. This versatility allows LLMs to bridge gaps between different data representations, enabling more holistic and integrated solutions for tasks involving diverse information types.

Transfer learning: Generative models often leverage transfer learning, where pre-trained models on large datasets can be fine-tuned for specific tasks with smaller datasets. This accelerates the training process and enhances performance.

LLMs often use transfer learning, where they are pre-trained on a large dataset for a general understanding of language. They can then be fine-tuned on smaller, domain-specific datasets for more targeted applications.

Human-like text generation: LLMs can generate text that closely resembles human-written content when appropriately trained. This is crucial in applications where a human touch is desired, such as content creation, dialogue generation, and storytelling.

Image generation and manipulation: Generative models, especially those based on neural networks like **Generative Adversarial Networks (GANs)**, can create realistic images and manipulate existing ones. This is widely used in image synthesis, style transfer, and deepfake technology.

LLMs like GPT-3 aid in image creation by leveraging their generative capabilities. While primarily designed for text, LLMs can be prompted to generate descriptive and contextual text corresponding to specific images. This textual guidance is a basis for developing images through collaboration with image generation models. Although LLMs are not inherently image generators, their ability to provide detailed instructions or captions contributes to the synthesis of images by guiding dedicated image generation algorithms in creating visual content aligned with the given textual prompts.

Unsupervised learning: Generative models often operate in unsupervised learning scenarios, where the algorithm learns patterns and structures in data without explicit labels. This makes them versatile for various applications.

LLMs contribute to unsupervised learning by learning patterns, structures, and relationships from unannotated data. LLMs acquire a broad understanding of language and context through pre-training on vast datasets. LLMs can be fine-tuned in unsupervised settings for specific tasks, leveraging the generalized knowledge gained during pre-training. Their ability to discern latent patterns in unlabeled data makes LLMs valuable for various unsupervised learning applications, where the model can infer meaningful insights, discover hidden correlations, and adapt to diverse domains without the need for labeled training examples.

In summary, LLMs are a powerful component of generative AI, particularly in natural language understanding and text generation. Their ability to understand context, generate coherent text, and exhibit creative behavior makes them valuable tools in content creation and various other applications.

Azure Cloud and generative AI

Azure Cloud's generative AI capabilities are primarily exemplified by services like Azure Cognitive Services and the integration of OpenAI's GPT-3 and GPT-4, a recent version of the OpenAI LLM engine. GPT-4 is GPT-4 is more advanced, and with this improvement, the model can better comprehend the context and recognize subtleties, producing more accurate and coherent results. With these offerings, Azure empowers developers and businesses to leverage advanced natural language processing and generation capabilities. Azure Cognitive Services includes language models for tasks like text analysis, translation, and sentiment analysis. OpenAI's GPT-3, integrated into Azure, enables users to generate human-like text based on given prompts, facilitating content creation and conversation simulations. These generative AI capabilities are instrumental in diverse applications, including chatbots, content generation, and creative writing. Azure's commitment to enhancing generative AI services aligns with the broader industry trend of leveraging Artificial Intelligence for innovative and practical purposes.

Azure Cloud Services for generative AI

Azure, Microsoft's cloud computing platform, offers various services and tools that support the development and deployment of generative AI models. Here are some critical Azure services relevant to generative AI:

Azure Machine Learning Service

Azure ML provides a cloud-based environment for building, training, and deploying Machine Learning models. It supports various frameworks and languages, making it versatile for generative AI projects. Azure Machine Learning Service is a comprehensive cloud-based platform by Microsoft for building, training, and deploying Machine Learning models. It offers a range of tools and services to streamline the end-to-end Machine Learning lifecycle. Users can prepare data, build models using popular frameworks like

TensorFlow and PyTorch, and deploy models at scale. Azure Machine Learning supports code-first and no-code/low-code experiences, catering to various skill levels.

Key features include AutoML, enabling automated model selection and hyperparameter tuning, and integration with Azure Notebooks for collaborative development. The platform provides powerful tools for model interpretation, version control, and monitoring. Azure Machine Learning also facilitates seamless deployment with containerization and integration with Azure Kubernetes Service.

With a focus on openness and interoperability, Azure Machine Learning supports Python and R languages, allowing data scientists and developers to leverage their preferred tools and libraries. Overall, Azure Machine Learning Service empowers organizations to accelerate their Machine Learning initiatives with a scalable and collaborative cloud-based environment.

Azure Cognitive Services

Azure Cognitive Services include pre-built AI models that can be easily integrated into applications. Services like Text Analytics, Computer Vision, and Speech APIs can be employed for generative AI. Azure Cognitive Services is a suite of AI services on the Azure cloud platform, offering pre-built models and APIs to enable developers to integrate advanced capabilities into applications easily without extensive machine learning expertise. The services cover various domains, including vision, speech, language, and decision-making. Below are the central Cognitive Services provided by the Azure cloud:

- **Vision services**: Azure Cognitive Services includes Computer Vision for image analysis, Face API for facial recognition, and Custom Vision for creating custom image classifiers.

- **Speech services**: Speech-to-text and Text-to-Speech APIs convert spoken language into written text and vice versa. Speaker recognition identifies and verifies speakers based on their voice.

- **Language services**: Text Analytics analyzes sentiment, extracts vital phrases, and performs language detection. **Language Understanding** (**LUIS**) helps in natural language understanding, while Translator API provides language translation capabilities.

- **Decision services**: Azure Cognitive Services offers services like Personalizer for personalized content recommendations and Anomaly Detector for detecting anomalies in time-series data.

  These services empower developers to enhance applications with AI features, from creating intelligent chatbots to implementing facial recognition in security systems. Azure Cognitive Services abstracts the complexity of Machine Learning models, making advanced AI accessible and easy to integrate for various applications across industries.

Azure Databricks

Azure Databricks is an Apache Spark-based analytics platform that facilitates large-scale data processing. It helps handle the vast datasets often required for training generative models. Azure Databricks is an Apache Spark-based analytics platform on Microsoft Azure. It provides a collaborative environment for big data analytics, Machine Learning, and data engineering. Azure Databricks seamlessly integrates with Azure services and offers features such as autoscaling, built-in notebooks, and a collaborative workspace. It accelerates data processing and analysis with a unified analytics platform, fostering collaboration between data scientists, engineers, and business analysts. With advanced analytics capabilities, including MLflow for Machine Learning lifecycle management, Azure Databricks empowers organizations to derive valuable insights from large datasets efficiently.

Azure GPU Virtual Machines

Generative AI models, especially Deep Learning models, benefit significantly from **graphics processing unit (GPU)** acceleration. Azure provides GPU virtual machines that enhance the training speed of complex models.

Azure GPU Virtual Machines offer powerful virtualized computing resources equipped with GPUs. These VMs are optimized for computationally intensive workloads such as AI, Deep Learning, and parallel processing tasks. They support various GPU types, including NVIDIA GPUs, providing the performance needed for demanding applications. Azure GPU Virtual Machines enable users to accelerate data processing, run complex simulations, and train Machine Learning models efficiently. With flexible configurations and access to GPU-optimized frameworks, these VMs are essential for organizations seeking high-performance computing capabilities in the cloud.

Azure Kubernetes Service

Azure Kubernetes Service (AKS) simplifies containerized applications' deployment, management, and scaling, including those hosting generative AI models. This ensures efficient and scalable deployment in production environments. We have covered AKS in Chapter 4, AzureKubernetes, *and Container Registry*.

Learning generative AI Azure services

Azure provides robust infrastructure support for generative AI through scalable and flexible cloud computing resources. Users can efficiently deploy and run generative AI models with services like Azure Virtual Machines. AKS allows for containerized deployments, optimizing resource utilization. Additionally, Azure's integration with GPU-accelerated instances enhances the performance of computationally intensive tasks in generative AI. The platform's infrastructure support enables users to scale resources based on demand, ensuring the efficient and reliable execution of generative AI workloads with the necessary computational power.

Access to generative AI services

Azure offers services like Azure Cognitive Services, which include language models for text generation. These services allow users to experiment with and understand the capabilities of generative AI without the need for extensive infrastructure setup.

Integration with OpenAI models

Azure has integrated OpenAI's advanced generative AI models, such as GPT-3, into its platform. This integration enables users to leverage state-of-the-art models for creative text generation and other applications.

Scalable infrastructure

Azure provides scalable cloud infrastructure, including virtual machines and AKS, allowing users to deploy and scale generative AI models based on their computational needs.

Development and experimentation

Azure Notebooks and Azure Machine Learning service offer environments for developing and experimenting with generative AI algorithms. These tools streamline the process of coding, testing, and refining models.

GPU Acceleration

Azure supports GPU-accelerated instances, enhancing the performance of computationally intensive tasks often associated with generative AI. This accelerates the learning process and experimentation with sophisticated models.

Comprehensive documentation and tutorials

Azure provides extensive documentation, tutorials, and learning resources on generative AI. This educational material supports users at various skill levels, from beginners to advanced practitioners, in understanding and applying generative AI concepts.

Scalability and ease of deployment

Azure's cloud infrastructure enables the scaling of computational resources as needed. This is crucial for training large, complex generative models requiring significant computational power.

Azure provides a seamless environment for deploying and managing machine learning models. With tools like Azure ML Service and AKS, deploying models becomes straightforward.

Collaboration and integration

Azure facilitates collaboration among data scientists, developers, and other stakeholders involved in generative AI projects. Integration with Azure DevOps ensures smooth workflows from development to deployment.

Data management

Generative AI models often demand extensive datasets for training. Azure's data storage and management services simplify handling large datasets, ensuring efficient training processes.

Security and Compliance

Azure Cloud is a conducive platform for individuals and organizations to explore, learn, and implement generative AI technologies, providing the necessary infrastructure, tools, and educational resources to support the learning journey. Azure offers robust security features and compliance certifications, making it suitable for handling sensitive data often involved in generative AI applications. This is crucial for industries like healthcare and finance.

Writing your first generative AI program

To use ChatGPT for Python, you can use the OpenAI API to request and receive responses from the ChatGPT model. Here are simple steps with a sample program using the OpenAI Python library:

1. Obtain an API key from OpenAI by signing up on their platform **https://platform.openai.com/playground**

2. Install the OpenAI Python library using pip:

   `pip install openai.`

3. Use the OpenAI API key in your Python program.

   Here is a simple example:

   ```
   import openai
   
   # Set your OpenAI API key
   openai.api_key = 'YOUR_API_KEY'
   ```

```python
# Define a prompt
prompt = "Tell me a joke"

# Make an API call to ChatGPT
response = openai.Completion.create(
    engine="text-davinci-003",
    prompt=prompt,
    max_tokens=150
)

# Extract and print the model's reply
reply = response['choices'][0]['text']
print("ChatGPT:", reply)
```

Here is another program using gpt-3.5-turbo engine:

```
import openai
openai.api_key = '<Access Key>'
model_engine = "gpt-3.5-turbo"
```

This specifies which GPT model to use, as several available models have different capabilities and performance characteristics.

In the below code, gpt-3.5-turbo model is being used to interact with the user and provide responses:

```
response = openai.ChatCompletion.create(
    model='gpt-3.5-turbo',
    messages=[
        {"role": "system", "content": "You are a helpful assistant."},
        {"role": "user", "content": "Hello, ChatGPT!"},
    ])

message = response.choices[0]['message']
print("{}: {}".format(message['role'], message['content']))
```

4. Run the program:

   Save your Python script and run it.

5. Receive ChatGPT's response:

ChatGPT will generate a response based on the provided prompt, and the program will print the model's reply.

Remember to handle API keys securely and be mindful of OpenAI's usage policies. Additionally, tailor the prompt and parameters based on your specific use case. The example above uses a simple prompt, but you can experiment with more complex prompts and parameters to achieve the desired results.

This provides a brief overview of generative AI and its features, along with the role of Azure Cloud in supporting it.

Future trends in cloud-native development

Cloud providers continuously deliver new services to help customers run their business efficiently. Here are some insights into potential future trends in cloud computing. Remember that the technology landscape is constantly evolving, so these trends may have further developed or evolved since then. Here are some key future trends in cloud computing:

Edge computing

Edge computing involves processing data closer to the source of data generation rather than relying on centralized cloud data centers. This trend is expected to grow as **Internet of Things (IoT)** devices become more prevalent, requiring real-time processing and reduced latency. Edge computing is a paradigm in cloud computing that involves processing data near the source of data generation rather than relying solely on centralized cloud servers. Traditional cloud computing sends data to a centralized data center for processing and analysis. Edge computing, however, brings computation and storage closer to the devices or edge of the network, reducing latency and improving overall system efficiency—a few of the emerging future trends in edge computing are as follows.

Helping 5G adoption

5G networks offer lightning-fast data transfer with minimal delays and ample bandwidth. According to Ericsson's recent report, global 5G mobile subscriptions are projected to hit 1.5 billion by the end of 2023. Integrating 5G and edge computing presents exciting opportunities to elevate digital experiences and enhance performance. As 5G adoption increases in 2024, previously limited edge computing applications due to connectivity issues will come to fruition.

Moreover, the swift and efficient data transfer enabled by 5G translates to cost savings. This dynamic duo of 5G and edge computing is poised to revolutionize business operations, allowing firms to deliver innovative, connected experiences seamlessly. Whether operating from a centralized on-premises setup or utilizing public or private cloud data centers, firms can leverage this synergy to unlock new data utilization and customer engagement potential.

Edge containers

Firms have witnessed a significant change in infrastructure technology, transitioning from **virtual machines** (**VMs**) in the past to edge containers today. Edge containers, a form of decentralized computing, reduce latency, conserve bandwidth, and improve digital experiences. By moving critical app components to the network's edge, firms can lower network expenses and enhance response times. In 2024, companies can deploy edge containers across various locations to cater to regional needs efficiently. This strategy also aids in directing traffic to the closest container using a single IP address.

Edge-as-a-Service

Edge-as-a-service (**EaaS**) revolutionizes how companies approach edge computing by offering subscription-based access to edge computing resources. This model allows firms to expand their edge computing capabilities without hefty investments in infrastructure. EaaS efficiently manages large-scale cross-node edge resources, promoting edge autonomy, collaboration, and resource flexibility.

It enables firms to deploy services, computing tasks, and intelligence flexibly. By leveraging EaaS, companies can harness the potential of edge computing without the initial costs associated with building and maintaining infrastructure. In 2024, EaaS is poised to unlock new opportunities for businesses, enabling them to fully realize the advantages of edge computing in delivering innovative services and experiences.

Advantages of edge computing

There are many benefits of edge computing, so companies are adopting it. Below are a few advantages of edge computing:

- **Low latency**: By processing data locally, edge computing reduces the round-trip time for data to travel between the source and the cloud. This is critical for applications where real-time responsiveness is essential, such as in autonomous vehicles or augmented reality.

- **Bandwidth efficiency**: Edge computing reduces the need to transmit large volumes of data to the cloud, optimizing bandwidth usage. This is particularly important in scenarios where network bandwidth is limited or expensive.

- **Privacy and security**: Processing sensitive data locally at the edge enhances privacy and security. Critical data can be processed and analyzed on-site, minimizing the need to transmit sensitive information over the network.

- **Scalability**: Edge computing complements cloud computing by distributing computing tasks. It enables horizontal scaling by deploying additional edge devices, providing scalability as the network of devices grows.

- **Reliability**: Edge computing enhances the reliability of applications by reducing dependence on a central cloud server. Local processing allows applications to continue functioning despite a temporary cloud connectivity loss.

Everyday use cases for edge computing include industrial IoT, smart cities, healthcare, retail, and autonomous vehicles. Combining cloud computing and edge computing creates a powerful and flexible architecture that can meet the diverse computational needs of modern applications.

Serverless computing

Serverless computing, also known as **Function-as-a-Service (FaaS)**, is gaining popularity. It allows developers to focus on writing code without worrying about server management. This trend is expected to continue as it simplifies development and reduces operational overhead. Many things are happening in serverless space to improve security, computing, monitoring, and trends, providing more maturity. Some of the future trends in this space are as follows:

Improved security in serverless computing: Security is increasingly crucial in serverless applications, with a notable percentage exhibiting critical vulnerabilities. This trend is prompting a shift towards a heightened emphasis on security, driven by client demand and developer awareness. Anticipate advancements in end-to-end security solutions and a stronger focus on securing serverless computing environments.

Enhanced observation and monitoring: Monitoring applications within serverless environments poses a significant challenge for developers, with observation and monitoring tools emerging as critical areas for improvement. Expect advancements in these tools, fueled by market demand and technological innovation. Commercial solutions and open-source initiatives like OpenTelemetry are poised to enhance the efficiency and effectiveness of observing and monitoring serverless applications.

Green future with serverless computing: Serverless computing presents an opportunity to promote environmental sustainability by reducing electricity over-utilization and eliminating physical servers. This approach decreases waste and energy consumption, making serverless setups more environmentally friendly than traditional server-heavy configurations. Moreover, serverless computing aligns with the growing trend of environmental consciousness and sustainable business practices in the IT sector.

Multi-cloud and hybrid cloud adoption

Many organizations are adopting multi-cloud and hybrid cloud strategies to avoid vendor lock-in, increase resilience, and optimize costs. Managing workloads across multiple cloud providers is becoming a standard practice. Companies increasingly adopt multi-cloud and hybrid cloud models to strategically maximize their IT infrastructure for diverse business needs. Multi-cloud deployment involves using services from multiple cloud providers, while hybrid cloud combines on-premises infrastructure with cloud services.

The key drivers for this adoption include:

- **Risk management**: Distributing workloads across multiple clouds mitigates the risk of service outages or disruptions. If one provider faces issues, others can maintain operations, enhancing overall system reliability.

- **Flexibility and vendor independence**: Multi-cloud strategies provide the flexibility to select services from different providers, avoiding vendor lock-in. This approach allows organizations to choose the best-fit solutions based on performance, pricing, and innovation.

- **Compliance and data control**: Hybrid and multi-cloud setups enable companies to meet regulatory compliance by keeping sensitive data on-premises or in specific geographic regions. This addresses concerns related to data sovereignty and compliance requirements.

- **Cost optimization**: Companies can optimize costs by selecting providers based on pricing models and service offerings that align with their budget and performance requirements. This flexibility supports efficient resource allocation.

- **Scalability and performance**: Multi-cloud environments facilitate resource scaling and performance optimization. Organizations can scale horizontally across providers or leverage cloud resources for non-sensitive workloads while maintaining critical functions on-premises.

- **Innovation and best-of-breed services**: Leveraging services from different cloud providers allows organizations to tap into unique innovations and adopt best-of-breed solutions for specific business needs without compromising capabilities.

- **Disaster recovery and business continuity**: Multi-cloud strategies enhance disaster recovery capabilities. Organizations can quickly switch to another provider in case of a significant outage, ensuring business continuity and minimizing downtime.

- **Edge computing integration**: Hybrid cloud supports edge computing by extending cloud services to the network's edge, enabling real-time data processing for applications requiring low-latency responses.

AI and Machine Learning integration

Cloud providers offer more AI and Machine Learning services, making it easier for businesses to leverage these technologies without significant expertise. Expect to see more AI-driven automation and analytics in the cloud.

Quantum computing in the cloud

While still in its early stages, quantum computing is making strides. Cloud providers are exploring ways to offer quantum computing services, which could open up new possibilities for solving complex problems.

Containerization and Kubernetes

Containers and orchestration tools like Kubernetes continue to gain popularity for deploying and managing applications in the cloud. This trend is expected to grow as more organizations modernize their infrastructure.

Serverless databases

As serverless computing is rising, serverless databases are becoming more prevalent. These databases automatically scale and manage resources, making it easier to handle dynamic workloads.

Security and compliance

Security and compliance remain top concerns with the increasing reliance on the cloud. Expect advancements in cloud security tools and practices to address evolving threats and regulatory requirements.

Green cloud computing

Sustainability is becoming a significant concern. Cloud providers are working to make their data centers more energy-efficient and are offering carbon-neutral or green cloud services to meet sustainability goals. Azure has been actively engaged in sustainability efforts to reduce its environmental impact.

Some of the key initiatives include:

- **Carbon neutrality**: Microsoft has committed to being carbon negative by 2030, meaning they aim to remove more carbon from the atmosphere than they emit. This includes direct and indirect emissions associated with their operations since their founding in 1975.

- **Renewable energy**: Azure has invested heavily in renewable energy sources to power its data centers. Microsoft has a goal to rely on 100% renewable energy by 2025.

- **Water conservation**: Azure is working on sustainable water practices to replenish more water than it consumes in water-stressed regions by 2030.

- **Zero waste**: Microsoft is committed to achieving zero-waste certification at its Puget Sound campus, and Azure is likely to adopt similar waste reduction initiatives.
- **Circular economy**: Azure is exploring circular economy principles, including designing products for reuse, recycling, and minimizing waste.
- **AI for Earth**: Microsoft's AI for Earth program, although not specific to Azure, promotes using artificial intelligence to address environmental challenges, including climate change, agriculture, and biodiversity.

Blockchain integration

Blockchain technology is being integrated into cloud platforms for various applications, such as supply chain management and secure data sharing. This trend is likely to continue as blockchain matures.

Cloud computing enhances blockchain implementations by providing scalable infrastructure and services. Cloud platforms offer the necessary computational power, storage, and networking capabilities for blockchain networks, supporting **decentralized applications (DApps)** and smart contracts. Cloud services simplify the deployment and management of blockchain nodes, ensuring reliability and accessibility. Additionally, cloud-based solutions enable cost-effective scalability, facilitating the growth of blockchain networks without significant upfront investments. This synergy between cloud computing and blockchain technology fosters innovation, accelerates development, and makes blockchain solutions accessible to various organizations.

5G and cloud

The rollout of 5G networks is expected to accelerate the adoption of cloud computing for applications that require high-speed, low-latency connectivity. Cloud computing is pivotal in 5G networks by providing the necessary infrastructure for advanced services. It enables the deployment of virtualized network functions, allowing for greater flexibility and scalability. Cloud-based solutions facilitate the rapid deployment of new services, efficient resource allocation, and dynamic scaling to meet varying demands. Additionally, edge computing in the cloud brings processing closer to the network edge, reducing latency and enhancing the performance of applications in 5G environments. This synergy between cloud computing and 5G technology optimizes network efficiency and supports the proliferation of innovative applications and services.

Serverless IoT

Combining serverless computing with IoT applications can streamline the development and managing IoT devices and services.

Data analytics and big data

Cloud providers are enhancing their data analytics and extensive data offerings, making it easier for businesses to derive insights from large datasets.

Container security

With the rise of containers, container security is becoming increasingly important. Expect to see more tools and practices focused on securing containerized applications. Cloud providers implement robust container security measures to protect containerized applications. Critical practices include image scanning for vulnerabilities, runtime security with features like isolation and privilege management, network segmentation to control container communication and continuous monitoring for anomalous behavior. Cloud services also offer identity and access management for secure container orchestration. Integration with security tools, like Azure Security Center, enhances threat detection and response. Regular updates and adherence to security best practices ensure a comprehensive defense against potential container exploits, securing applications throughout their lifecycle in the cloud environment.

Mature cloud-native ecosystem

The cloud-native ecosystem, including technologies like microservices and DevOps practices, will continue to evolve, making it easier to develop, deploy, and manage applications in the cloud. Building a mature cloud ecosystem involves concerted interoperability, standardization, and innovation efforts. Collaborative initiatives among cloud providers promote open standards, easing data portability and application development. Industry-wide collaborations, like the **Cloud Native Computing Foundation (CNCF)**, drive the adoption of cloud-native technologies. Continuous security, compliance, and governance advancements ensure trust and regulatory adherence. Training programs and certifications empower a skilled workforce. Integrating emerging technologies, such as AI and edge computing, fosters a holistic ecosystem. The collective focus on these elements facilitates a mature cloud environment supporting diverse workloads and promoting innovation across industries.

These trends reflect the ongoing evolution of cloud computing to meet the changing needs of businesses and technology landscapes. It is essential to stay current with the latest developments in the cloud computing industry.

Azure Cloud future trends

We have covered how the cloud landscape is changing. Now, we will see how Azure Cloud is coping with the changes and in which direction it is moving. We will cover some insights into the latest developments in Microsoft Azure cloud computing up to that point.

However, remember that the Azure ecosystem constantly evolves, and there may have been further developments since then. Here are the following vital advancements are happening in the Azure cloud field:

Azure Arc

Azure Arc allows organizations to extend Azure services and management to any infrastructure, including on-premises, multi-cloud, and edge environments. It provides a unified management platform for all resources, regardless of location. Azure Arc extends Azure's capabilities to on-premises, multi-cloud environments, and edge locations, providing a unified management experience. Azure Arc enables organizations to seamlessly manage and govern resources across diverse environments, ensuring consistency and compliance. It offers Azure Arc-enabled services, such as Azure Arc-enabled Kubernetes, allowing the management of Kubernetes clusters across different infrastructures. This extends to servers, databases, and other resources, allowing for central monitoring, policy enforcement, and application deployment. With Azure Arc, businesses gain flexibility and control over their hybrid and multi-cloud architectures, simplifying operations and enhancing the scalability of their applications and infrastructure. Azure Arc is critical to Microsoft's commitment to delivering a consistent and holistic cloud experience across various deployment scenarios.

Azure Quantum

Addressing some of the most challenging global issues, like climate change and food insecurity, necessitates groundbreaking scientific discoveries in chemistry and materials science. Progress in these domains holds the potential to influence 96 percent of products and impact the entirety of humanity. Azure Quantum applications have been crafted to support quantum chemists and researchers in swiftly expanding and accelerating their scientific investigations. Empower your journey in building influential applications for quantum chemistry and materials science, contributing to the collective effort in tackling pressing global challenges. Commence your impactful endeavors in this realm today.

There is a lot of work going on in Quantum Space, and it is going to be the future of computing. Microsoft has been working on quantum computing technologies and offers Azure Quantum, a cloud service that allows researchers and developers to experiment with quantum computing.

Azure Quantum is a Microsoft cloud service that brings the power of quantum computing to researchers, developers, and organizations. It aims to revolutionize computation by leveraging the principles of quantum mechanics to solve complex problems that classical computers struggle with. Azure Quantum provides a comprehensive platform comprising quantum hardware, simulators, and development tools.

Key components include the Quantum Development Kit, which features the Q# programming language and quantum simulators for algorithm testing. Developers can access diverse quantum computing hardware from partners like IonQ and Honeywell through Azure Quantum. The platform integrates seamlessly with Visual Studio, providing familiar tools for quantum development.

Azure Quantum targets many applications, including optimization, cryptography, and material science. It empowers users to harness the potential of quantum computing to address real-world challenges. With a commitment to advancing quantum computing accessibility, Azure Quantum is a significant player in the evolving landscape of quantum technologies, offering learning resources, community engagement, and practical tools for the quantum computing ecosystem.

Microsoft offers a Quantum Development Kit to help developers start with quantum programming and explore quantum computing concepts.

Azure Percept

Azure Percept is a comprehensive platform for building and deploying AI solutions at the edge. It is designed for scenarios like industrial IoT and includes hardware and services for edge AI. It is an end-to-end platform by Microsoft designed for building and deploying edge AI solutions. It integrates hardware, services, and AI models to enable organizations to implement intelligent edge devices quickly. Azure Percept includes Azure Percept Studio for creating and managing AI models, **Azure Percept DK (Development Kit)** for building prototypes, and Azure Percept Edge for deploying solutions at scale. The platform supports a variety of AI scenarios, such as object detection and classification, in industries like manufacturing, retail, and healthcare. By offering a streamlined approach to implementing edge AI, Azure Percept empowers businesses to derive insights and intelligence directly at the edge, enhancing efficiency and enabling new possibilities in real-world applications.

Generative AI and Azure AI

We have covered above that generative AI is all about creation. It can generate new product ideas, design customized marketing campaigns, and even help develop new drug treatments. The emergence of Artificial Intelligence technologies such as LLMs, natural language processing, and computer vision is far from just business; it is a game changer that continues to expand our horizons. Microsoft continues to invest in Azure AI services, including Azure Cognitive Services, Azure Machine Learning, and Azure Bot Service, making it easier for developers to integrate AI capabilities into their applications.

The future of generative AI holds exciting possibilities with continuous advancements in models, algorithms, and applications. Anticipate the development of more sophisticated models, potentially surpassing current benchmarks like GPT-3, with increased capacities for understanding context and nuances and generating diverse content. Multimodal models, combining text, images, and audio, will likely become more prevalent, enabling a holistic approach to content generation. Ethical considerations will remain at the forefront, driving efforts to address biases, fairness, and responsible AI practices.

Customization and personalization will grow significantly, tailoring generative models to individual user preferences and needs. Industries will witness a surge in domain-specific generative AI applications, optimizing healthcare, finance, education solutions, and beyond. Collaboration between generative AI and humans will intensify, fostering creativity, problem-solving, and content creation synergies. The emergence of real-time generative systems will enable dynamic responsiveness to changing contexts, enhancing the interactive nature of applications.

Moreover, exploration into quantum-inspired computing for generative AI could open new frontiers. The future promises a rich landscape of innovative applications, shaping how we interact with AI-generated content and expanding the boundaries of what generative AI can achieve across various domains. Stay tuned for an era of ever-evolving possibilities and transformative advancements in generative AI.

Azure Virtual Desktop

Azure Virtual Desktop (formerly Windows Virtual Desktop) has gained popularity as a cloud-based virtual desktop infrastructure solution, particularly with the increase in remote work scenarios. Azure Virtual Desktop is a cloud-based **virtual desktop infrastructure** (**VDI**) service by Microsoft Azure. It enables organizations to deploy and manage Windows desktops and applications in the Azure cloud. Users can access these virtualized resources from various devices, providing flexibility and scalability. Azure Virtual Desktop supports Windows 10 multi-session, optimizing resource utilization. It offers personalized user experiences, seamless integration with Microsoft 365, and robust security measures. Organizations can rapidly scale resources based on demand and reduce infrastructure costs. With Azure Virtual Desktop, businesses can enhance remote work capabilities, streamline desktop management, and provide a secure and efficient virtualized computing environment for their workforce.

Azure Data Explorer

Azure Data Explorer is a fast and highly scalable data exploration service by Microsoft. It enables users to analyze and visualize large volumes of diverse data in real time. Users can perform complex analytics on streaming and historical data with a powerful query language called **Kusto Query Language** (**KQL**). Azure Data Explorer is designed for scenarios with high volumes of data, making it ideal for IoT, telemetry, monitoring, and log analytics applications. It offers seamless integration with other Azure services and tools, providing a comprehensive ecosystem for data analytics. Its capabilities include data ingestion, storage, and visualization, making it a versatile solution for extracting valuable insights from massive datasets in real time.

Azure IoT

Azure IoT (Internet of Things) services have seen updates to improve IoT devices and data management and security. Azure IoT is a comprehensive set of cloud services offered by Microsoft to build, deploy, and manage end-to-end IoT solutions. It facilitates the seamless integration of devices, data, analytics, and application services, empowering organizations to harness the power of connected devices and unlock new possibilities across industries.

The following are the key components and features:

- **Device provisioning and management**:
  - **Azure IoT Hub**: A scalable and fully managed IoT messaging service that enables bidirectional communication between IoT applications and devices. It supports device registration, provisioning, and management at scale.
  - **Azure IoT Central**: A fully managed IoT application platform simplifies the development, deployment, and scaling of IoT solutions without extensive coding or infrastructure management.
  - **Azure IoT Device Management**: Offers capabilities for monitoring, configuring, and updating IoT devices at scale, ensuring efficient management and maintenance.

- **Edge computing**:
  - **Azure IoT Edge**: Extends cloud intelligence to edge devices, allowing data processing, analytics, and Machine Learning to occur locally on IoT devices. This minimizes latency, reduces bandwidth usage, and enhances privacy and security.
  - **Azure IoT Edge modules**: Containers that encapsulate different functionalities, enabling users to deploy custom code or pre-built modules on edge devices for specific processing needs.

- **Data and analytics**:
  - **Azure Time Series Insights**: A fully managed analytics, storage, and visualization service for IoT-scale time-series data. It enables users to explore and analyze large volumes of IoT data quickly.
  - **Azure Stream Analytics**: Real-time analytics service that processes streaming data from devices and integrates with various Azure services for further analysis and visualization.

- **Security and identity**:
  - **Azure IoT Security**: Provides comprehensive security measures, including device provisioning, authentication, and monitoring. Features like Azure Sphere enhance security for microcontroller-based devices.

- o **Azure IoT Hub Device Provisioning Service**: Automates the enrollment of IoT devices at scale, ensuring secure onboarding.

- **Integration with Azure services**:
    - o Integration with Azure services like Azure Functions, Logic Apps, and Cosmos DB allows seamless data flow and interoperability with other cloud services.

- **Development tools**:
    - o **Azure IoT SDKs**: Software development kits for various programming languages, easing the development of IoT applications on different platforms.
    - o **Azure IoT Workbench**: An extension for Visual Studio Code that simplifies IoT application development by providing project templates, code samples, and debugging capabilities.

Azure IoT empowers organizations to build innovative IoT solutions, monitor and manage devices efficiently, and derive actionable insights from IoT data. Whether for predictive maintenance, asset tracking, or innovative city applications, Azure IoT provides a scalable and secure foundation for realizing the full potential of the Internet of Things.

The Azure platform has likely seen further enhancements and new features since then. To stay updated with the latest developments in Azure cloud computing, visiting the official Azure website and monitoring Microsoft's announcements and blogs related to Azure services and updates is recommended.

Conclusion

The future of Azure and the broader cloud industry is marked by ongoing innovation and transformative trends. Azure, Microsoft's cloud computing platform, is set to play a significant role in shaping this evolution. Key industry trends include the growing adoption of hybrid and multi-cloud strategies, emphasizing combining on-premises infrastructure with cloud services. Edge computing, where data processing occurs closer to the source, is gaining prominence, with Azure actively participating in this space through initiatives like Azure IoT Edge.

AI and ML integration are becoming integral to cloud platforms, and Azure's AI services and Azure Machine Learning contribute to the rise of intelligent applications. Containerization, mainly through technologies like Kubernetes, is a crucial aspect of cloud-native development, with AKS solidifying Azure's position in container orchestration.

The industry is witnessing increased attention to cybersecurity, compliance, and sustainable practices. Azure's robust security features, compliance certifications, and commitment to green computing align with these priorities. Additionally, serverless computing models, exemplified by Azure Functions, are gaining traction for their efficiency and cost-effectiveness. Azure is expected to continue driving innovation and addressing diverse business needs in this dynamic cloud landscape.

Questions

1. How is Azure positioned to contribute to the growing hybrid and multi-cloud adoption trend?
2. In what ways does Azure actively participate in the evolution of edge computing?
3. How does Azure address the increasing emphasis on Artificial Intelligence and Machine Learning integration in cloud platforms?
4. Can you elaborate on the role of AKS in the context of container orchestration and cloud-native development?
5. What initiatives and features make Azure a key player in addressing cybersecurity and compliance concerns in the cloud industry?
6. How does Azure demonstrate its commitment to sustainability and green computing practices?
7. Explain the significance of serverless computing models, particularly Azure Functions, in the context of efficiency and cost-effectiveness.
8. How does Azure align with the industry's focus on reducing the carbon footprint of data centers?
9. What key trends in the cloud industry does the summary highlight as significant for the future?
10. In what ways is Azure expected to continue driving innovation and meeting diverse business needs in the evolving cloud landscape?

Join our book's Discord space

Join the book's Discord Workspace for Latest updates, Offers, Tech happenings around the world, New Release and Sessions with the Authors:

https://discord.bpbonline.com

Index

A

access control and identity management 127, 128
ACID properties 33
Airbnb 189
Amazon 188
Amazon Web Services (AWS) 3, 5
append-only file (AOF) 45
Application Insights SDK 107
application performance monitoring (APM) tools 176
application programming interfaces (APIs) 67
applications
  developing, with Java and .Net 95
Argo CD 144
ARM templates 126
Artificial Intelligence (AI) 162, 164

automated QA process
  implementing 141-143
auto scalability 195
Azure 1
  monitoring and logging services 102
  security and governance features 119, 120
  virtual machines (VMs) 8
Azure Active Directory (AAD) 13, 18, 119
  features 18
Azure AD Connect 18
Azure AD logs 123
Azure API Gateway 68, 69
Azure API Management 64, 67
  features 64-68
Azure application
  issues, troubleshooting 114, 115
Azure Application Gateway 123

Azure Application Insights 104, 139
  auto instrumentation 107
  availability testing 106
  dependency tracking 106
  exception tracking 106
  features 104, 105
  performance monitoring 105
  using 106, 107
Azure applications
  deployment best practices 150-152
  issues, troubleshooting 113
  security best practices 120, 121
Azure App Service 8, 13, 23
  features 23, 24
Azure Archive Storage 36, 40, 130
  features 40, 41
Azure Artifacts 138
Azure Bastion and VPN Gateway 124
Azure Batch 17
Azure Blob Storage 35, 50
  features 50, 51
Azure Blob Storage Lifecycle Management 130
Azure Blueprints 126
Azure Boards 138
Azure Cache for Redis 36, 44
  features 45
Azure Cloud 7
  benefits for development 9, 10
  offerings 7-9
  problems 110, 111
Azure Cloud future trends 214
  Azure Arc 215
  Azure Data Explorer 217
  Azure IoT (Internet of Things) 218, 219
  Azure Percept 216
  Azure Quantum 215, 216

Azure Virtual Desktop 217
  generative AI and Azure AI 216, 217
Azure Cloud Services for generative AI 202
  Azure Cognitive Services 203
  Azure Databricks 204
  Azure GPU Virtual Machines 204
  Azure Kubernetes Service (AKS) 204
  Azure Machine Learning Service 202, 203
Azure Cognitive Services 162
  components 163, 164
  practical use cases 163, 164
Azure Compliance Center 126
Azure Compliance Manager 130
Azure Compute 13-15
Azure Container Instances (ACI) 17
Azure Container Registry (ACR) 57, 63, 65, 80, 133, 139, 144
  features 66
Azure Cosmos DB 9, 36, 41
  features 42, 43
  using, for NoSQL databases 89-91
Azure Cost Management 184
Azure cost management + billing 126
Azure Databricks 51, 52
  architecture 52, 53
  features 53, 54
Azure Data Catalog 129
Azure Data Factory 129
Azure Data Lake Storage 36, 48
  features 49, 50
Azure Data Masking 129
Azure DDoS Protection 119, 124
Azure DevOps 9, 120, 133, 138
  DevOps, setting up with 139-141
  using 143

Index

Azure Event Bus 21
  features 22
Azure Event Grid 14, 21
  features 21
  using 92
Azure Event Hubs 14, 19
  features 20
Azure Files 36, 47
  features 47, 48
Azure Firewall 119
Azure Functions 9, 17, 19
  example 87-89
  features 19
  serverless development 86, 87
Azure Functions and Logic Apps 148
  using 148-150
Azure GitHub Actions 133
Azure governance policies 126, 127
Azure HDInsight 36, 46
  features 46, 47
Azure Identity and Access Management (IAM) 13
Azure Information Protection (AIP) 119, 129
Azure IoT Hub 167
  components 167-169
  features 167-169
Azure Key Vault 119, 129
Azure Key Vault Auditing 124
Azure Kubernetes 57
Azure Kubernetes Service (AKS) 9, 17, 63, 139, 144
  microservices, building with 80-85
  using 146-148
Azure Log Analytics 107
  log collection 107
  log search and analysis 108

log types 109, 110
visualization and dashboards 108
Azure Logic Apps 22
  features 22, 23
  workflows, working with 93-95
Azure Machine Learning 158
  architecture 158, 159
  collaboration 161
  data preparation 159
  experimentation and version control 161
  integration 161
  model deployment 160
  model training 159
  monitoring and management 160, 161
  security and compliance 161, 162
  use cases 162
Azure management groups 126
Azure Mobile Apps 14
Azure Mobile Services 25
  features 25, 26
Azure Monitor 102, 139, 144
  and Log Analytics 123
  high-level architecture 103, 104
  monitoring, setting up 111, 112
Azure Pipelines 133, 138
Azure Policy 119, 126
Azure Policy and Azure Blueprints 130
Azure Purview 129
Azure RBAC 126, 130
Azure Repos 138
Azure Resource Manager (ARM) 79, 120
Azure Security Center (ASC) 119, 123, 127
Azure Security Logs 124
Azure Security Policy and Compliance Center 124
Azure Sentinel 119, 124
Azure Service Bus 14

using 92
Azure Service Fabric 14, 26
　features 26, 27
Azure SignalR 27
　features 27, 28
Azure SignalR Service 14
Azure SQL Database 9, 36, 37, 40
　benefits 38
　purchasing models 38, 39
Azure Storage Service Encryption (SSE) 129
Azure Support website 115
Azure Synapse Analytics 165
　components 165, 166
　features 165, 166
Azure Table Storage 36, 43
　features 43, 44
Azure Test Plans 139
Azure Virtual Machines 15
　features 15-17
　types 16
Azure WebJobs 24
　features 24, 25

B
business critical service tier 39

C
CI/CD pipelines 79
CI/CD process 144-146
cloud computing 1
　evolution 2, 3
　history 2
cloud deployment models 196
cloud-native best practices 171, 178-184
Cloud Native Computing Foundation (CNCF) 214
cloud-native design
　best practices 73-75
　challenges 73-75
cloud-native development 2
cloud-native development, future trends 208
　5G networks 213
　AI and Machine Learning integration 211
　blockchain integration 213
　containerization and Kubernetes 212
　container security 214
　data analytics and big data 214
　edge computing 208-210
　green cloud computing 212, 213
　mature cloud-native ecosystem 214
　multi-cloud and hybrid cloud adoption 210, 211
　quantum computing 212
　security and compliance 212
　serverless computing 210
　serverless databases 212
　serverless IoT 213
cloud-native technologies 2
cloud service models 3
　Infrastructure-as-a-Service (IaaS) 5
　Platform-as-a-Service (PaaS) 4
　Software-as-a-Service (SaaS) 4, 5
Coca-Cola 190
Command Query Responsibility Segregation (CQRS) 174
compute tiers 39
　provisioned compute tier 39
　serverless compute tier 40
Conditional Access 17
container 58
containerization 78
　deployment strategies 78-80
containerized applications 58
container orchestration 60

key capabilities 60, 61
continuous delivery 136
continuous deployment 136
continuous integration (CI) 136
  key practices 136
continuous integration/continuous deployment (CI/CD) 134, 135, 198
  benefits 137
  tools and practices 137
customer relationship management (CRM) 3

D
data analysis 156
data center locations 197
Datadog 176
data governance 118
  methodologies 129, 130
Data-Information-Knowledge-Wisdom (DIKW) 156
data storage options 197
data storage services 35
data transfer costs 198
decentralized applications (DApps) 213
Delta Sharing 118
DevOps 134, 135
  fundamental principles 137, 138
  practices 198
DevOps culture 180
DevOps pipeline
  setting up, with Azure DevOps 139-141
DIKW Pyramid 156-158
distributed denial of service (DDoS) attacks 119
Docker 59
  benefits 59, 60
DTU-based purchasing model 39

E
Edge-as-a-service (EaaS) 209
edge computing 208
  5G adoption, helping 208
  advantages 209
  Edge-as-a-service (EaaS) 209
  edge containers 209
Elastic Compute Cloud (EC2) 3-5
elastic load balancing 197
Etsy 189
event-driven applications
  building 92, 93

F
Function-as-a-Service (FaaS) 210

G
general-purpose service tier 39
generative adversarial networks (GANs) 198
generative AI 198
generative AI Azure services
  accessing 205
  collaboration and integration 206
  comprehensive documentation and tutorials 205
  data management 206
  deployment 205, 206
  development and experimentation 205
  GPU acceleration 205
  learning 204
  OpenAI model integration 205
  scalability 205, 206
  scalable cloud infrastructure 205
  security and compliance 206
generative AI program
  writing 206-208
GitHub 144

GitHub Action 143, 144
   working 144
graph processing (GraphX) 53
green cloud computing 212

H
Health Insurance Portability and Accountability Act (HIPAA) 10
HIPAA Business Associate Agreement (BAA) 161
Horizontal Pod Autoscaler (HPA) 80
Hyperscale service tier 39

I
Identity and Access Management (IAM) 17
   features 17, 18
Incident Response Plan 124
Infrastructure-as-a-Service (IaaS) 3, 5
Infrastructure as Code (IaC) 175
input/output operations per second (IOPS) 48
International Organization for Standardization (ISO) 10
Internet of Things (IoT) 155

J
Java (Spring Boot) 95-97

K
Kubernetes 61
   features 62, 63
Kusto Query Language (KQL) 108, 217

L
Language Understanding (LUIS) 203
large language model (LLM) 199
   chatbots and conversational agents 200
   creativity and innovation 200
   for generative AI and content creation 199, 200
   human-like text generation 201
   image generation and manipulation 201
   knowledge synthesis 200
   multi-modal capabilities 201
   natural language processing (NLP) 200
   text generation 200
   transfer learning 201
   unsupervised learning 201, 202
LinkedIn 189

M
machine learning library (MLlib) 53
microservices
   building, with AKS 80-85
microservices architecture 7, 75, 76
   patterns 76, 77
Microsoft Azure 1
monitoring and managing tools 198
monitoring, Azure ML
   alerting and notifications 160
   data drift monitoring 160
   endpoint monitoring 160
   explainability and fairness monitoring 160
   integration, with Azure Monitor 160
   model monitoring 160
   model retraining 160
monolithic application
   best practices 172-177
   considerations 172
   transforming 172-177
monolithic architecture 6
multi-factor authentication (MFA) 17

N

National Institute of Standards and Technology (NIST) 3
NET (ASP.NET Core) 97, 98
Netflix 186
network access 197
Network File System (NFS) protocol 48
Network Security Groups (NSG) 123
New Relic 176
non-relational data 32
normalization forms 33
   Boyce-Codd normal form (BCNF) 34
   domain-key normal form (DK/NF) 34
   fifth normal form (5NF) 34
   first normal form (1NF) 33
   fourth normal form (4NF) 34
   second normal form (2NF) 33
   sixth normal form (6NF) 34
   third normal form (3NF) 33
NoSQL databases
   Cosmos DB, using for 89-91

O

on-demand self-service 194, 195
OpenAI's Generative Pre-trained Transformer (GPT) series 199
Open Container Initiative (OCI) 63
orchestration 198

P

pay-as-you-go pricing model 196
Payment Card Industry Data Security Standard (PCI-DSS) 10
PEN testing 117
Persistent Volume Claims (PVCs) 62
Persistent Volumes (PVs) 62
Platform-as-a-Service (PaaS) 3, 4
Pod 62
Privileged Identity Management (PIM) 17
protected health information (PHI) 161
provisioned compute tier 39
purchasing models
   compute tiers 39, 40
   DTU-based purchasing model 39
   service tiers 39
   vCore-based purchasing model 39

Q

quantum computing 212

R

real-world cloud-native applications 184-186
   Airbnb 189
   Amazon 188
   Coca-Cola 190
   Etsy 189
   LinkedIn 189
   microservices usage 188
   Netflix 186, 187
   Spotify 187
   Twitter 189
   Uber 187
   Walmart 190
redundancy and high availability 197
relational databases
   essential property 33
   normalization forms 33
relational data format 32
ReplicaSet 62
resource pooling 197
role-based access control (RBAC) 17

S

security and compliance 197
security information and event management (SIEM) 119

semi-structured data 35
serverless compute tier 40
Server Message Block (SMB) protocol 48
Service Level Agreements (SLAs) 197
service models 195
  IaaS 195
  PaaS 195
  SaaS 195
service tiers 39
  business critical service tier 39
  general-purpose service tier 39
  Hyperscale service tier 39
shared access signatures (SAS) 41
Simple Storage Service (S3) 3
Single Sign-On (SSO) 18
Software-as-a-Service (SaaS) 3, 4
Spotify 187
structured data 32, 33
surface attacks
  identifying 122-124

T

Team Foundation Version Control (TFVC) 138
technical account manager (TAM) 114
Terraform 79
threat intelligence feeds 124
threat modeling 124, 125
twelve-factor applications 77, 78
Twitter 189

U

Uber 187
Unity Catalog 118
unstructured data 34, 35
User and Entity Behavior Analytics (UEBA) 124

V

vCore-based purchasing model 39
virtual desktop infrastructure (VDI) 217
virtualization 194

W

Walmart 190
Web Application Firewall (WAF) 123
workflows
  building, with Azure Logic Apps 93-95

Made in United States
North Haven, CT
31 March 2024

50312364R00135